TECHNICAL ANALYSIS

AIM, LOCK & EXECUTE

Practical Technical Analysis for Stocks, F&O, Crypto, Commodities & More

AMIT R CHARAN

notionpress.com

INDIA • SINGAPORE • MALAYSIA

ISBN
Paperback 979-8-90479-541-2
Hardcase 979-8-90560-854-4

About the Author

Amit R Charan is a distinguished corporate lawyer with nearly two decades of experience specializing in Banking & Finance law, developed through his association with some of India's leading law firms. He has led the BFSI practice of a reputed legal firm as a Partner, with his professional expertise deeply rooted in financial products, securities, structured finance, and capital markets. His academic background spans Law, Business Administration, and Software Programming, reflecting his multidisciplinary approach toward finance, technology, and problem-solving.

Over the course of his professional journey, Amit has advised prominent domestic and international financial institutions, private equity investors, and corporates on complex debt and equity transactions. This extensive exposure to the financial ecosystem provided him with a deep practical understanding of financial markets, investment structures, and market behaviour. Alongside his legal career, his passion for independent research, analytical thinking, and practical market study led him to undertake an in-depth exploration of trading psychology, technical analysis, derivatives, investment strategies, and broader financial planning concepts. His writing therefore reflects a unique blend of corporate precision, practical market understanding, and a strong focus on simplifying complex concepts for everyday market participants.

Amit is also the author of the widely appreciated ***The Intelligent F&O Trader*** **series comprising Volumes I, II & III**, designed to provide comprehensive and practical insights into Futures & Options trading for traders and investors alike. In addition, he has authored numerous articles on law, finance, and financial markets for various journals and publications, as well as a book on Letters of Credit.

Driven by his vision to democratize financial knowledge through technology, Amit founded **Aineura**, a startup focused on building innovative Generative AI-powered financial learning solutions. Through this venture, he is spearheading the development of **FnKnowBot**, a multilingual AI-powered platform aimed at making practical personal finance and market education accessible to people globally. FnKnowBot can be accessed at **https://fnknowbot.in** and is designed to serve as an intelligent financial knowledge companion covering a wide spectrum of money matters including investing, trading, F&O, crypto, technical and fundamental analysis, budgeting, debt management, succession planning, and financial report and chart analysis.

Through his books, research, and technology initiatives, Amit continues his mission of empowering individuals with practical financial knowledge and decision-making capabilities across capital markets and personal finance.

To explore his literary work and initiatives, you may visit: **https://amitrcharan.com**

Dedication

This book is lovingly dedicated to my family, whose sacrificial love and unwavering support have carried me through my every endeavour.

To my beloved wife, Sharon, and my precious daughter, Jessica—my treasures and my daily joy—your love fills my life with meaning and strength.

To my dearest mother, Elizabeth Charan, whose prayers and nurturing spirit have been my foundation, and to my late father, K. B Charan, who fought a good fight of faith and was promoted to glory to be with the Lord.

Each of you is God's special gift to me, and this work is as much yours as it is mine.

This work is born from the grace of the Almighty and the cherished prayers of loved ones who have stood beside me in all seasons.

Acknowledgment

I extend my heartfelt thanks and deep gratitude to ***Mr. Nitish Kumar Singh*** *of NK* ***Stock Talk****, from whom I have drawn valuable inspiration and profound insights into the practical aspects of Technical Analysis for investments and trading.*

His rich experience of over 25 years as a successful trader and investor has illuminated significant dimensions of insightful analysis for investment and trading.

His vast knowledge and generous guidance to the retail trading community have been instrumental in inspiring me to author this book as a comprehensive knowledge resource for all traders, investors and market enthusiasts.

Disclaimer

This book on Technical Analysis (the "Book") is intended solely for informational and educational purposes. The information, concepts, strategies, techniques, charts, illustrations, market views, and risk management discussions presented in this Book are based on the author's personal studies, research, observations, learning, and market experience up to the time of writing and publishing. Nothing contained in this Book should be construed as financial, investment, trading, legal, tax, or professional advice, nor as any recommendation, solicitation, or assurance to buy, sell, or hold any financial instrument or participate in any specific market activity.

Trading and investing in financial markets — including equities, derivatives, Futures & Options, commodities, currencies, debt instruments, cryptocurrencies, and other asset classes — involve substantial risk and may not be suitable for all individuals. Financial markets are inherently uncertain and volatile, and past performance is not indicative of future results. The author makes no representation or warranty, express or implied, regarding the accuracy, completeness, reliability, or profitability of any information, strategy, technique, or viewpoint discussed in this Book. No assurance or guarantee is provided that the use of the contents of this Book will result in profits or avoidance of losses.

Readers are advised to exercise independent judgment and carefully evaluate their financial condition, investment objectives, risk appetite, and suitability before making any trading or investment decisions. Readers should consult qualified financial or professional advisors before acting upon any information contained in this Book. Any action taken by the reader based on the contents of this Book shall be entirely at the reader's own discretion, risk, and responsibility.

The discussions, examples, charts, patterns, technicals, lot sizes, expiry cycles, instruments, regulations, and market-related information referred to in this Book are based primarily on the Indian financial markets and the prevailing framework at the relevant time of writing. Such information and regulations may change over time pursuant to actions by regulators, stock exchanges, or other authorities. Readers are advised to refer to official and updated sources for the latest information.

This Book and its contents are provided on an "as is" basis without warranties of any kind. To the fullest extent permitted by applicable law, the author shall not be liable for any direct, indirect, incidental, consequential, special, or other damages or losses arising from the use of or reliance upon the contents of this Book.

Why Technical Analysis?

Financial markets are driven by a continuous interaction of price, volume, liquidity, momentum, sentiment, macroeconomic developments, geopolitical events, institutional participation, and human psychology. Every movement in the market reflects the collective behaviour of buyers and sellers responding to changing expectations, risk perception, opportunity, fear, and greed. In such a dynamic and ever-evolving environment, Technical Analysis serves as a practical framework to study, interpret, and understand market behaviour through price action, charts, volume dynamics, momentum, and trend structure.

Technical Analysis is essentially the study of market-generated data — primarily price and volume — to understand the probable direction, strength, momentum, sustainability, and behaviour of a financial instrument. It helps market participants identify trends, reversals, support and resistance zones, accumulation and distribution phases, volatility expansion, momentum shifts, overbought and oversold conditions, and changing market sentiment. Rather than depending purely on assumptions, emotions, opinions, or speculation, Technical Analysis enables traders and investors to make more structured and probability-based decisions by understanding what the market itself may be communicating through its behaviour.

One of the most powerful aspects of Technical Analysis is that its principles are universally applicable across virtually all segments of financial markets and asset classes. Whether one participates in equities, indices, Futures & Options, commodities, precious metals such as gold and silver, energy products like crude oil and natural gas, currencies, debt instruments, global markets, ETFs, or even digital assets and cryptocurrencies such as Bitcoin and Ethereum — Technical Analysis remains relevant wherever price and volume exist. The charts may belong to different instruments, but the underlying principles of trend, momentum, accumulation, distribution, support, resistance, volatility, and human behaviour remain remarkably similar across all markets.

Similarly, Technical Analysis is not restricted to any one style of market participation. It remains highly useful for intraday traders, swing traders, positional traders, scalpers, derivatives traders, long-term investors, value investors, growth investors, and portfolio managers alike. Although the time horizon, objectives, and risk appetite may differ from one participant to another, the need to understand market structure, trend direction, momentum strength, and risk remains common across all approaches.

For investors, Technical Analysis can significantly improve the quality of investment decisions by helping identify favourable entry zones, strong sectors, market leaders, accumulation phases, trend reversals, and broader market direction. It complements fundamental analysis by helping determine *when* to enter, accumulate, reduce exposure, or remain patient. Even fundamentally strong stocks can underperform for extended periods if purchased at technically unfavourable levels, whereas technically well-timed entries may improve conviction, risk management, and return potential.

For traders, Technical Analysis becomes even more crucial because trading decisions depend heavily upon timing, momentum, volatility, liquidity, trend continuation, and risk management. Concepts such as moving averages, VWAP and AVWAP, support and resistance, candlestick patterns, Relative Strength, price-volume analysis, demand and supply zones, momentum studies, and price action analysis help traders identify high-probability opportunities and align themselves with prevailing market direction. More importantly, Technical Analysis helps traders protect capital, manage drawdowns, control losses, identify exits, and quickly adapt whenever market dynamics begin to change.

Markets are inherently uncertain, and no indicator, strategy, or chart pattern can guarantee success with certainty. However, Technical Analysis helps improve probabilities and decision quality by providing a structured framework for understanding market behaviour. It teaches market participants to think in terms of discipline, adaptability, probabilities, and risk management rather than emotional reaction or blind prediction. Over time, consistent study of charts and market behaviour trains the mind to recognize recurring structures, momentum shifts, trend transitions, and behavioural tendencies that often precede significant market moves.

Technical Analysis also reflects the psychology of market participants. Every breakout, reversal, consolidation, volume surge, or failed move represents changing conviction between buyers and sellers. In many situations, price action and volume behaviour begin reflecting evolving sentiment much before broader news or public perception changes. This is why experienced market participants often believe that "price discounts everything," and therefore carefully study charts to understand underlying market strength, weakness, institutional participation, and sentiment dynamics.

It is equally important to understand that Technical Analysis is not merely about memorizing indicators or patterns. It is a practical skill developed gradually through observation, discipline, patience, emotional control, and continuous learning. Over time, charts begin to communicate a story to those who consistently study and respect market behaviour. Technical Analysis therefore evolves from being merely a collection of tools into a structured way of reading the market and participating with greater clarity, preparedness, and confidence.

In today's fast-moving and highly interconnected financial world, a sound understanding of Technical Analysis can provide a meaningful edge to both traders and investors across all market segments and asset classes. Whether the objective is wealth creation, active trading, hedging, capital preservation, or risk management, Technical Analysis can become an invaluable framework for understanding market behaviour and navigating financial markets with greater discipline, clarity, and conviction.

Preface

The financial markets are a fascinating blend of opportunity, uncertainty, psychology, discipline, and continuous learning. Over the years, I have come to realize that while markets may appear chaotic on the surface, they often leave behind meaningful footprints through price action, volume behaviour, momentum shifts, and trend structures. The ability to understand and interpret these footprints through Technical Analysis can significantly enhance the quality of trading and investing decisions.

After the encouraging response and grand success of my earlier series on Futures & Options trading — ***The Intelligent F&O Trader: Vol I, II & III*** — I felt motivated to further contribute toward empowering retail market participants with deeper and more practical market knowledge. Through this book, my sincere effort is to further arm and equip traders and investors alike — whether beginners, intermediate learners, or experienced market participants — with practical insights and a structured understanding of Technical Analysis that can help add an important edge to their journey through the financial markets.

Technical Analysis is not merely about indicators or chart patterns; it is about understanding market behaviour, identifying changing dynamics, recognizing opportunity, managing risk, and adapting intelligently to evolving market conditions. Whether one participates as an investor, swing trader, positional trader, intraday trader, scalper, or options trader, the principles of Technical Analysis remain highly relevant and practically valuable across all market segments and time frames.

One of my key objectives while writing this book has been to simplify complex concepts and present them in a practical and easily understandable manner without distancing them from real-market applicability. The discussions throughout this book are intentionally grounded in practical market behaviour and actionable insights so that readers can relate the concepts directly to live trading and investing situations. It is my belief that knowledge becomes truly meaningful only when it can be applied with clarity and confidence in real-world conditions.

This book attempts to cover Technical Analysis not only from a theoretical perspective, but also from the standpoint of practical decision-making — helping readers understand price action, momentum, moving averages, VWAP and AVWAP, Relative Strength, accumulation and distribution, demand and supply, candlestick behaviour, volatility, trend structure, market psychology, and many other important aspects that shape financial markets. My sincere hope is that these concepts help readers improve their observation skills, strengthen discipline, refine entries and exits, and become more adaptive and risk-aware participants in the market.

I strongly believe that Technical Analysis is a skill that develops gradually with observation, patience, emotional control, and continuous practice. The charts begin to communicate more clearly over time to those who consistently study and respect market behaviour. While no strategy or indicator can guarantee certainty in the markets, a disciplined understanding of Technical Analysis can help improve probabilities, manage risk more intelligently, and navigate uncertainty with greater confidence.

I hope this book becomes a meaningful guide and practical companion in your trading and investing journey, helping you strengthen your understanding of market behaviour and sharpen your decision-making process over time. If this effort contributes even in a small way toward helping readers become more informed, disciplined, and confident market participants, it would truly fulfil its purpose.

I wish you all the very best in your journey through the ever-evolving and fascinating world of financial markets.

Wishing you success,

With Best Wishes & Compliments,

Amit

Happy Learning!

Contents

Chapter – 1

Technical Analysis

Getting Started

Retail participants often enter the stock market with the belief that success comes from frequent trading or chasing quick profits. In reality, meaningful and consistent profitability comes from **structured participation**, not activity. The biggest advantage a retail participant has over large institutions is **flexibility**—they can enter and exit quickly, focus on select opportunities, and avoid the pressure of deploying large capital. To benefit from the market, a retail trader or investor must shift from a "trading mindset" to a **decision-making mindset**, where every action is based on logic, planning, and discipline rather than impulse.

A key foundation for profitable participation is **clarity of approach**—whether one is an investor, swing trader, or intraday trader. Each approach requires different timeframes, expectations, and risk management. For instance, an investor aligning with broader trends of indices like NIFTY 50 focuses on long-term wealth creation through fundamentally strong companies, while a trader focuses on price action, momentum, and technical structures. Mixing these approaches often leads to confusion and losses. Therefore, defining one's style and sticking to it is critical.

Another crucial aspect is **risk management and capital preservation**. Retail participants must understand that survival in the market is more important than aggressive profit-making. Limiting capital deployment, using disciplined stop losses, and avoiding over-leverage—especially in derivatives—ensures longevity. The idea is simple: if capital is preserved, opportunities can always be captured later. Many retail traders fail not because they cannot identify opportunities, but because they **lose capital before the opportunity arrives**.

Retail participants can significantly improve their outcomes by focusing on **high-probability setups rather than frequent trades**. Markets offer countless movements, but only a few meaningful opportunities. Identifying structured setups—such as trend continuation, reversals at key support/resistance, or volatility expansions—can tilt probabilities in one's favour. The goal should be to trade less, but trade better. A single well-executed trade, aligned with trend and supported by conviction, can outperform multiple random trades.

Equally important is developing the skill of **reading price action and market context**. Price reflects all available information—news, sentiment, institutional activity—and learning to interpret it provides a real edge. Retail traders should focus on understanding how price behaves around key levels, how trends form and reverse, and how volatility expands and contracts. Over time, this builds intuition backed by logic, allowing traders to act decisively rather than react emotionally.

The psychological aspect cannot be overstated. Retail participants often struggle with fear, greed, and impatience—leading to early exits, late entries, or overtrading. Profitable participation requires **emotional discipline**—the ability to follow a plan even when the market tests conviction. Accepting losses as part of the process, booking profits systematically, and avoiding the urge to "win back losses" are essential traits of a successful participant.

Finally, retail investors and traders must embrace the idea that the market is a **continuous learning environment**. There is no fixed formula or guaranteed system. Success comes from adapting to changing market conditions, refining strategies, and learning from both profits and losses. Over time, with consistent effort, disciplined execution, and a focus on quality over quantity, retail participants can not only participate meaningfully in the stock market but also build sustainable and rewarding profitability.

INVESTING IN SHARES

Meaningful participation in the stock market is built on a disciplined, structured, and long-term approach, rather than chasing quick gains. Broad indices like NIFTY 50 and SENSEX reflect the economy's growth over time, but this journey is uneven and filled with volatility. Investors who stay patient, focus on quality businesses, and avoid emotional decisions improve their probability of success significantly. The key is to think like a participant in business growth, not a speculator reacting to daily price movements.

Equally important is aligning investments with one's risk profile, financial situation, and stage of life. Younger investors can take higher exposure and ride volatility, while conservative investors must prioritize capital protection. Avoiding common mistakes—such as over-concentration, deploying all capital at once, or reacting to market noise—is critical. A balanced approach through diversification, phased investing, and maintaining liquidity helps manage uncertainty and take advantage of opportunities during market corrections.

Finally, preparation is what separates successful investors from the rest. While fundamental analysis helps identify strong businesses, it is incomplete without understanding technical analysis, which guides timing, trend identification, and risk management. Learning to read charts, interpret price action, and make informed entry and exit decisions adds precision to investing. Combining both approaches enables investors to participate with greater clarity, confidence, and consistency in the market.

TRADING

An individual can participate in the market not only by trading equities and indices, but also by actively engaging in the derivatives segment across asset classes such as commodities and precious metals. Markets like gold, silver, crude oil, natural gas, and base metals offer ample trading opportunities alongside instruments linked to indices such as NIFTY 50 and Bank Nifty. These segments provide significant leverage and liquidity, enabling traders to capitalize on both rising and falling markets.

However, while the potential for profitability in trading—especially in the F&O segment—is undeniably high, it comes with equally high risk. Derivatives trading is largely a zero-sum game, where one participant's gain is another's loss. This makes it a highly competitive and unforgiving space, where lack of preparation can quickly lead to capital erosion. Success in such an environment is not driven by chance, but by consistent discipline, structured thinking, and continuous skill development.

To become proficient in trading, one must go beyond basic knowledge and cultivate deep expertise. To learn and truly understand Futures & Options trading, you may consider reading my book: *The Intelligent F&O Trader* (Vol I, II & III), available on all major online platforms, including Amazon.

A trader fundamentally relies on technical analysis—understanding price action, trends, patterns, and market behaviour across timeframes. Therefore, mastering technical analysis is not optional; it is a non-negotiable foundation for any aspiring trader. In fact, whether one is an investor or a trader, the ability to read and interpret charts effectively becomes a critical edge in navigating markets with confidence and precision.

ABOUT TECHNICAL ANALYSIS

Technical analysis is the study of price, volume, and market behaviour to understand how and why prices move. It is built on the idea that all known information—fundamental, economic, and psychological—is ultimately reflected in price. By analysing charts, trends, support–resistance levels, and indicators, technical analysis helps market participants interpret the ongoing battle between demand and supply. Its real strength lies not in prediction, but in improving probability, timing, and decision-making based on observable price action.

For both investing and trading, technical analysis serves as a common and essential framework. Investors use it on higher timeframes to identify long-term trends, accumulation zones, and optimal entry points in fundamentally strong stocks, thereby enhancing returns and reducing risk. Traders, on the other hand, rely on it across multiple timeframes—daily, hourly, and intraday—to capture shorter-term opportunities through momentum, breakouts, reversals, and patterns. Whether it is identifying a trend, spotting a reversal near key levels, or aligning with market momentum, technical analysis provides the structure required to act with clarity rather than emotion.

Its significance lies in **its universality and adaptability—it** works across asset classes such as equities, indices, commodities, currencies, crypto and derivatives, and remains relevant in different market conditions. However, it is not a certainty-driven tool; it is a probability-based approach that requires discipline, practice, and continuous learning. When combined with sound risk management and emotional control, technical analysis becomes a powerful edge—helping both investors and traders participate in the market more confidently, protect capital, and consistently improve their outcomes.

KEY TERMS & CONCEPTS

Before we delve deeper into the detailed concepts of technical analysis, it is important to first take a step back and familiarize ourselves with the key terms and foundational concepts of the financial markets. A clear understanding of these essential building blocks—ranging from price behaviour and market dynamics to trading and risk-related terminology—will provide the necessary context and clarity as we progress further. This overview will serve as a strong base, enabling readers to better grasp and apply the more advanced aspects of technical analysis with confidence and precision.

Get a good grasp of the following terms:

Accumulation: A phase where smart money quietly buys stocks over time at lower prices. Price usually moves in a range during this period before a potential rise.

Alpha: Alpha refers to the extra return generated by an investment or trader compared to the overall market or a benchmark index. It represents the ability to outperform the market through superior stock selection, strategy, timing, or skill. For example, if the market gives a return of 10% and a portfolio generates 15%, then the additional 5% return is considered alpha.

Beta: Beta measures the volatility or sensitivity of a stock or portfolio in comparison to the overall market, indicating how strongly it reacts to market movements. A beta value of around 1 means the stock generally moves in line with the market, a beta above 1 indicates the stock is more volatile and tends to move more aggressively than the market, while a beta below 1 suggests the stock is relatively less volatile and moves more moderately compared to the broader market.

Breakout / Breakdown: A *breakout* occurs when price moves above a resistance level, indicating potential upward movement. A *breakdown* occurs when price falls below a support level, indicating potential downward movement.

Buyer vs Seller Dynamics: This reflects the constant battle between buyers (who push price up) and sellers (who push price down). Price moves in the direction of whoever is stronger at that moment.

Capital Allocation: Distributing your total capital across different trades or investments to manage risk and optimize returns.

Candlestick Patterns: These are patterns formed by individual or multiple candles that show the behaviour of buyers and sellers during a time period. They help in understanding whether the market may rise, fall, or pause.

Chart Patterns: These are larger formations created over many candles that reflect market psychology. They help identify possible trend reversals or continuation based on repeating price structures.

Consolidation / Range-bound Market: A phase where price moves within a fixed range between support and resistance, showing no clear trend.

Demand Zones: Areas where strong buying has happened in the past, indicating potential support in future.

Distribution: A phase where smart money gradually sells their holdings at higher prices. Price often moves sideways before a possible decline.

Divergence (Bullish / Bearish): Divergence happens when price and an indicator (like RSI) move in opposite directions. Bullish divergence may signal a rise, while bearish divergence may signal a fall.

Drawdown: The decline in your trading capital from its peak to a lower level. It reflects the losses experienced during a period.

Dynamic Support / Resistance: Support or resistance levels that move with price, such as moving averages or trendlines.

Exhaustion: Exhaustion occurs when a trend is losing energy after a strong move. It suggests that buyers or sellers are getting tired, and a reversal or pause may happen.

Expansion / Contraction: Expansion refers to increasing volatility (big price moves), while contraction refers to decreasing volatility (tight range movement).

Expansion Phase: A phase where price breaks out of a range and starts moving strongly in one direction with increased momentum and participation.

Fear & Greed: These are the two main emotions driving markets. *Greed* pushes traders to buy at higher prices expecting more gains, while *fear* makes them sell quickly to avoid losses—often at the wrong time.

Geopolitics: Geopolitics relates to global political events and relationships between countries—such as wars, trade tensions, elections, and policy decisions. These events can create uncertainty or opportunity in financial markets, often leading to sudden movements in prices.

Hedging: Taking an opposite or protective position to reduce potential loss in an existing trade or investment.

Higher Highs / Higher Lows: In an uptrend, price keeps making higher peaks (higher highs) and higher bottoms (higher lows). This shows that buyers are in control and pushing prices upward.

Intraday Trading: Positions are opened and closed within the same day. Traders typically use 5-min, 10-min, or 15-min charts, often aligning with the hourly trend.

Liquidity Zones: These are areas where large buy or sell orders exist, often near support, resistance, or previous highs/lows. Price tends to move toward these zones as big players operate there.

Long Build-up: When price rises along with increasing Open Interest—indicating new buyers entering the market.

Long Unwinding: When traders who were holding long (buy) positions start selling to exit, leading to a fall in price along with a decrease in Open Interest.

Lower Highs / Lower Lows: In a downtrend, price forms lower peaks (lower highs) and lower bottoms (lower lows). This indicates that sellers are dominating and driving prices downward.

Macroeconomics: Macroeconomics refers to the study of the overall economy, including factors like inflation, interest rates, GDP growth, employment, and government policies. These factors influence the broader direction of markets and impact all sectors and asset classes.

Market Correction: A temporary fall in price during an uptrend (or rise during a downtrend) to adjust or "cool off" before the main trend continues.

Market Sentiment: The overall mood of the market—whether participants are generally optimistic (bullish) or pessimistic (bearish). It influences price movement beyond just technical or fundamental factors.

Markup / Markdown Phases: Markup is when price moves upward after accumulation. Markdown is when price falls after distribution.

Momentum: Momentum refers to the speed at which price is moving. Strong momentum means price is moving quickly in one direction, while weak momentum indicates slow or struggling movement.

Open Interest (OI): Open Interest represents the total number of active (unsettled) contracts in the market. It shows how much participation is there. Rising OI with price movement indicates strength in the trend.

Overbought / Oversold: Overbought means price has risen too much and may correct or fall. Oversold means price has fallen too much and may bounce or rise. These conditions help identify potential reversal zones.

PCR (Put-Call Ratio): PCR is the ratio of total Put option volume or OI to Call option volume or OI. It helps gauge market sentiment—high PCR may indicate fear (potential bullish reversal), while low PCR may indicate greed (potential bearish reversal).

Pivot Points (PR / PS): Pre-calculated levels used to identify potential support (PS) and resistance (PR) areas for intraday or short-term trading.

Positional Trading: Positions are held for weeks to months. Traders rely on daily and weekly charts to ride larger trends.

Position Sizing: Deciding how much capital to use in a trade. Proper sizing ensures that no single trade causes major damage to your overall capital.

Price Structure: Price structure refers to the way price moves—whether it is making higher highs, lower lows, or moving in a range. It helps in identifying the trend and overall market direction.

Pullback / Retracement: A pullback or retracement is a temporary move against the main trend. For example, in an uptrend, price may fall slightly before continuing upward—this is a pullback.

Rejection / Acceptance of Price: Rejection happens when price tries to move to a level but fails and quickly moves away (showing strong opposition).

Acceptance means price sustains at a level, indicating comfort and potential continuation in that direction.

Resistance: A price level where selling pressure is strong enough to stop price from rising further.

Risk-Reward Ratio: This compares how much you are risking in a trade to how much you expect to gain. A good trade usually has higher potential reward than risk.

Role Reversal (Support becomes Resistance & vice versa): When a broken support level starts acting as resistance, or a broken resistance level starts acting as support.

Scalping: Very short-term trading where positions are held for seconds to a few minutes. Traders aim to capture small price movements using very low time frames like 1-min or 5-min charts.

Short Build-up: When price falls along with increasing Open Interest—indicating new sellers entering the market.

Short Covering: When traders who earlier sold (shorted) the market start buying back their positions, causing price to rise. This often leads to sharp upward moves.

Smart Money vs Retail Participation: Smart money refers to institutional or experienced players with large capital and better information. Retail participants are individual traders. Markets often move in ways that benefit smart money while trapping uninformed retail traders.

Stop Loss (SL): A pre-decided level where you exit a trade to limit losses. It protects your capital if the market moves against you.

Stop Loss Hunting: This happens when price briefly moves to trigger common stop-loss levels (set by many traders) and then reverses. It is often driven by large players seeking liquidity.

Strength / Weakness: Strength shows how powerful a trend is—whether buyers (in an uptrend) or sellers (in a downtrend) are in firm control. Weakness indicates that the trend may slow down or reverse.

Supply Zones: Areas where strong selling has happened earlier, indicating potential resistance ahead.

Support: A price level where buying interest is strong enough to stop price from falling further.

Swing High: A swing high is a price point where the market reaches a temporary peak before reversing downward. It is typically formed when a candle (or a group of candles) has a higher high than the candles immediately before and after it. Swing highs represent areas where selling pressure has overcome buying pressure, often acting as resistance levels in the market.

Swing Low: A swing low is a price point where the market reaches a temporary bottom before reversing upward. It is formed when a candle (or group of candles) has a lower low than the candles immediately before and after it. Swing lows indicate areas where buying interest has emerged, often acting as support levels.

Swing Trading: Trades are held for a few days to a few weeks. Traders use daily charts and sometimes hourly charts to capture short- to medium-term price swings.

Technical Indicators: Technical indicators are mathematical tools applied on price and volume data to help understand trend, momentum, and strength. Examples include moving averages, RSI, MACD, and Bollinger Bands. They do not predict the market but help in making more informed trading decisions.

Time Frame: A time frame refers to the duration of each price bar or candle on a chart—such as 1 minute, 5 minutes, 15 minutes, 1 hour, daily, weekly, or monthly. It defines how price data is viewed and analysed over a specific period.

Trade Management: The process of handling a trade after entry—adjusting stop loss, booking profits, or exiting based on changing market conditions.

Traps (Bull Trap / Bear Trap): A bull trap occurs when price appears to break upward but quickly reverses down, trapping buyers. A bear trap is the opposite—price breaks down but reverses up, trapping sellers.

Trend (Uptrend, Downtrend, Sideways): A trend is the overall direction in which the market is moving. If prices are generally rising, it is an *uptrend*; if falling, a *downtrend*; and if moving within a range without clear direction, it is *sideways* or range-bound.

Trend Continuation: Trend continuation means the market pauses briefly (through consolidation or small pullbacks) and then continues moving in the same direction as before.

Trendline: A trendline is a straight line drawn on a chart connecting key highs or lows to show the direction of the trend. It helps identify support in an uptrend and resistance in a downtrend.

Trend Reversal: A trend reversal happens when the market changes its direction—for example, from uptrend to downtrend or vice versa. It signals a shift in control from buyers to sellers or sellers to buyers.

VIX (Volatility Index): An index that measures market volatility or fear. Higher VIX indicates higher uncertainty and sharp movements, while lower VIX suggests calm and stable markets.

Volatility: The degree of price movement—high volatility means big and fast price swings, while low volatility means slow and small movements.

Volume: The number of shares or contracts traded during a period. It shows the level of participation in the market.

Volume Breakout: A sudden increase in volume, usually confirming a strong move or breakout in price.

Volume Climax: A very high-volume spike, often marking the end of a strong trend (either buying climax or selling climax).

Volume Divergence: When price moves in one direction but volume does not support it, indicating possible weakness in the move.

Volume Dry-up: A period of very low volume, indicating lack of interest and often seen before a big move.

LET US EXPLORE

Given the critical role that technical analysis plays in both investing and trading—across all financial markets where price and volume exist—it becomes not just useful, but indispensable for anyone seeking consistent success. The real edge, however, lies not in knowing many indicators, but in deeply understanding how price behaves, how patterns repeat, and how market structure evolves across timeframes.

As we progress, the focus should be on diving deeper into the practical world of technical analysis—uncovering unique concepts, refined techniques, high-probability patterns, and those rare "golden nuggets" of insight that separate an average participant from a consistently profitable one. These are the elements that bring clarity amidst noise, confidence amidst uncertainty, and discipline amidst volatility.

Equipped with this deeper understanding, a trader or investor is not merely reacting to the market but is prepared, structured, and strategically aligned. This knowledge becomes your armour, your edge, and your arsenal—helping you stay ahead of the curve and make sharper, more informed decisions, ultimately guiding you toward achieving your investment and trading goals with greater consistency and conviction.

Chapter – 2

Price Action

The Building Blocks

Technical analysis is built on a few foundational pillars that together help decode market behaviour. At its core lies **price**, which reflects the collective action of all market participants, followed by **volume**, which indicates the **strength** and conviction behind that price movement. Surrounding these are essential elements such as trend identification, support and resistance levels, and timeframes, all of which help in understanding whether a market is trending, consolidating, or reversing. These components form the basic language of charts—once understood, they allow a participant to "read" the market rather than merely observe it.

Another key constituent of technical analysis is the use of indicators and patterns. Moving averages, Bollinger Bands, RSI, and VWAP help simplify complex price data into actionable insights, while candlestick patterns and chart formations reveal recurring behavioural tendencies of the market. Importantly, these tools are not meant to predict with certainty, but to provide probability-based guidance. When multiple elements align—price structure, trend, volume, and indicators—they create high-confidence setups that can significantly improve decision-making for both investors and traders.

With these fundamentals in place, the journey into technical analysis becomes both practical and powerful. The real learning begins when we move beyond theory and start connecting these elements in real market scenarios. So, get ready to dive deeper into this fascinating world—where charts tell stories, patterns reveal intent, and disciplined interpretation creates opportunity. Let us begin.

PRICE

Price, as the core element of technical analysis, is expressed through its fundamental **OHLC structure—Open, High, Low, and Close**—for every trading session or timeframe. This OHLC framework captures the complete story of market behaviour within a given period: the open reflects initial sentiment, the high and low define the battle range between buyers and sellers, and the close reveals the final dominance and conviction.

Whether viewed on intraday, daily, weekly, or monthly timeframes, this OHLC data forms the foundation upon which all price interpretation, pattern recognition, and trading decisions are built.

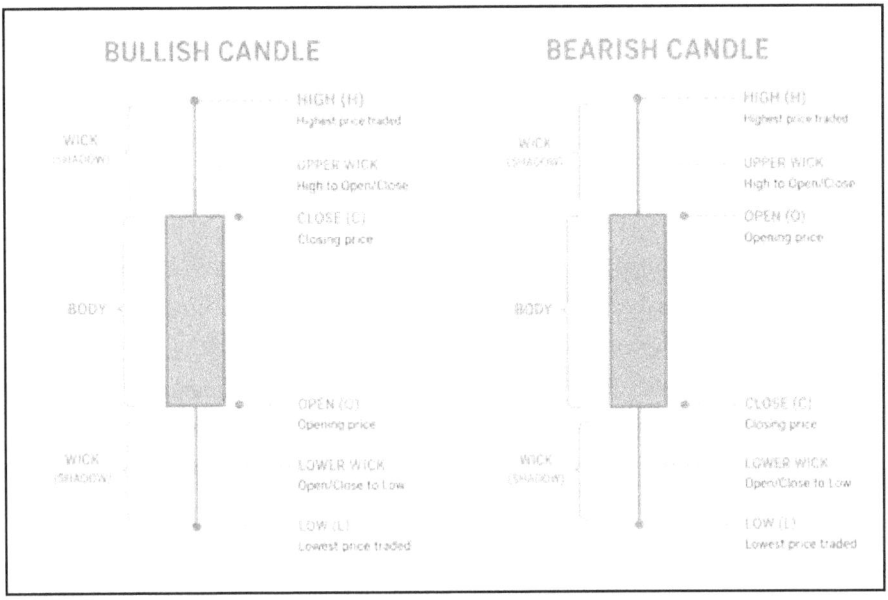

To interpret this price data effectively, traders and investors rely on different charting formats, each offering a unique lens. **Candlestick charts**, built directly from OHLC data, are the most widely used as they visually represent market psychology and enable identification of patterns like doji, hammer, and engulfing formations. **Heikin-Ashi charts** smooth out price action to highlight trends more clearly, making them useful for trend-following strategies. **Line charts**, typically based on closing prices, provide a simplified view for long-term investors. Meanwhile, **Renko charts** filter out noise by focusing only on price movement, ignoring time, and are helpful in identifying strong trends. **Point & Figure (P&F) charts** further abstract price action by emphasizing supply-demand imbalances, making them effective for spotting breakouts and reversals.

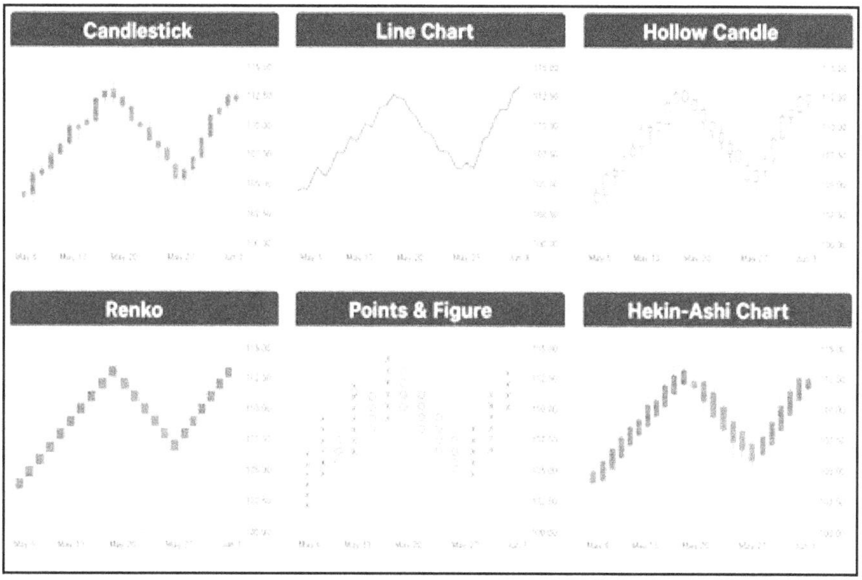

Each of these chart types derives its essence from the same OHLC data but serves different purposes depending on the trader's objective and style. While candlestick charts are ideal for detailed price action analysis, Heikin-Ashi aids in clarity of trend, Renko and P&F help eliminate noise, and line charts simplify broader direction. Mastering how to read and interpret OHLC-based price across these charting methods is fundamental—because regardless of the tool used, it is ultimately the understanding of price behaviour that lies at the heart of successful investing and trading.

We have discussed about different tradable Chart Patterns in Chapter 12.

How Price is Determined:

Price discovery in financial markets is essentially the process through which buyers and sellers agree on a fair value for an asset. In the cash (non-derivative) segment—whether it is shares, cryptocurrencies, or commodities—this happens through continuous interaction between **bid prices** (what buyers are willing to pay) and **ask prices** (what sellers are willing to accept). The order book reflects this dynamic: when a buyer's bid matches a seller's ask, a transaction occurs, and that traded price becomes the latest market price.

When demand is strong, buyers are willing to place bids at progressively higher levels to secure the asset. As these higher bids match with sellers' asks, the traded price moves upward—this is how an **uptrend** forms. Conversely, when supply dominates, sellers lower their asking prices to attract buyers. As bids meet these lower asks, **prices decline**. Thus, price movement is nothing but a continuous balancing act between demand and supply, reflected through bid-ask matching.

In the F&O (Futures & Options) segment, however, price discovery involves additional layers of complexity. For futures, prices are influenced not only by spot demand and supply but also by factors such as cost of carry, interest rates, and expectations of future price movements.

Options introduce even more dimensions—premiums are shaped by intrinsic value and time value, along with key variables known as "Greeks" (such as delta, theta, and vega), which capture sensitivity to price, time decay, and volatility. Expiry timelines and volatility expectations further play a critical role in how option prices evolve.

If you wish to gain a deeper and practical understanding of F&O concepts and trading, you may consider reading *The Intelligent F&O Trader: Volume I, II & III*, which presents these ideas in a comprehensive yet simplified manner. It is available on all major online platforms like Amazon and its ebook version is available on kindle and google play.

VOLUME

Volume is the second pillar of technical analysis after price, and in many ways, it is the **force behind price movement**. While price tells us *what* is happening, volume tells us *how strongly* it is happening. Every traded unit represents participation—hence volume reflects the intensity of buyer–seller interaction in a given timeframe. A price move supported by strong volume carries conviction, whereas a similar move on weak volume often lacks sustainability. Thus, volume is not just a confirming indicator—it is a **truth detector** of price action.

At its core, volume reflects the ongoing battle between buyers and sellers. Every transaction has both a buyer and a seller, but what matters is **who is more aggressive**. When buyers are willing to transact at higher prices, volume pushes price upward; when sellers dominate and accept lower prices, volume drives price downward. The **net effect of volume in a timeframe or trading session** is therefore seen in the price spread and closing position—wide-range candles with high volume indicate strong dominance, while narrow-range candles with high volume may indicate absorption or indecision. This interplay reveals whether smart money is accumulating (buying quietly within a range) or distributing (selling into strength), often before a visible price breakout or breakdown.

Volume is typically measured and visualized using **volume bars**, which show the total traded quantity for each candle or timeframe. A sudden spike in volume often signals a **shift in market participation**, such as breakout, climax, or reversal zones. Study of price candles with volume bars gives very insightful information, like:

- rising price with rising volume suggests strength and continuation;
- rising price with falling volume hints at exhaustion;
- falling price with increasing volume signals panic or strong selling;
- declining volume during a fall may indicate weakening momentum.

Beyond simple volume bars, advanced tools like **volume profile** provide deeper insights by mapping volume across price levels rather than time. This helps identify high-volume zones (areas of acceptance or fair value) and low-volume zones (areas of rejection or fast movement), enabling traders to understand where the market has spent the most time and built positions.

In essence, volume acts as a **magnifying glass for price action**, helping traders decode hidden activity, validate trends, anticipate reversals, and align themselves with informed market participants. Mastering volume analysis, therefore, adds depth and clarity to trading decisions, making it an indispensable tool for both investors and traders.

We have further discussed in detail about volume and price-volume analysis in Chapter 4.

STRENGTH

Strength in technical analysis represents the **quality and sustainability of a price move**. While momentum reflects the *speed* of price movement, strength reflects the *conviction* behind that movement. A market may move up or down quickly, but unless that move is backed by strength, it is unlikely to sustain. Thus, strength is what converts a mere price move into a **trend**—an uptrend when buyers consistently dominate, and a downtrend when sellers maintain control over time.

Strength is deeply interconnected with both **price and volume**. Price shows direction, volume shows participation, and strength emerges from the **alignment of both**. For instance, a rising market with expanding volume, strong bullish candles (closing near highs), and shallow pullbacks indicates strong buying pressure—hence a strong uptrend. Conversely, falling prices accompanied by increasing volume, long bearish candles, and weak bounces reflect strong selling pressure. If price moves but volume contracts, or candles show rejection (long wicks), it signals weakening strength, even if direction appears intact.

At a micro level, strength is a reflection of **buyer vs seller dominance**. When buyers are aggressive—absorbing supply and pushing prices higher despite resistance—the market exhibits strength. When sellers overpower demand and consistently push prices lower, strength shifts to the downside. Importantly, strength is not just about who is active, but *who is in control at the close of each timeframe*. Repeated strong closes in one direction indicate sustained control, which is the hallmark of a trending market.

Strength can be measured using a combination of tools and observations. Indicators like Relative Strength Index (RSI), moving averages (like 20 SMA or 50 SMA), and price structure (higher highs/higher lows or vice versa) help gauge trend strength. Additionally, observing how price behaves around key levels—such as VWAP, support/resistance, or AVWAP—provides insight into whether strength is building or fading. Strong trends respect moving averages and continue in their direction, while weak trends frequently violate these levels.

Ultimately, strength conveys a powerful message: it tells us whether a trend is likely to **continue, exhaust, or reverse**. A strong market tends to move with clarity, offers better follow-through, and rewards trend-following strategies. A weak market, on the other hand, is prone to whipsaws, false breakouts, and traps. Therefore, understanding and aligning with strength—rather than just direction—enables traders and investors to participate with higher conviction, better timing, and improved probability of success.

MOMENTUM

Momentum in technical analysis refers to the **speed and acceleration of price movement**—it tells us how fast and forcefully price is moving in a particular direction. While trend defines *direction* (uptrend or downtrend), momentum defines *intensity*. A strong uptrend with rising momentum reflects aggressive buying, whereas a downtrend with increasing momentum indicates panic or forceful selling. Momentum is what **drives price away from its averages**, creating expansions, breakouts, and directional moves that traders seek to capture.

Momentum is closely linked with **price and volume**. Price provides direction, volume reflects participation, and momentum emerges when **both align with force**. For example, a breakout accompanied by rising volume and expanding candle bodies indicates strong momentum—buyers are chasing price higher. On the other hand, if price moves upward but candles shrink and volume dries up, it signals weakening momentum despite the upward direction. Thus, momentum is not just about movement—it is about **the quality and urgency of that movement**.

From a buyer–seller dynamics perspective, momentum reflects **aggression imbalance**. In a high-momentum upmove, buyers are willing to buy at higher prices without waiting, overpowering sellers decisively. In a strong downmove, sellers hit bids aggressively, forcing prices lower. Momentum becomes sustainable when this imbalance continues over multiple candles and timeframes. However, when the opposing side begins to absorb this aggression—visible through long wicks, smaller candle bodies, or divergence—momentum starts weakening, often preceding consolidation or reversal.

Momentum can be measured using both **visual price action and indicators**. Indicators like RSI (Relative Strength Index), MACD, and rate-of-change tools help quantify momentum. Rising RSI with price indicates strengthening momentum, while divergence (price rising but RSI falling) signals weakening momentum. Similarly, observing candle structure—wide-range candles, consecutive directional closes, and minimal pullbacks—indicates strong momentum. In contrast, choppy candles, overlapping ranges, and frequent reversals suggest weak or fading momentum.

Distinguishing between **real and fake momentum** is critical. Real momentum is supported by volume expansion, clean breakouts, and follow-through in subsequent candles. Fake momentum often appears as sudden spikes (news-driven or trap moves) with little follow-through, often reversing quickly. Sustainable momentum respects key levels like VWAP or moving averages, whereas unsustainable momentum tends to overshoot and snap back.

Ultimately, momentum acts as the engine of the trend. Strong momentum creates opportunities for trend continuation trades, while weakening momentum provides early signals for exits or reversals. Understanding momentum—how it builds, sustains, and fades—enables traders to align with powerful moves, avoid traps, and participate with higher precision and confidence.

ABOUT PRICE ACTION

Price action is the **purest form of technical analysis**—it is the direct study of how price moves over time without heavy dependence on lagging indicators. It reflects the real-time interaction between buyers and sellers and captures the **collective psychology of the market**. Every tick, every candle, every breakout or rejection is a footprint of decision-making by market participants. In essence, price action is not just about price—it is about **behaviour, intent, and conviction** embedded within price movement.

The core constituents of price action include OHLC (Open, High, Low, Close) of each candle, candle structure (body and wicks), market structure (higher highs, lower lows), and key levels such as support, resistance, VWAP, and moving averages. These elements together form a narrative. For example, strong bullish candles closing near their highs indicate buyer dominance, while long upper wicks near resistance signal selling pressure. Thus, price action is a language—and candles, patterns, and levels are its vocabulary.

Price action is deeply correlated with **volume, strength, and momentum**. Price gives direction, volume gives participation, strength gives sustainability, and momentum gives speed. When all align—for instance, price breakout with rising volume, strong candle closes, and expanding momentum—it signifies a high-quality, sustainable move. Conversely, if price moves without volume support or shows repeated rejection (long wicks), it indicates weak or fake moves. Hence, price action helps distinguish between real vs false breakouts, strong vs weak trends, and sustainable vs exhausted moves.

From a buyer–seller dynamics perspective, price action reveals who is in control. If buyers consistently push price higher with minimal pullbacks, it reflects strength and control. If sellers repeatedly reject higher prices and force price lower, it indicates supply dominance. The key lies in observing how price behaves at important zones—does it break through with conviction or get rejected sharply? Does it sustain above/below levels or quickly revert? These observations help form a clear trading or investment view.

Reading price action effectively involves a **top-down approach**—starting from higher timeframes to identify the broader trend, then refining entries on lower timeframes. Tools like trendlines, support/resistance, VWAP, moving averages, Bollinger Bands, and volume analysis complement price action but do not replace it. The goal is not to overload charts with indicators, but to interpret price behaviour in context—structure, location, and reaction.

Mastering price action is a skill developed over time through observation, screen time, and disciplined practice. It requires training the eye to recognize patterns, understanding the context behind movements, and aligning one's emotions with what price is communicating. There is no shortcut or holy grail—only consistency in learning, patience in execution, and discipline in risk management. Once mastered, price action becomes a powerful edge, enabling traders and investors to read the market with clarity, act with conviction, and navigate uncertainty with confidence.

MASTERING PRICE ACTION

Technical analysis stands as one of the most practical and widely applicable approaches to understanding financial markets. It is built on the foundational belief that **price discounts everything** and that recurring patterns in price behaviour can offer meaningful insights into future movement. Its core constituents—**price, volume, strength, and momentum**—work together to form a comprehensive framework through which market participants can interpret trends, identify opportunities, and manage risk. Unlike purely theoretical models, technical analysis is rooted in observable data and evolving market behaviour, making it highly relevant across asset classes, timeframes, and trading styles.

At the heart of technical analysis lies **price action**, which serves as the most direct and reliable expression of market sentiment. Price action encapsulates the ongoing battle between buyers and sellers, revealing not just direction but also conviction, exhaustion, and intent. It helps traders distinguish between strong and weak trends, sustainable and fragile moves, and genuine breakouts versus deceptive traps. By studying how price reacts at key levels and how it behaves over time, one can develop a deeper, more intuitive understanding of market dynamics—far beyond what standalone indicators can provide.

Among the many tools available, certain elements form the **core pillars of price action analysis**—notably **moving averages, VWAP / AVWAP, and support and resistance levels**. These are not merely indicators but dynamic reference points that reflect where price finds balance, momentum, and reaction. Moving averages help identify trend direction and dynamic support/resistance; VWAP and AVWAP provide insights into institutional positioning and fair value zones; and support/resistance levels highlight critical areas of demand and supply where decisions are made. Together, these elements create a structured lens through which price action can be read with clarity and confidence.

Given their significance, it becomes essential to first build a strong foundation by deeply understanding these fundamental aspects. Mastery of moving averages, VWAP/AVWAP, and support/resistance will not only sharpen one's ability to read charts but also enhance decision-making in both trading and investing.

However, before we venture into understanding the various aspects of price action—such as moving averages, VWAP/AVWAP, and key levels like PR/PS—it is essential to first lay a strong foundational understanding of **deciphering candlestick patterns**.

Candlesticks are the most basic yet powerful building blocks of chart reading, as they directly reflect the ongoing battle between buyers and sellers in every timeframe. A clear grasp of how different candles form, what they signify, and how they behave in different market contexts will go a long way in helping us interpret price movement with clarity. This foundational skill will seamlessly integrate into all other aspects of technical analysis—be it price action, chart patterns, or indicator-based strategies—making our overall market understanding sharper, more structured, and far more effective.

Chapter – 3

Candlestick Patterns

The Footprints

Candlestick patterns form one of the most fundamental pillars of technical analysis. Each candlestick represents the open, high, low, and close (OHLC) of price over a specific timeframe, but more importantly, it reflects the **underlying sentiment and psychology of market participants** during that period. The shape, size, and position of a candle reveal whether buyers were in control, sellers dominated, or if the market remained undecided. In essence, candlesticks are not just visual representations of price—they are **real-time footprints of demand and supply dynamics**, capturing the ongoing battle between fear and greed.

The significance of candlestick patterns lies in their ability to provide **early signals of trend continuation, reversal, or indecision**. A single candle, or a combination of candles, can indicate exhaustion of a trend, emergence of momentum, or a pause before the next move. When these patterns appear at key locations—such as near support and resistance, moving averages, or VWAP / AVWAP—they become even more powerful and actionable. This makes candlestick analysis an indispensable tool for traders and investors alike, helping them anticipate potential market moves rather than reacting late.

Studying candlestick patterns is therefore essential for anyone seeking to develop a strong foundation in technical analysis. They serve as the **building blocks for understanding price action**, which in turn forms the basis for interpreting chart patterns, trend structures, and indicator behaviour. Whether one is analysing breakouts, reversals, or range-bound markets, the ability to read and interpret candlesticks adds depth and clarity to decision-making. In many ways, mastering candlestick patterns is akin to learning the language of the market—once understood, it enables a trader or investor to read charts with confidence, precision, and a deeper sense of insight.

The study of candlestick patterns can be effectively categorized based on what they represent in terms of market sentiment—namely, patterns that indicate:

- **bullish bias**,
- **bearish outlook**,
- **indecision or uncertainty.**

Each category conveys a distinct message about the balance of power between buyers and sellers. Bullish patterns signal potential upward movement as buying strength emerges, bearish patterns indicate possible downside pressure driven by sellers, while indecision patterns highlight a temporary equilibrium where neither side has clear control. This classification helps simplify the understanding of candlesticks and enables traders and investors to interpret market behaviour more systematically and contextually.

Let us study some of the prominent candle stick patterns under each of the aforesaid categories.

BULLISH CANDLE-STICK PATTERNS

Bullish candlestick patterns represent situations where buying interest begins to dominate selling pressure, often signalling a potential upward move or reversal in price.

These patterns typically emerge after a decline or near important support zones, indicating that buyers are stepping in with conviction and absorbing supply. The structure, size, and positioning of these candles help reveal the strength of demand and the likelihood of continuation in the upward direction. When **supported by factors such as volume, trend context, or key technical levels**, bullish candlestick patterns become powerful tools for identifying potential buying opportunities.

There are many bullish candlestick patterns that one can explore and understand over time with deeper study and practice. For now, we will focus on a few prominent bullish candlestick patterns to build a strong foundational understanding. Some of the most important candle-stick patterns indicating bullish bias / reversal typically emerging after a decline or near support – thus signalling potential buying strength are discussed below:

Hammer:

The Hammer is a single-candle bullish reversal pattern that typically appears after a decline. It has a small real body near the top and a long lower shadow, indicating that sellers initially pushed prices down but buyers stepped in strongly to recover most of the losses.

Shows rejection of lower prices and potential bullish reversal.

This rejection of lower prices suggests emerging buying strength and a potential reversal, especially when formed near a key support level.

Inverted Hammer:

The Inverted Hammer forms after a downtrend and features a small body with a long upper shadow and little to no lower shadow.

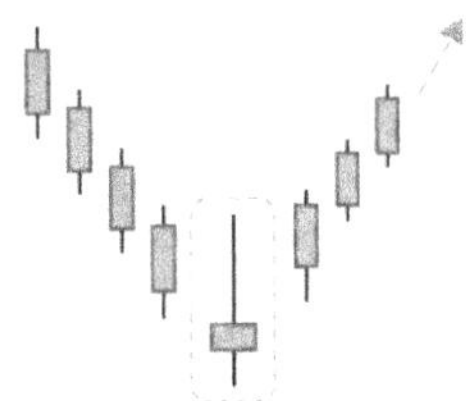

Shows rejection of higher prices and potential bullish reversal.

It indicates that buyers attempted to push prices higher during the session, showing early signs of strength. Although confirmation is required in the next candle, this pattern often signals a possible shift from bearish to bullish sentiment.

Bullish Engulfing:

The Bullish Engulfing pattern is a strong two-candle reversal formation. It occurs when a small bearish candle is followed by a larger bullish candle that completely engulfs the previous one.

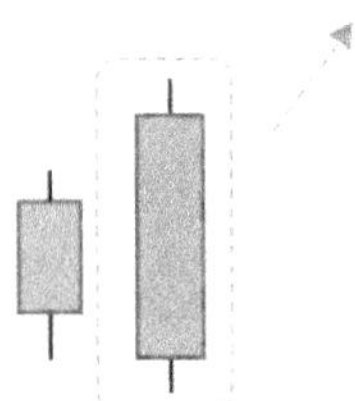

Bullish candle engulfs the previous bearish candle.

This pattern reflects a decisive shift in control from sellers to buyers, often indicating the start of a new upward trend when formed after a decline.

Piercing Pattern:

The Piercing Pattern is a two-candle bullish reversal pattern seen after a downtrend. The first candle is bearish, followed by a bullish candle that opens lower but closes more than halfway into the body of the previous candle.

This indicates that buyers are regaining control and suggests a potential upward reversal.

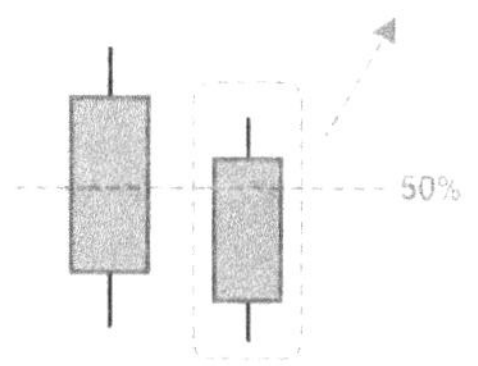

Bullish candle closes above the 50% level of the previous bearish candle.

Morning Star:

The Morning Star is a three-candle bullish reversal pattern that appears at the bottom of a downtrend. It consists of a strong bearish candle, followed by a small-bodied candle (indecision), and then a strong bullish candle that closes well into the first candle's body.

This formation reflects a transition from selling pressure to buying dominance, signalling a likely trend reversal.

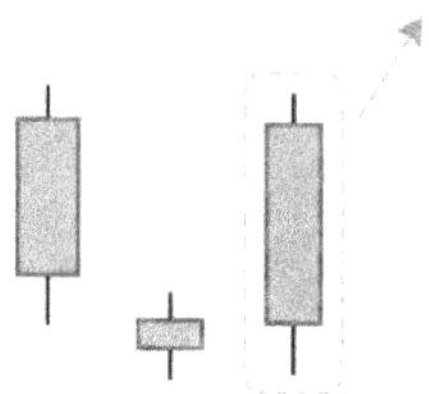
Three-candle pattern that signals a bullish reversal.

Three White Soldiers:

The Three White Soldiers pattern is a powerful bullish continuation or reversal signal, consisting of three consecutive long bullish candles with higher closes.

It indicates sustained buying pressure and strong momentum, often marking the beginning of a significant upward move when formed after a downtrend or consolidation.

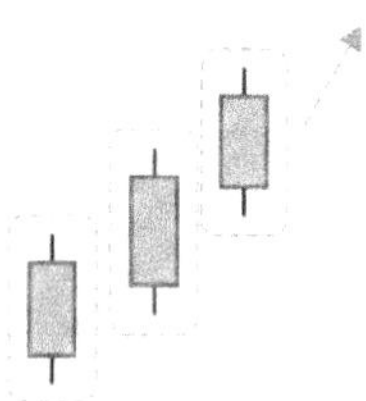
Three strong bullish candles in a row. Indicates continued bullish momentum.

Bullish Harami:

The Bullish Harami is a two-candle pattern where a small bullish candle forms completely within the body of a preceding large bearish candle.

It reflects a slowdown in selling pressure and the emergence of buying interest.

While not as strong as engulfing patterns, it signals a potential reversal, especially when supported by other indicators.

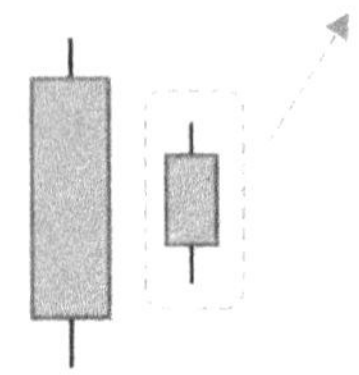

Small bullish candle inside a larger bearish candle. Signals potential bullish reversal.

Rising Three Methods:

The Rising Three Methods is a continuation pattern that occurs during an uptrend. It consists of a strong bullish candle, followed by a series of smaller bearish or neutral candles that remain within the range of the first candle, and then another strong bullish candle.

This pattern indicates a temporary pause or consolidation before the uptrend resumes with renewed strength.

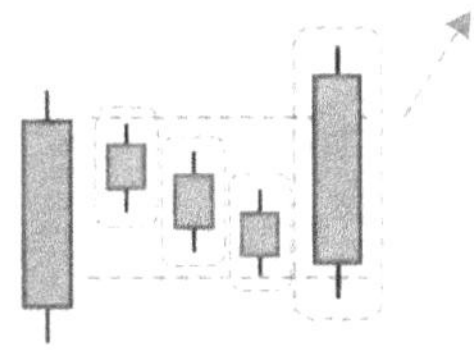

Bullish continuation pattern. Three small bearish candles within the range of a big bullish candle, followed by another strong bullish candle.

Bullish Marubozu:

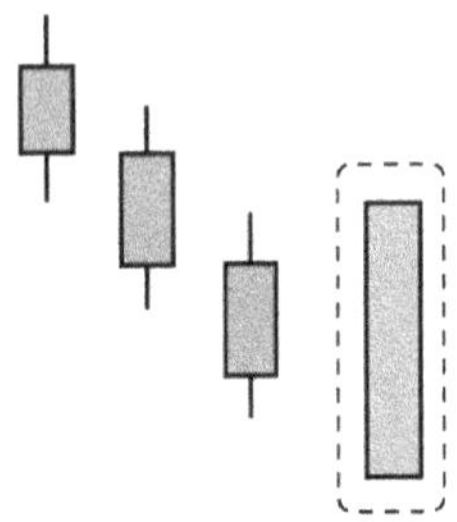

Bullish Marubozu

The Bullish Marubozu is a strong bullish candle with little to no shadows on either side, indicating that price opened near the low and closed near the high of the session.

It reflects complete dominance of buyers throughout the period and often signals strong upward momentum or continuation of an uptrend.

BEARISH CANDLE-STICK PATTERNS

Bearish candlestick patterns represent scenarios where selling pressure begins to dominate buying interest, often signalling a potential downward move or reversal in price.

These patterns typically emerge after an uptrend or near important resistance levels, indicating that buyers are losing control and sellers are stepping in with strength. The structure and positioning of these candles help identify weakening momentum, distribution, or exhaustion of an uptrend. When **supported by volume, resistance zones, or broader trend context**, bearish candlestick patterns become powerful tools for identifying potential selling opportunities or cautioning against further long positions.

There are many bearish candlestick patterns that can be explored and understood with deeper learning and experience over time. For now, we will focus on a few prominent bearish candlestick patterns to build a strong and practical foundation.

Some of the most important candle-stick patterns indicating bearish bias/ reversal typically emerging after a decline or near support – thus signalling potential selling strength are discussed below:

Shooting Star:

The Shooting Star is a bearish reversal pattern that appears after an uptrend. It has a small real body near the lower end of the candle with a long upper shadow, indicating that buyers pushed prices higher during the session but sellers eventually took control and forced prices down.

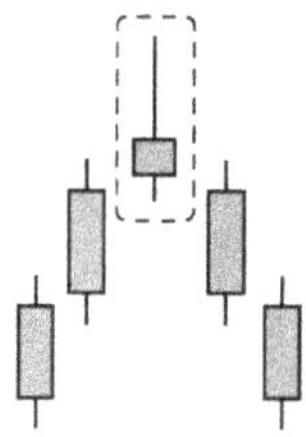

Shooting Star

This rejection of higher levels signals potential weakness and a possible reversal.

Hanging Man:

The Hanging Man forms at the top of an uptrend and resembles a Hammer in structure, with a small body and a long lower shadow.

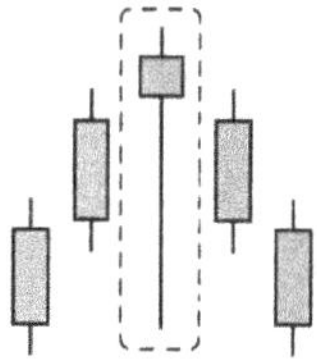

Hanging Man

It indicates that despite the upward trend, selling pressure emerged during the session.

Although buyers managed to push the price back up, the presence of strong selling suggests vulnerability and a potential trend reversal.

Bearish Engulfing:

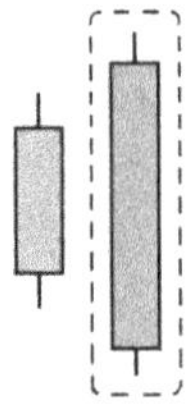

Bearish Engulfing

The Bearish Engulfing pattern is a strong two-candle reversal formation. It occurs when a small bullish candle is followed by a larger bearish candle that completely engulfs the previous candle's body.

This pattern reflects a clear shift in control from buyers to sellers, often indicating the beginning of a downward move.

Dark Cloud Cover:

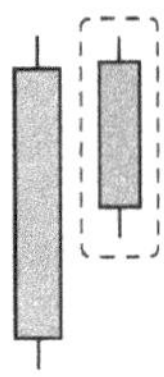

Dark Cloud Cover

The Dark Cloud Cover is a two-candle bearish reversal pattern seen after an uptrend. The first candle is bullish, followed by a bearish candle that opens higher but closes below the midpoint of the previous candle's body.

This indicates that sellers are gaining control and suggests a potential reversal to the downside.

Evening Star:

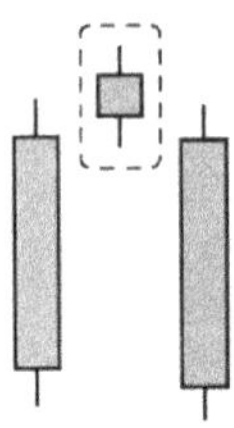

Evening Star

The Evening Star is a three-candle bearish reversal pattern that appears at the top of an uptrend. It consists of a strong bullish candle, followed by a small-bodied candle (indicating indecision), and then a strong bearish candle that closes well into the first candle's body.

This formation signals a shift from buying strength to selling dominance.

Three Black Crows:

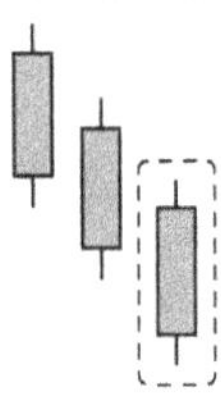

Three Black Crows

The Three Black Crows pattern consists of three consecutive long bearish candles with lower closes.

It indicates sustained selling pressure and strong downward momentum.

When formed after an uptrend or consolidation, it often signals the start of a significant bearish move.

Bearish Harami:

The Bearish Harami is a two-candle pattern where a small bearish candle forms within the body of a preceding large bullish candle.

It indicates a slowdown in buying momentum and the possible emergence of selling pressure.

While not as strong as engulfing patterns, it suggests a potential reversal when supported by other signals.

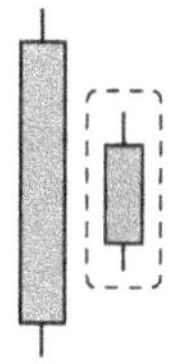

Bearish Harami

Falling Three Methods:

The Falling Three Methods is a continuation pattern that occurs during a downtrend. It consists of a strong bearish candle, followed by a series of smaller bullish or neutral candles that remain within the range of the first candle, and then another strong bearish candle.

This pattern reflects a temporary pause before the downtrend resumes with renewed selling strength.

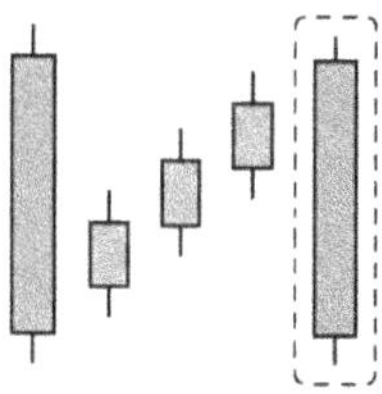

Falling Three Methods (continuation bearish)

Bearish Marubozu:

The Bearish Marubozu is the opposite of a bullish one, with little to no shadows and a full-bodied red candle. It shows that price opened near the high and closed near the low, indicating sustained selling pressure throughout the session.

This pattern signals strong bearish momentum or continuation of a downtrend.

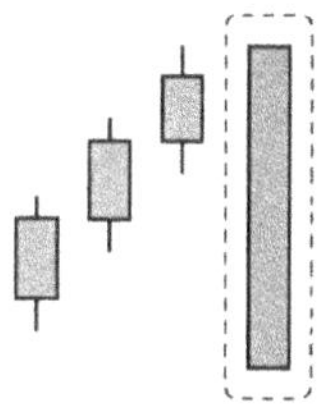

Bearish Marubozu

CANDLE-STICK PATTERNS INDICATING UNCERTAINITY

Candlestick patterns that indicate indecisiveness or uncertainty reflect a temporary balance between buyers and sellers, where neither side is able to establish clear control over price. These patterns often emerge during phases of consolidation, near key support or resistance levels, or after a strong trending move where the market begins to pause and reassess direction. Structurally, they are typically characterized by small real bodies, long wicks on either or both sides, or overlapping price action—signalling hesitation and lack of conviction.

Such patterns serve as an important caution signal for traders and investors. They suggest that the prevailing trend may be losing momentum, and that a potential reversal, continuation pause, or breakout setup could be forming. However, by themselves, these patterns do not provide a definitive directional bias. Instead, they call for patience, observation, and confirmation through subsequent price action, volume behaviour, or alignment with broader technical factors such as support/resistance or moving averages.

From a practical standpoint, indecisive candlestick patterns advise market participants to avoid aggressive entries and instead wait for clarity. They are often precursors to significant moves, especially when followed by strong breakout or breakdown candles. Therefore, rather than being signals for immediate action, **they are signals to prepare, to watch closely, and to let the market reveal its next intention** before committing capital.

While there are many candlestick patterns that indicate indecision or uncertainty, we will focus on a few important and widely observed ones in the discussion below.

Doji:

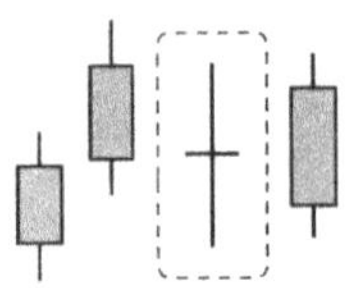

Doji

A Doji is formed when the open and close prices are nearly equal, resulting in a very small or non-existent body. It reflects indecision between buyers and sellers.

Depending on its position (after an uptrend or downtrend) and surrounding context, it may signal a potential reversal or simply a pause in the trend.

Spinning Top:

The Spinning Top has a small real body with relatively long upper and lower shadows. It indicates indecision and a balance between buying and selling forces.

While it does not confirm a reversal on its own, it suggests that the current trend may be losing strength and a potential shift could be near.

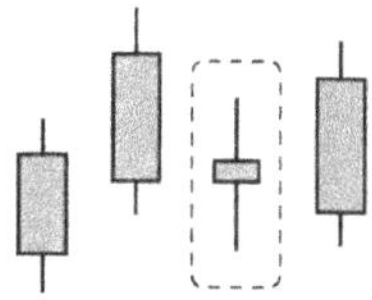

Spinning Top

Inside Bar:

An Inside Bar is a candle that forms completely within the range (high and low) of the previous candle. It represents consolidation and reduced volatility.

This pattern often precedes a breakout, and traders watch for a move beyond the high or low of the mother candle to determine direction.

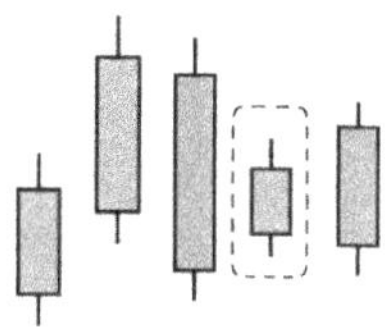

Inside Bar

Outside Bar:

An Outside Bar, also known as an engulfing bar, occurs when the current candle's range fully engulfs the previous candle's high and low.

It indicates increased volatility and strong participation. Depending on the direction of the close, it can signal either a bullish or bearish reversal or continuation.

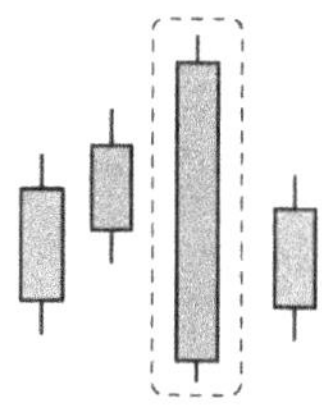

Outside Bar

UNDERSTANDING THE FOOTPRINTS

Understanding and remembering candlestick patterns is not merely an academic exercise—it is a practical skill that significantly enhances one's ability to read and interpret price action. Each pattern represents a story of buyer–seller interaction within a given timeframe, and when observed in the right context—near support, resistance, or within a trend—they provide meaningful clues about potential market direction. A trader or investor who becomes familiar with these patterns begins to "see" the market more clearly, as price movements start to convey intent rather than appear random.

While we have discussed some of the more prominent candlestick patterns, it is important to recognise that there are many more variations and combinations that exist. True mastery comes not from memorisation alone, but from consistent observation—both during live market sessions and through post-market chart analysis. Over time, this practice sharpens one's ability to identify patterns quickly, understand their reliability in different market conditions, and integrate them effectively with other technical tools. This continuous learning process transforms candlestick patterns into a powerful lens through which price action can be interpreted with greater depth and confidence.

With this foundational understanding of price and its behavioural patterns now in place, we are better prepared to move forward into more advanced aspects of price action. In the sections ahead, we will explore key tools such as VWAP, AVWAP, and moving averages—each of which plays a critical role in defining trend, support and resistance, and market equilibrium. These concepts, when combined with candlestick insights, will further strengthen our ability to make informed and precise trading and investment decisions.

Chapter – 4

Price & Volume

Volume Rules the Price

In technical analysis, price is the visible outcome of market action, but **volume is the underlying force** that gives that action meaning. While price reflects the direction in which the market / asset is moving, volume reveals the level of participation and commitment behind that move. A price trend without volume is often fragile, whereas a trend supported by expanding volume carries conviction and is more likely to sustain. For any trader or investor, understanding this relationship is essential to separating meaningful moves from noise.

Why volume is important? It is important because volume reveals multiple critical facets of price behaviour that are highly significant from both a trading and investment perspective. It provides deep insights into the **momentum within a trend**, helping assess whether a move is gaining strength or losing steam; it reflects phases of **accumulation and distribution**, where smart money quietly builds or exits positions; it captures the underlying **demand–supply dynamics**, indicating whether buying or selling pressure is dominant; and it plays a crucial role in identifying the strength and reliability of **breakouts and breakdowns**. In essence, volume acts as a lens through which the true intent and strength behind price movements can be understood.

SIGNIFICANCE OF VOLUME

Volume represents the number of shares or contracts traded over a given period and serves as a direct measure of market/asset participation. High volume indicates strong involvement from market participants, often including institutional players, while low volume suggests limited interest. The key idea is that **price movements backed by high volume carry conviction**, whereas those occurring on low volume are often weak and unreliable. In this sense, volume acts as a validator of price action, confirming whether a move is supported by real demand or supply.

Let us now explore these key aspects in detail.

Institutional Participation: The Real Driver Behind Volume:

Volume is often the **footprint of institutional activity**. Large market participants—such as mutual funds, hedge funds, and proprietary desks—cannot execute large orders without impacting price. Their buying and selling naturally create spikes and expansions in volume. When a price move is accompanied by a noticeable increase in volume, it often suggests institutional involvement. This is important because institutional money tends to drive sustained trends.

Conversely, price movements on **low volume are often retail-driven** and lack the strength to continue for long. Learning to identify where institutions are likely participating allows traders to align themselves with the dominant force in the market rather than trading against it.

Momentum and Volume: Measuring the Strength of a Move:

Momentum in the market is not just about the **speed of price movement**, but also about the **strength** behind it—and volume plays a crucial role in validating that strength.

When price accelerates in a particular direction and volume expands simultaneously, it indicates strong momentum and increasing participation. This suggests that traders are not only agreeing with the direction but are actively committing capital to it.

On the other hand, if price moves sharply but volume remains subdued or starts declining, the momentum is questionable. Such moves are often short-lived and may result in sharp reversals once the limited participation dries up.

Breakout and Breakdown Dynamics: Volume as a Validator:

Breakouts and breakdowns are among the most traded setups in technical analysis, and volume is critical in validating them.

A breakout above a resistance level or a breakdown below support becomes meaningful only when **supported by a surge in volume**. High volume at these levels indicates that a large number of participants are willing to transact at new price zones, confirming a shift in market consensus.

In contrast, breakouts or breakdowns that occur on low volume are often deceptive. These "false moves" lack participation and can quickly reverse, trapping traders who entered prematurely.

Thus, volume acts as a filter to distinguish genuine moves from market noise.

Accumulation and Distribution: The Silent Action of Smart Money:

Markets often move through phases of accumulation and distribution before major trends begin or end.

During accumulation, **institutional players gradually build** positions at lower price levels without causing significant price increases. This phase is typically characterized by sideways price movement with subtle increases in volume on up moves.

Conversely, during distribution, institutions begin offloading their holdings near the top of a trend. Price may still move sideways or slightly upward, but volume often increases on down moves, signalling selling pressure beneath the surface. Recognizing these phases through price–volume behaviour allows traders to anticipate future breakouts or reversals with greater confidence.

Demand and Supply Dynamics: Volume as a Reflection of Imbalance:

At its core, the market is driven by demand and supply.

Price rises when demand exceeds supply and falls when supply exceeds demand. Volume provides insight into **how strong this imbalance is**.

For example, a sharp rise in price with high volume suggests aggressive buying, where demand is overwhelming supply—indicating imbalance is favouring demand. Similarly, a sharp fall with high volume indicates aggressive selling, where supply dominates demand—indicating imbalance is favouring supply.

When price moves occur on low volume, it suggests that the **imbalance is weak** and may not sustain. Understanding volume in this context helps traders assess whether a move is backed by genuine demand or merely a temporary fluctuation.

Candlestick Patterns and Volume Confirmation:

Candlestick patterns offer visual clues about market sentiment, but their reliability increases significantly when combined with volume analysis.

A bullish candlestick pattern, such as an engulfing pattern or a strong breakout candle, gains credibility when accompanied by high volume, indicating strong buying interest. Similarly, bearish patterns become more meaningful when supported by increased selling volume.

On the other hand, candlestick patterns that form on low volume often lack conviction and may fail to produce the expected outcome.

Volume, therefore, acts as a confirmation layer that enhances the effectiveness of price-based signals.

Climax Volume: Identifying Market Extremes:

Climax volume represents a sudden and **significant spike in volume**, often occurring at the end of a strong trend.

At market tops, this may appear as extremely high volume with limited upward price progress, indicating that buying is being absorbed by selling—often a sign of distribution.

At market bottoms, climax volume may accompany sharp declines followed by stabilization, reflecting panic selling or capitulation.

These moments often mark turning points in the market, where the prevailing trend exhausts itself and reverses.

Volume Divergence: Early Signals of Weakness or Strength:

One of the most insightful aspects of volume analysis is divergence between price and volume.

When price continues to rise but volume starts to decline, it suggests that buying interest is fading, even though price is still moving upward. This often precedes a reversal or consolidation. Similarly, when price declines but volume decreases, it indicates that selling pressure is weakening, potentially signalling the formation of a bottom.

These divergences provide early warning signs, allowing traders to prepare for possible changes in trend before they become obvious. It is therefore absolutely necessary to understand the price-volume co-relation. Discussed below are the different aspects of price-volume analysis.

PRICE-VOLUME ANALYSIS

As already highlighted, price and volume together form a complete narrative of market behaviour. While price reflects direction, volume reveals the intensity, participation, and conviction behind that direction.

Price–volume analysis is one of the most fundamental and insightful tools in technical analysis. While price reflects the outcome of market activity, volume reveals the intensity and participation behind that activity. Together, they form a powerful framework for understanding not just what the market is doing, but *why* it is doing so. Every price movement—whether a trend, reversal, or consolidation—carries a deeper meaning when interpreted alongside volume. For a trader, mastering this relationship is essential to distinguishing genuine moves from deceptive ones.

Thus, the real depth of understanding comes from studying the different permutations and combinations between price movement and volume behaviour. Each **combination of price candle and volume bar** tells a different story about trend strength, weakness, continuation, or reversal combinations of the price-volume relationship are discussed below.

Price Rising with Increasing Volume: Strong Bullish Participation:

When price rises along with expanding volume, it signals strong demand and increasing participation. This is typically driven by institutional buying, where large players are actively accumulating positions.

The alignment of price and volume confirms that the trend has strength and is likely to continue. Momentum builds as more participants join the move, reinforcing the uptrend.

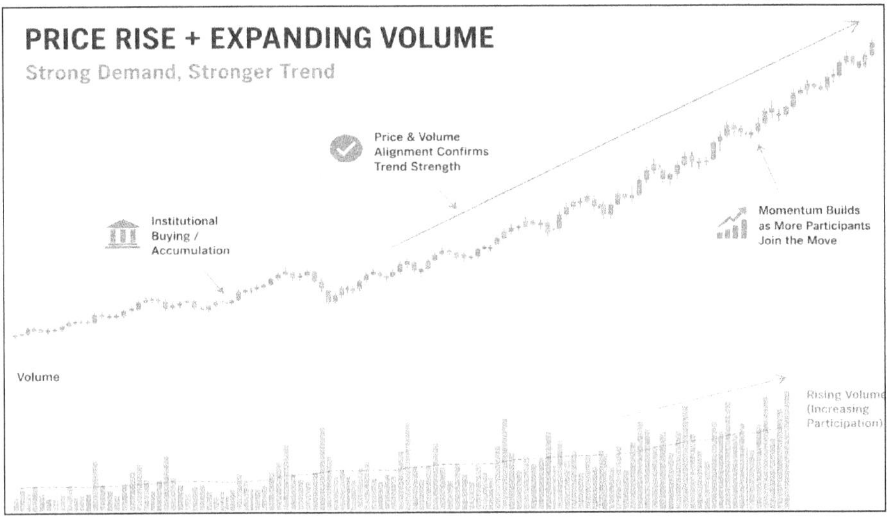

Price Rising with Decreasing Volume: Weakening Uptrend:

A rising price accompanied by declining volume reflects a lack of conviction. While the market is still moving upward, fewer participants are supporting the move. This often indicates that the rally is losing strength and may be driven by short covering or limited buying interest rather than fresh accumulation.

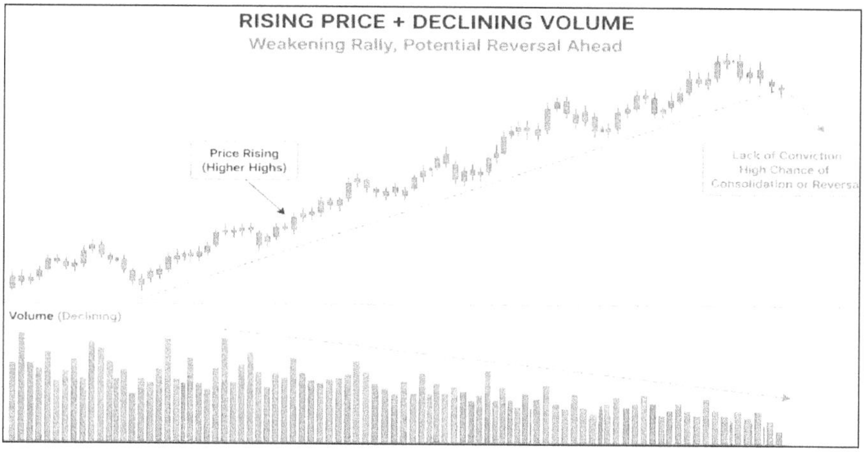

Such conditions frequently precede consolidation or reversal, making this a critical warning signal for traders.

Price Falling with Increasing Volume: Strong Bearish Pressure:

When price declines and volume increases, it indicates aggressive selling. This often reflects institutional distribution or panic selling among market participants. The high volume confirms that supply is overwhelming demand, and the downtrend is likely to persist. This combination is typically seen during strong bearish phases or breakdowns.

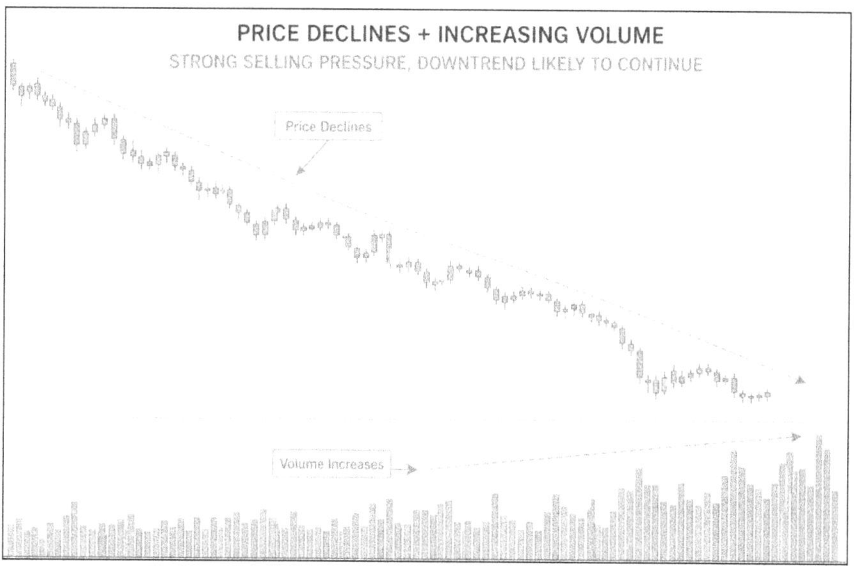

Price Falling with Decreasing Volume: Weak Downtrend and Possible Bottoming:

A falling price with declining volume suggests that selling pressure is reducing. Fewer participants are willing to sell at lower levels, indicating that the bearish momentum is weakening.

This often occurs during the later stages of a downtrend and may signal the beginning of accumulation or a potential reversal zone.

Sideways Price with Increasing Volume: Accumulation or Distribution in Progress:

When price moves within a range but volume gradually increases, it indicates that significant activity is taking place beneath the surface. This could represent accumulation (buying) or distribution (selling) by institutional players.

The direction of the eventual breakout depends on whether demand or supply dominates during this phase.

This setup often precedes a strong directional move.

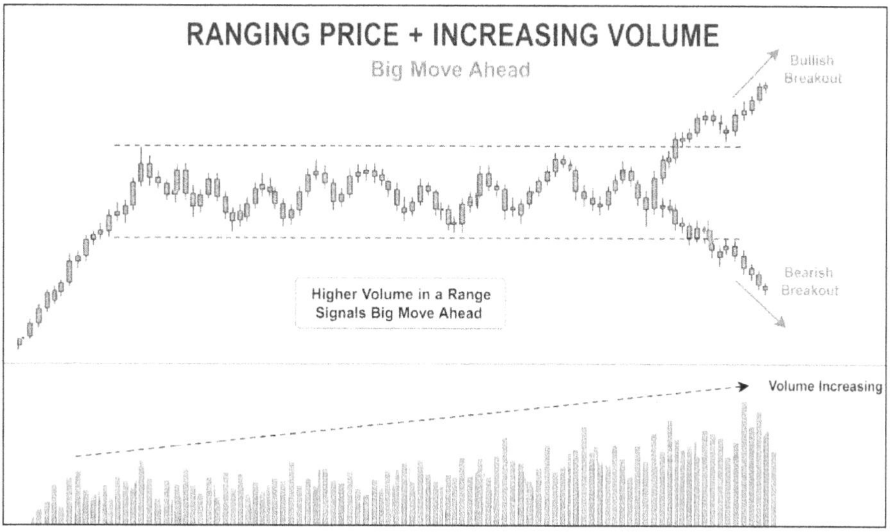

Sideways Price with Decreasing Volume: Market Indecision:

A range-bound market with declining volume reflects a lack of interest and participation. Neither buyers nor sellers are in control, and the market is essentially waiting for a trigger.

Such conditions are typically low-probability trading environments and often precede a volatility expansion once participation returns.

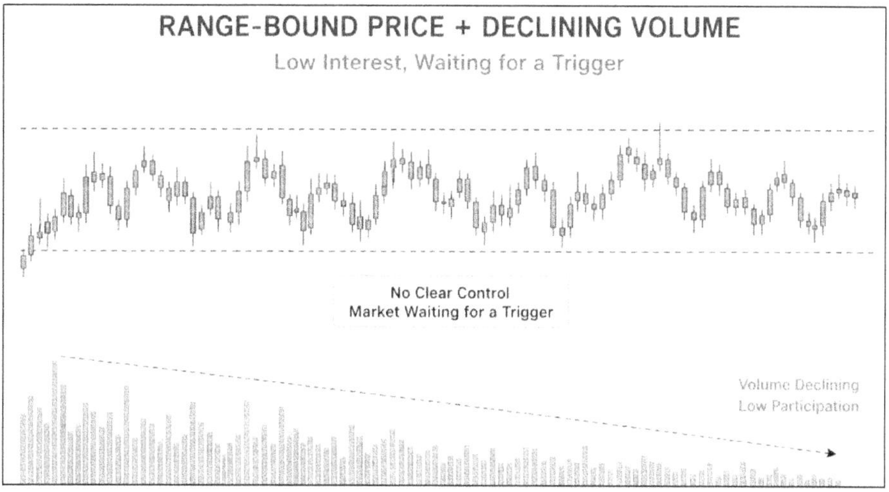

Breakout with High Volume: Confirmation of Strength:

A breakout above resistance or below support becomes highly reliable when accompanied by a surge in volume. This indicates strong participation and acceptance of new price levels.

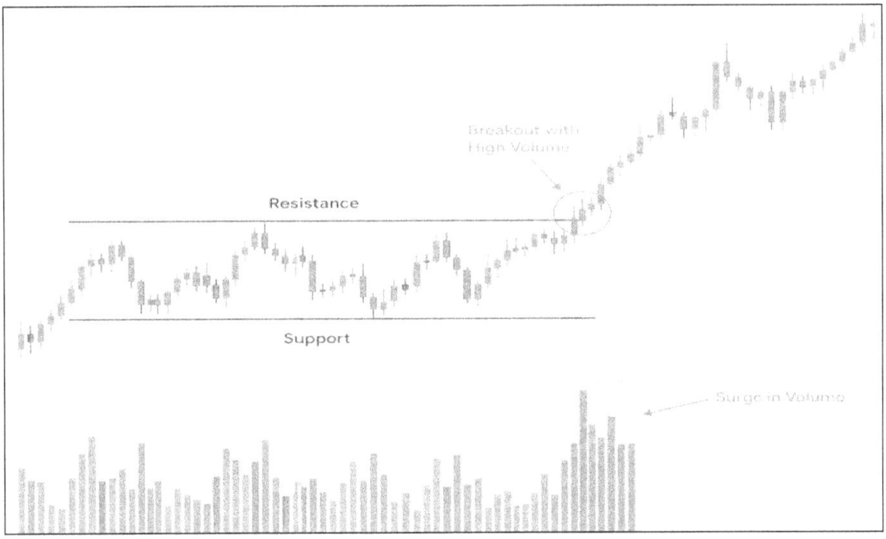

High volume confirms that the breakout is supported by conviction, reducing the likelihood of failure and increasing the probability of trend continuation.

Breakout with Low Volume: False Move and Trap Risk:

When a breakout occurs on low volume, it lacks participation and conviction. Such moves are often unsustainable and can quickly reverse, trapping traders who entered based on price alone.

These false breakouts highlight the importance of volume as a validation tool.

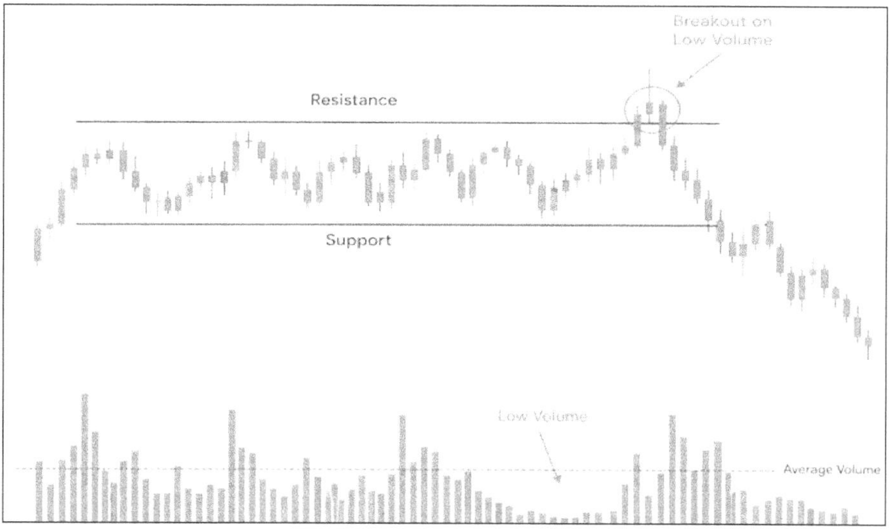

Volume Spikes and Climax Behaviour: Signs of Exhaustion:

Sudden spikes in volume often indicate climactic phases in the market. At the top of an uptrend, extremely high volume (it may be a green or a red volume bar) with limited price progress may signal distribution, where smart money exits positions. At the bottom of a downtrend, high volume (usually a red colour volume bar) combined with sharp declines may indicate capitulation, where panic selling exhausts itself. These moments often mark turning points in the market.

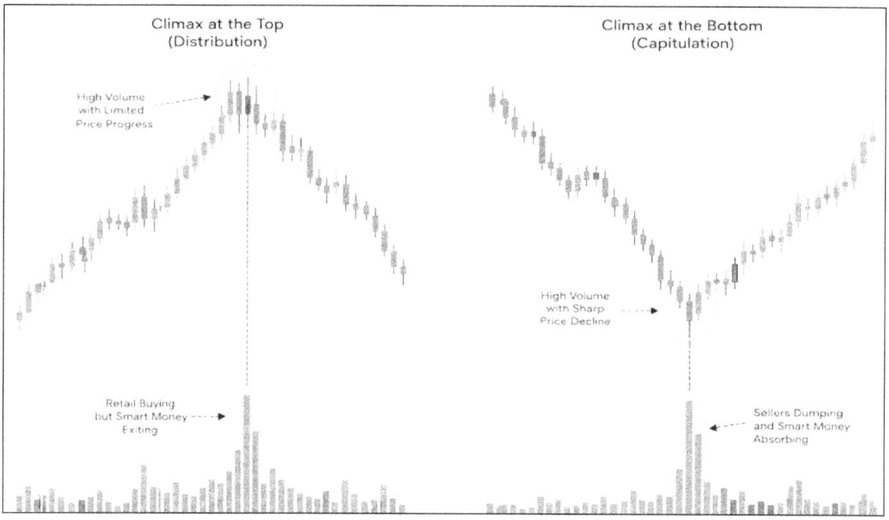

COLOUR OF THE VOLUME BARS

Every price candle, on every time frame, represents a continuous negotiation between buyers and sellers. For every transaction that occurs, there is always **both a buyer and a seller**—no trade can exist without this exchange. What the candle ultimately shows is who was more aggressive during that period: buyers (resulting in a bullish/green candle) or sellers (resulting in a bearish/red candle).

In this context, the colour of the volume bar is typically derived from the candle's close relative to its open—green if price closes higher, red if it closes lower. However, this colour does **not** mean that only buying or only selling occurred; it merely reflects which side had marginal control at the close of that time frame.

Therefore, the significance of volume bar colour should be interpreted with caution. A **green volume bar** indicates that buyers had the upper hand by the end of that interval, but it does not imply the absence of selling—often, significant selling may have been absorbed within that same candle. Similarly, a **red volume bar** suggests selling dominance, but strong buying may have been present beneath the surface, especially at key levels.

This is why, in many critical situations—such as distribution at market tops or capitulation at bottoms—the **colour of the volume bar can be misleading if viewed in isolation**. In such cases, the focus should shift from colour to context:

- the size of the volume bar
- the structure of the price candle
- position of price candle within the trend; and
- location price candle relative to support and resistance

In essence, volume colour has relevance in understanding immediate control within a candle, but its true significance emerges only when combined with price action and market context. Traders should give less importance to volume colour during extreme conditions or key turning points and instead focus on **volume magnitude, price behaviour, and broader market structure** to derive meaningful insights.

UNDERSTANDING OF VOLUME PROFILE

Volume bars and Volume Profile both represent trading activity, but they differ fundamentally in **how that activity is organized and interpreted.**

Volume bars display the total traded volume over a specific time period (per candle), helping traders understand participation and momentum *over time.* In contrast, Volume Profile organizes volume **across price levels**, showing where the most trading has actually occurred regardless of time.

While volume bars are useful for confirming trends, breakouts, and momentum within a given timeframe, Volume Profile provides deeper insight into **market structure**, highlighting key areas of value, support, resistance, and price acceptance or rejection.

Volume Profile is an advanced form of volume analysis that shows how much trading activity has occurred at different price levels, rather than over time. Unlike traditional volume bars plotted below a chart, Volume Profile is displayed horizontally along the price axis, revealing where the market has spent the most time and conducted the most transactions. This provides a far richer insight into market behaviour, as it highlights the **true areas of interest and agreement between buyers and sellers**.

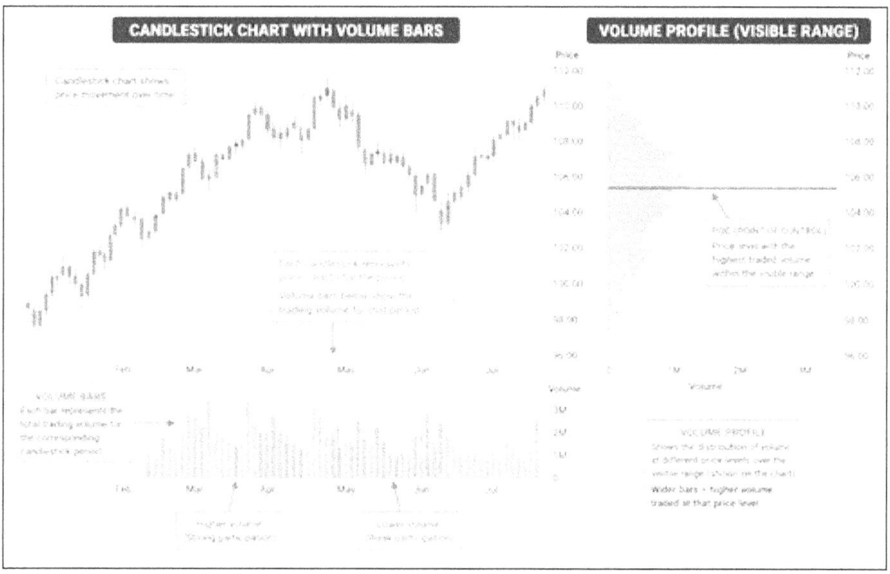

The significance of volume lies in the message it forcefully conveys: **it reveals intent**.

In essence, volume bars answer *"how much activity happened during this time?"*, whereas Volume Profile answers *"at which price levels did the most meaningful activity occur?"*

Volume profile and its usage and interpretation is discussed separately under Technical Indicators in Chapter 8.

DRY-VOLUME SIGNIFICANCE

Dry volume refers to periods in the market where trading activity is noticeably low, indicating a lack of participation from both buyers and sellers. Unlike high-volume phases that reflect strong conviction and active engagement, dry volume represents a state of indifference, hesitation, or temporary equilibrium.

It is not merely low volume in absolute terms, but low volume relative to the instrument's historical activity, making it a contextual concept rather than a fixed threshold. **Dry volume often appears during consolidation phases**, pauses within trends, or just before significant market moves.

Identification of Dry Volume on Charts:

Dry volume can be identified by observing **consistently shrinking or below-average volume bars** over a period of time. On charts, this often coincides with:

- Narrow price ranges or small-bodied candles
- Reduced volatility
- Lack of strong directional movement

On higher time frames such as **weekly and monthly charts**, dry volume becomes even more meaningful. A series of low-volume weeks or months indicates that the market is not attracting meaningful participation, especially from institutional players. This **absence of activity is often a precursor to a larger move** once participation returns.

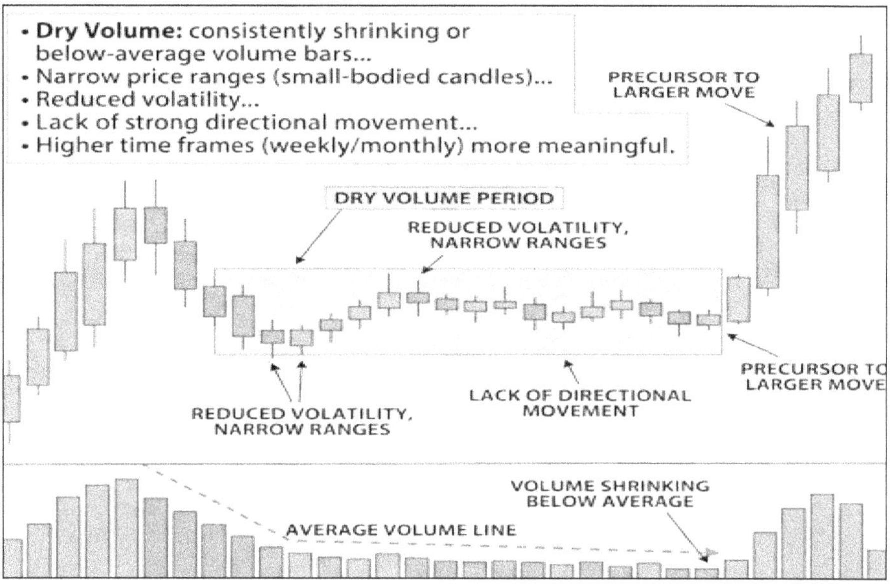

Drying volume is often best identified when combined with structural and volatility-based tools such as **Bollinger Bands** and patterns like the **Volatility Contraction Pattern (VCP)**. When volume begins to consistently decline while price trades in a tightening range, and the Bollinger Bands start to contract or squeeze, it reflects a reduction in volatility and participation—both key signs of drying volume. In a VCP setup, this is seen as a series of progressively smaller price contractions accompanied by lower volume on each pullback, indicating that selling pressure is getting absorbed and supply is diminishing.

This combination—shrinking volume, narrowing price swings, and contracting bands—signals that the market is entering a phase of compression, where energy is building beneath the surface. Such conditions are highly significant because they often precede strong directional moves or breakouts, especially when volume expands again, confirming renewed participation.

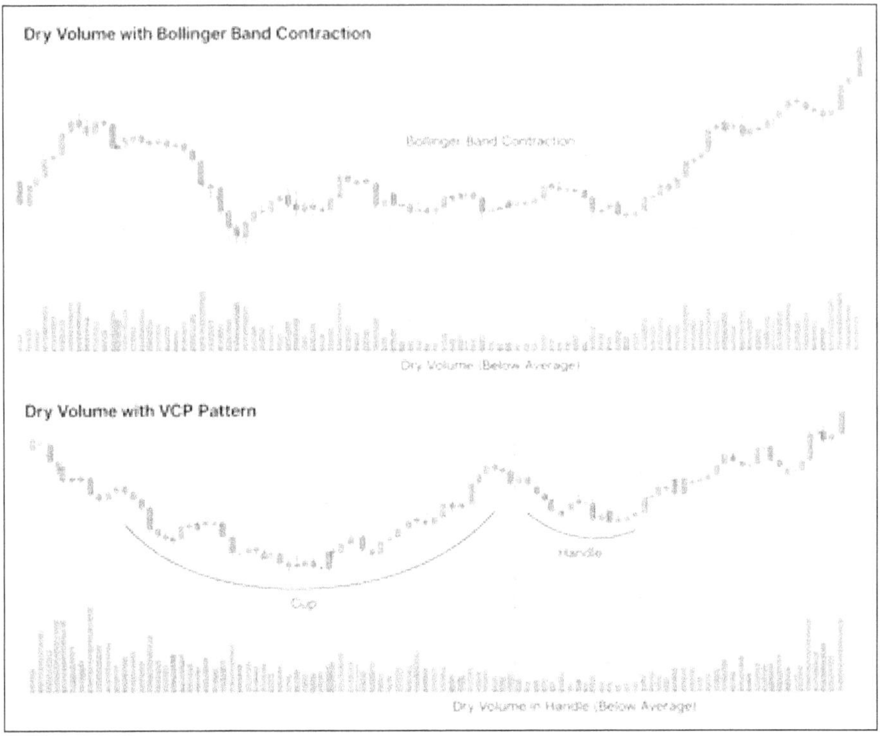

Relevance: The Calm Before the Move:

Dry volume is highly relevant because it often represents the **"quiet phase" before expansion**. Markets tend to alternate between periods of low activity (contraction) and high activity (expansion). When volume dries up, it suggests that both buying and selling pressure are subdued, and the market is waiting for a trigger.

From a demand–supply perspective, dry volume indicates a temporary balance or lack of urgency on either side. There is no aggressive buying (demand) or selling (supply), which leads to subdued price action. However, this balance is usually temporary. Once either demand or supply begins to dominate, volume expands and price moves accordingly. Thus, dry volume represents a latent imbalance waiting to emerge.

Once new information or interest enters the market, volume expands and price moves decisively. Thus, dry volume is not a signal in isolation but a setup condition that prepares the ground for future volatility.

Dry volume carries greater weight on higher time frames because it reflects longer-term participation trends. When volume dries up on a weekly or monthly chart:

- It may indicate long-term consolidation or base formation
- It often reflects a phase where institutions are either inactive or accumulating very gradually
- It can precede major breakouts or breakdowns once volume returns

For investors, such phases are critical because they often represent **early stages of accumulation before large trends begin**.

Dry Volume - Trading & Investing Opportunity:

For traders, dry volume is a signal to be patient rather than reactive. Low-volume environments often produce false moves and lack follow-through. However, they also provide opportunities to prepare for high-probability setups, such as breakouts from consolidation. Traders can use dry volume phases to identify key levels and wait for volume expansion as confirmation before entering trades.

From an investing standpoint, dry volume phases can be highly valuable. Extended periods of low volume on higher time frames may indicate that a stock is quietly forming a base. Investors who recognize these conditions can begin accumulating positions gradually, often at relatively stable prices, before broader market interest returns. Additionally, low-volume declines may signal that selling pressure is weakening, offering potential entry points for long-term investments.

Dry volume therefore represents the market in a state of silence—where activity is low, but potential is building. While it may appear uneventful, it often holds the key to understanding upcoming moves. Whether viewed from a trading or investing perspective, recognizing dry volume helps in identifying periods of consolidation, assessing the strength of trends, and preparing for future volatility. In many cases, it is this quiet phase that precedes the most meaningful market opportunities.

READING PRICE THROUGH VOLUME

For an investor/ trader, the true value of volume lies in its ability to validate and interpret price action. Every price movement should be viewed through the lens of volume—asking whether the move is supported by participation or not. Strong trends, reliable breakouts, and meaningful reversals are almost always accompanied by corresponding changes in volume.

By integrating volume analysis into their decision-making process, traders/ investors can improve the accuracy of their trades and avoid being misled by weak or deceptive price movements. The relationship between price and volume is not limited to a single rule but is best understood through its various combinations. Each permutation—whether confirming or diverging—provides insight into market strength, weakness, and intent. By learning to interpret these combinations in the context of institutional activity, momentum, demand–supply dynamics, and price structure, traders can develop a deeper and more accurate understanding of market behaviour.

Chapter – 5

Moving Averages

Tendency of Price

Understanding the average of price and its movement is the foundation—and often the first step—of effective chart reading. A well-informed trade should primarily be driven by chart interpretation, where approximately **70% weight is given to price action**, and the remaining 30% to supporting parameters such as indicators or external factors. Price reflects visible market behaviour, but its average provides deeper insight into the underlying trend and equilibrium.

In essence, **price can be seen as the body, while its average represents the soul**—giving direction, balance, and meaning to raw price movements. While there are numerous chart types and moving averages available to traders, the objective is not to use many, but to use the right ones effectively.

To truly understand price action, one must first understand where the **average price lies and how price behaves around it**. Tools such as VWAP, AVWAP, and key moving averages like the 20 SMA and 50 SMA help in identifying this average. These act as dynamic reference points, enabling traders to assess whether price is trading at a premium or discount, and whether it is likely to revert, continue, or consolidate.

PRICE AVERAGING NEAR 20 SMA

The 20 SMA serves as a key reference point for the average price, around which price action tends to revolve. In most market conditions, price and the 20 SMA move in close alignment—price frequently returns to this average, consolidates, and then resumes its directional move. This repeated interaction makes the 20 SMA a crucial guide for understanding short-term equilibrium and trend behaviour.

When there is a significant gap or distance between price and the 20 SMA, it is generally not an ideal time to initiate a trade. Such divergence is typically unsustainable, and the market tends to rebalance itself—either through price moving back toward the 20 SMA (often indicating distribution) or the 20 SMA catching up to price (often indicating accumulation). Therefore, it is advisable to wait for price to realign or "average out" near the 20 SMA and then observe the next directional move before entering a trade.

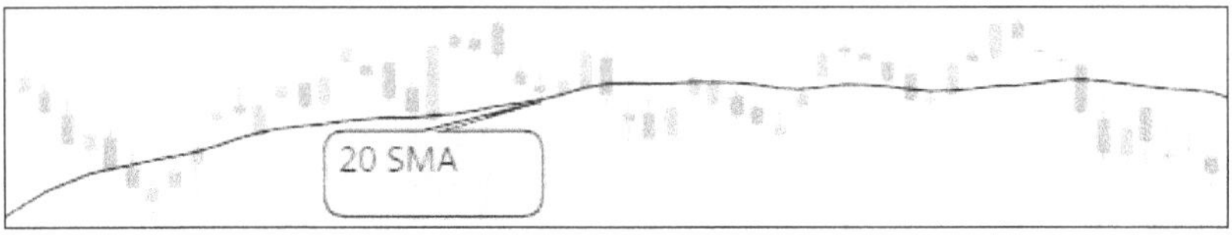

While the 20 SMA is widely used, the 20 EMA can also serve a similar purpose, offering a slightly more responsive view of price behaviour.

20 SMA For Trend Identification:

The 20 SMA is a reliable indicator for identifying the prevailing market trend, especially on higher timeframes such as the daily chart. When price consistently trades **below the 20 SMA**, it reflects a bearish bias, whereas sustained trading **above the 20 SMA** indicates a bullish trend. For a shift in trend, price must not only cross the 20 SMA but also **hold and sustain above or below it**, confirming a change in market direction.

A clear trend is observed when both **price and the 20 SMA move in the same direction**. If both are rising steadily, it indicates a strong uptrend; if both are declining, it reflects a downtrend. On the other hand, when the 20 SMA moves sideways or flattens, it signals a **range-bound or consolidating market**, where price oscillates around the average. During such phases, price typically moves between the upper and lower bands of volatility (such as Bollinger Bands), which often begin to contract, indicating reduced volatility and a tightening range.

For price to break out of this range—either above the upper band or below the lower band—it must be supported by **strong momentum and significant volume**. Once such a breakout occurs, often referred to as a "volatility expansion" or "band blast," price tends to move decisively in that direction, establishing a new trend with increased momentum.

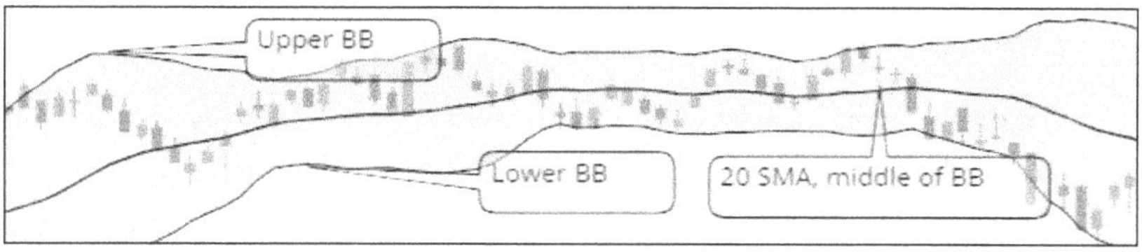

20 SMA Monthly TF For Investment:

20 SMA on the monthly timeframe is a powerful indicator of the broader market trend and long-term stability. When price consistently **trades and sustains above the 20 SMA on the monthly chart**, it generally indicates that the market is not in a major or sharp downtrend, providing a level of confidence for long-term participants. However, even a correction toward the 20 SMA on the monthly timeframe can result in a **significant decline in prices**, as such moves reflect deeper, time-based corrections within an overall trend.

After a prolonged uptrend, markets often undergo **time-wise consolidation or correction**, during which price tends to gravitate back toward the 20 SMA on the monthly chart to re-establish equilibrium. If, however, price decisively **breaks below the 20 SMA on the monthly timeframe and sustains below it**, it may signal the onset of a more pronounced bearish phase or a sharp downward move.

In scenarios where price moves sideways on the monthly timeframe while continuing to respect the 20 SMA—and the lower band (such as the LBB) gradually trends upward—it often indicates **accumulation by institutional or smart money** during a consolidation phase.

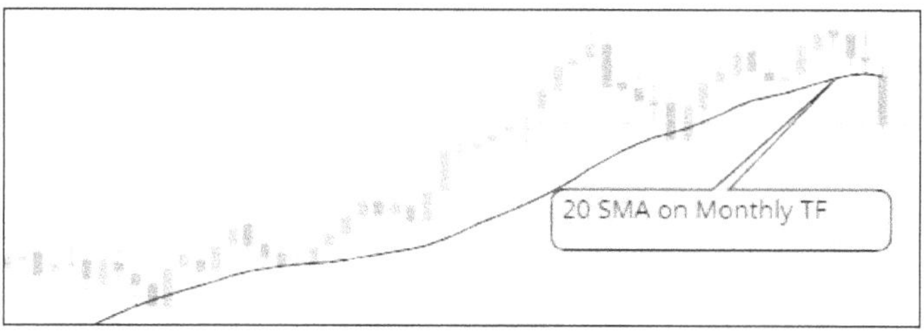

From an investment perspective, the 20 SMA on the monthly chart serves as a strong and relatively safer zone for long-term entry. That said, among all such levels, **AVWAP on the monthly timeframe is often considered an even more optimal zone** for identifying high-quality investment opportunities. We have discussed about AVWAP in detail in Chapter 6.

Price Averaging Near 20 SMA Monthly TF:

When a significant gap develops between price and the 20 SMA on the monthly timeframe, it signals an unsustainable extension. Over time, this imbalance is corrected—either through **price moving down toward the 20 SMA** or the **20 SMA gradually catching up with price**. This rebalancing phase is a natural part of market behaviour.

On the monthly timeframe, indices and stocks, after reaching an **overbought zone or the "maximum optimism" level—tend to correct downward to rebalance themselves.** This process of averaging typically unfolds in stages. The first level of mean reversion is the **20 SMA on the monthly chart**, and if the correction deepens further, price may gravitate toward the **lower Bollinger band and during extreme fall towards lowest AVWAP levels** (i.e. AVWAP anchored at the lowest level of price during the most recent extreme fear events, for example, like price bottom formed during events like Russia-Ukraine or US-Iran War).

Chart below shows AVWAP anchored at the lowest price point of Lehman crisis of 2008 – which was respected by the price fall during Covid crash after price dropped below lower Bollinger band on Monthly TF.

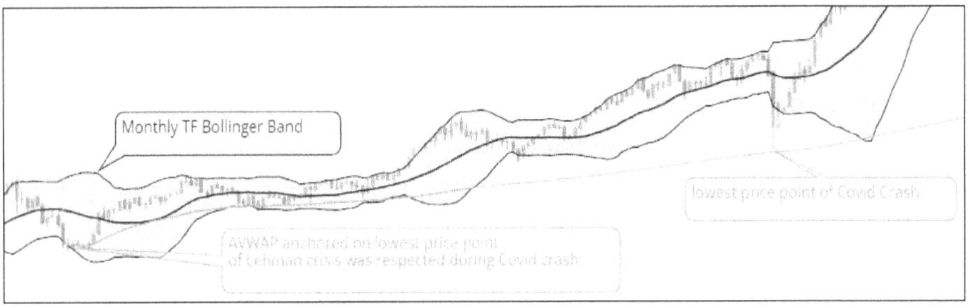

A key early indication of this process begins when price **moves from upper Bollinger band starts moving towards monthly 20 SMA inside the Bollinger Bands and thereby starts closing lower on the monthly timeframe**. Such behaviour often suggests the start of an averaging phase, which may manifest either as a **price correction** or a **time-wise consolidation**, where price oscillates within a broad range (often spanning thousands of points in indices) while the averages adjust. For tracking broader market correction, higher timeframe like Monthly TF is very much suitable.

This phase of correction or consolidation typically continues until price aligns on a monthly TF with the **20 SMA or deeper AVWAP-based support levels**, restoring equilibrium. Only after this averaging process is complete does the market tend to **resume its fresh directional move**, often marking the beginning of a fresh upward trend post-correction. The concept and application of AVWAP will be discussed in greater detail in Chapter 6.

Exiting Long Positions Near 20 SMA Daily TF:

On the daily timeframe, the 20 SMA often acts as a **one-time exit zone**, particularly for trades taken in the opposite direction of the prevailing move. For instance, if a trader has initiated a long position and price moves upward toward the 20 SMA, this zone can act as a resistance, making it prudent to consider exiting the position.

A fresh directional trade should ideally be taken only after a **decisive breach and sustained move beyond the 20 SMA**. Such breaches are typically strong in nature and often occur either through a **large momentum candle during intraday** or, in a majority of cases, via a **gap-up or gap-down on the next trading session**, followed by at least an hour of sustained price action beyond the level.

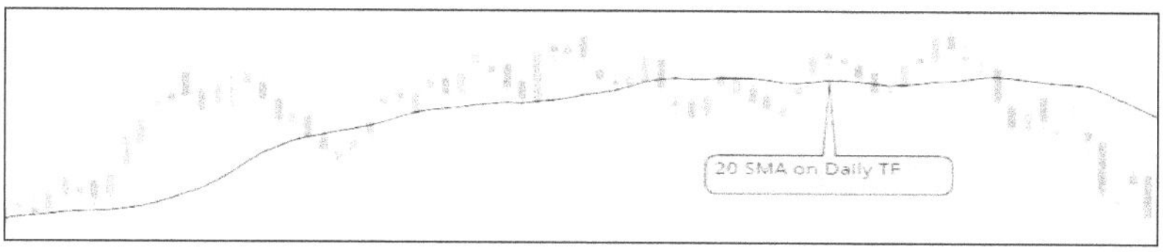

Additionally, if price on the daily timeframe fails to break above the 20 SMA, and on the hourly timeframe a sell signal is observed (e.g., through HM indicator or similar indicators), along with price trading below VWAP, it can present an opportunity for an **intraday short trade**. In such cases, the 20 SMA on the daily chart acts as a strong resistance reference, with the stop loss placed on a closing basis above this level (preferably on the hourly timeframe).

When price consistently trades **below the 20 SMA on the hourly or daily timeframe** and continues to consolidate beneath it, it reflects underlying weakness in the market. During such phases, the 20 SMA gradually slopes downward, while price intermittently moves up to touch or approach the average—essentially "rebalancing" itself. This interaction often represents a phase of distribution before the next directional move.

Once price repeatedly approaches the 20 SMA from below and fails to sustain above it, the likelihood of a **sharp downward move increase**. This setup becomes even stronger if there is an additional resistance factor—such as a pivot level—positioned below or around the 20 SMA, preventing price from moving higher. Such confluence provides added confirmation that the market may struggle to break above the average and is likely to resume its downward trend after this averaging phase.

From a trading perspective, if this pattern forms on the **hourly timeframe**, short trades can be considered when price approaches the 20 SMA and shows signs of reversal on a lower timeframe, or through strategies like STBT. If the same structure appears on the **daily timeframe**, it offers an opportunity for a **positional short trade** near the 20 SMA, with appropriate confirmation and risk management.

Trend Reversal From 20 SMA:

In a declining market, price often rallies back toward the 20 SMA on the daily timeframe, averages itself around this level, and then resumes its downward trend.

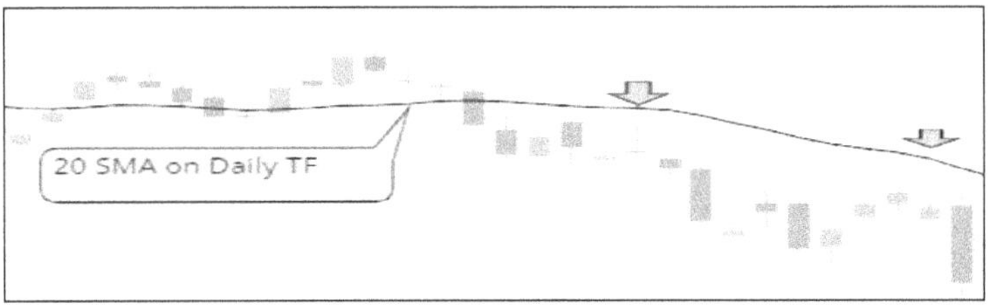

However, a potential shift in trend emerges when price not only crosses the 20 SMA but also **sustains above it with multiple closes**. Typically, **three consecutive closes above the 20 SMA** provide a stronger indication that the downtrend may be reversing into an uptrend. The same principle applies in reverse during a rising market—sustained closes below the 20 SMA can signal the beginning of a bearish reversal.

The 20 EMA can also be used in place of the 20 SMA for similar analysis, offering a slightly more responsive indication of price movement.

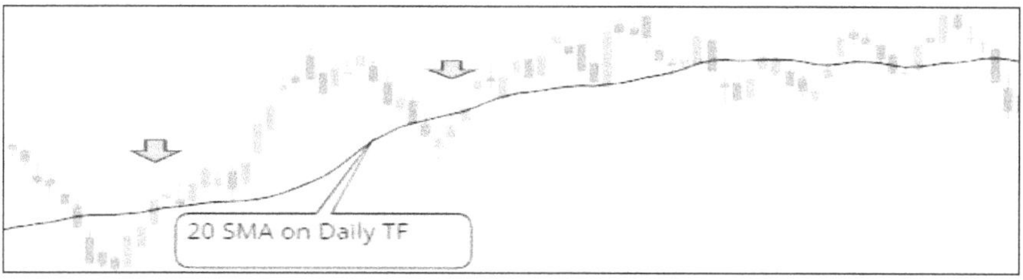

Conviction in the trend reversal strengthens further when price sustains above both the **20 SMA and 50 SMA on the daily timeframe**, and these moving averages begin to curve upward. This alignment reflects improving market structure and increasing bullish momentum, confirming a potential transition into an uptrend.

CROSS-OVER OF 20 & 50 SMA

The combination of the 20 SMA and 50 SMA provides a simple yet effective framework for identifying the market trend. When price **sustains and consistently trades above both the 20 SMA and the 50 SMA**, it indicates a bullish market structure, reflecting strength and upward momentum.

Conversely, when price **remains below both the 20 SMA and 50 SMA**, it signifies a bearish trend, highlighting weakness and downward pressure.

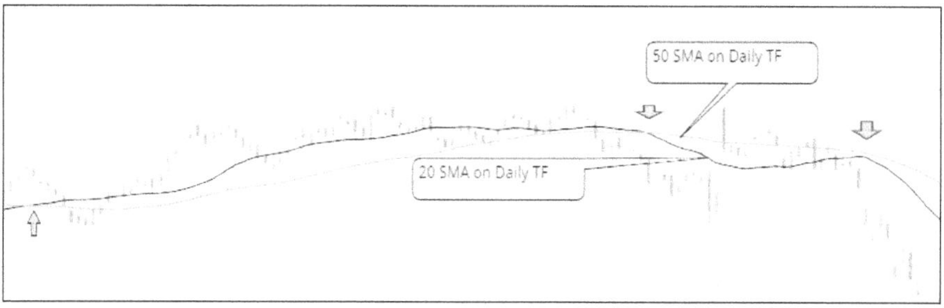

The reliability of this trend identification increases significantly on higher timeframes. If the same alignment is observed on the **weekly timeframe**, it provides even stronger confirmation of the prevailing trend, as it reflects broader market participation and long-term directional bias.

Convergence of 20 & 50 SMA:

When the 20 SMA and 50 SMA begin to **converge closely**, it often serves as an early warning sign of a potential shift in market dynamics (refer chart above – both lines running into each other closely). Such convergence indicates a loss of clear trend direction and typically precedes a **strong price reaction or expansion in volatility**.

At these convergence zones, price is likely to make a decisive move—either continuing the existing trend or reversing it. In many cases, if price fails to hold above these averages and begins to **close and sustain below both,** it may signal a transition toward a bearish trend. This signal becomes even more significant when observed on **higher timeframes, particularly the weekly chart**, as it reflects a broader shift in market sentiment and structure.

Price Deviation From 20 & 50 SMA:

Whenever price moves significantly **away from the 20 SMA and 50 SMA**, it serves as a cautionary signal. Such extended moves are often unsustainable, as price tends to revert back toward its averages to restore equilibrium. This phase of reversion reflects the market's natural tendency to **"average out" after excessive expansion**.

Once price returns and stabilizes near these moving averages, it typically decides its next directional move. A fresh trend then emerges depending on whether price **sustains above both the 20 and 50 SMA (indicating bullish continuation)** or **falls below and holds under these levels (indicating bearish continuation)**. Therefore, chasing price when it is far from its averages can be risky, and it is generally more prudent to wait for this rebalancing phase before initiating new positions.

Golden Cross-over of 20 & 50 SMA:

In a bearish market, the 20 SMA typically trends below the 50 SMA, often with a visible gap between the two, reflecting sustained downward momentum. A potential bullish reversal begins when the **20 SMA starts forming an upward "U-shaped" curve**, indicating a shift in short-term momentum. As this strength builds, the 20 SMA eventually **crosses above the 50 SMA**, forming what is commonly known as a **golden crossover**. This transition phase often creates a rounded, base-like or "boat-shaped" structure formed by the candles on the chart.

The reversal gains confirmation when price begins to **close and sustain above both the 20 SMA and 50 SMA**, particularly above the crossover zone. Over time, the 50 SMA also starts curving upward, reinforcing the change in trend. As the bullish structure develops, price typically continues to respect the 20 SMA—pulling back to it for averaging before moving higher—while both averages remain upward sloping with a healthy gap between them. This alignment confirms a well-established uptrend.

The **golden crossover zone** often serves as a high-probability area to initiate long positions, provided price sustains above it. This setup is effective across timeframes—on the **hourly chart for intraday trades**, and on the **daily or weekly charts for positional trades**. When observed on the weekly timeframe, the signal carries even greater reliability, reflecting a broader and more durable shift in market trend.

For **investment or long positional trades** with a holding period of around 20–30 days, the **20 SMA and 50 SMA** on a daily timeframe are more suitable, as they provide a smoother and more stable view of the trend. On the other hand, for **intraday long trade or short-term positional long trades with a holding period of 2–3 days**, the **20 EMA and 50 EMA** on hourly timeframe can be used, as they are more responsive to recent price movements and help capture quicker market shifts on the upward side.

Death Cross-over of 20 & 50 SMA:

In a bullish market, the 20 SMA typically trends above the 50 SMA, often with a clear gap between the two, reflecting sustained upward momentum. A potential bearish reversal begins when the **20 SMA starts forming a downward "U-shaped" curve**, signalling weakening strength. As this shift develops, the 20 SMA eventually **crosses below the 50 SMA**, forming what is known as a **death crossover**. This phase often marked by an inverted, top-like or "inverted boat" structure by the candles on the chart.

The reversal is confirmed when price begins to **close and sustain below both the 20 SMA and 50 SMA**, particularly below the crossover zone.

Over time, the 50 SMA also turns downward, reinforcing the bearish trend. As the structure matures, price typically continues to respect the 20 SMA from below—rallying up to it for averaging before declining again—while both averages slope downward with a widening gap between them, confirming a strong downtrend.

The **death crossover zone** is generally considered a high-probability area to initiate short positions, provided price sustains below it. This setup is effective across timeframes—on the **hourly chart for intraday trades**, and on the **daily or weekly charts for positional trades**. When observed on the **weekly timeframe**, the signal carries greater significance, often leading to sharp and extended declines, sometimes accompanied by consecutive gap-down moves.

For sell side **positional trades** with a holding period of around 20–30 days, the **20 SMA and 50 SMA** on a daily timeframe are more suitable, as they provide a smoother and more stable view of the bearish trend. On the other hand, for **intraday sell trade or short-term positional sell trades with a holding period of 2–3 days**, the **20 EMA and 50 EMA** on hourly timeframe can be used, as they are more responsive to recent bearish price movements and help capture quicker market shifts on the downward side.

Cross-over of 20 & 50 SMA on Weekly timeframe:

Greater importance should be given to **higher-period moving averages** compared to lower-period ones, as they reflect broader market trends and carry stronger reliability, like 50 SMA over 20 SMA for a longer-term view. Also, for longer time period view – the longer timeframe may be analysed.

On the **weekly timeframe**, the 50 SMA acts as a highly significant level, and any decisive move below it often triggers a strong market reaction. When price slips and sustains below the 50 SMA on the weekly chart, it signals growing weakness, and short positions can be considered—particularly around the **death crossover zone** for better confirmation.

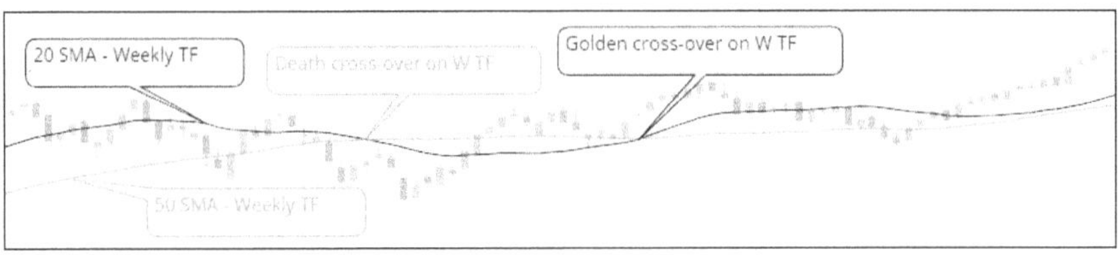

Conversely, when price consistently trades and sustains **above both the 20 SMA and 50 SMA on the weekly timeframe**, it reflects strong bullish momentum on a longer term. In such conditions, long positions can be considered, especially near the **golden crossover zone**, which often marks the beginning of a sustained uptrend.

Golden and death crossovers on the weekly timeframe require extended holding periods to capture the full price movement, often exposing traders to significant interim drawdowns. Therefore, while trading directly on weekly or monthly signals may be practically challenging, they are best used to form a broader market view and directional bias.

Cross-over of 20 & 200 SMA – a trend reversal signal:

The interaction between the 20 SMA and 200 SMA provides a powerful indication of trend strength and potential reversal. When price consistently trades **below the 20 SMA**, it reflects a bearish bias. However, if price declines further and **falls below the 200 SMA on the daily timeframe**, it indicates a phase of **extreme bearishness**, often associated with deeper and more sustained downtrends.

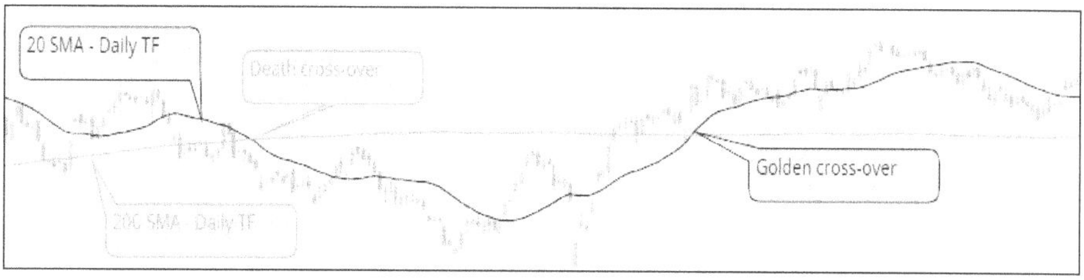

In a falling market, when the **20 SMA and 200 SMA begin to converge**, it signals a potential transition phase. If, during this period, price manages to **break above the 200 SMA and sustain**, it reflects emerging strength. Once this happens, the resistance from the 20 SMA—now in close proximity—tends to weaken, and price often proceeds to **cross above and sustain above the 20 SMA** For trade execution, the 5 SMA (Low) can be used as both an entry and risk management reference. **Long positions may be initiated just above the 5 SMA (Low)**, with a stop loss placed on a closing basis below it. Likewise, **short positions can be initiated just below the 5 SMA (Low)**, with a stop loss on a closing basis above it.**as well.**

When price successfully holds above both the **200 SMA and 20 SMA**, it indicates a meaningful **shift in market structure from bearish to bullish**, suggesting the possibility of a trend reversal and the beginning of a new upward phase.

Therefore, in crossover-based trading, the crossover junction becomes a critical entry zone, as it often marks a potential bottom or top formed over that period. Once price **sustains above the crossover level (golden crossover)**, it signals the beginning of a new upward move, making it a favourable area for initiating long positions. Conversely, if price **sustains below the death crossover level**, it indicates emerging weakness and provides a suitable entry point for initiating short trades. This is true for all timeframes: whether hourly, daily or weekly or monthly timeframe.

TREND CONFIRMATION WITH 5 SMA

On the daily timeframe, the **5 SMA (Low)** serves as a practical and responsive guide for short-term trade direction. As a general rule, **avoid initiating long trades when price is below the 5 SMA (Low)**, and similarly, **avoid short trades when price is above it**. When price consistently trends above the 5 SMA (Low), it reflects underlying bullishness; conversely, sustained trading below it indicates a bearish bias.

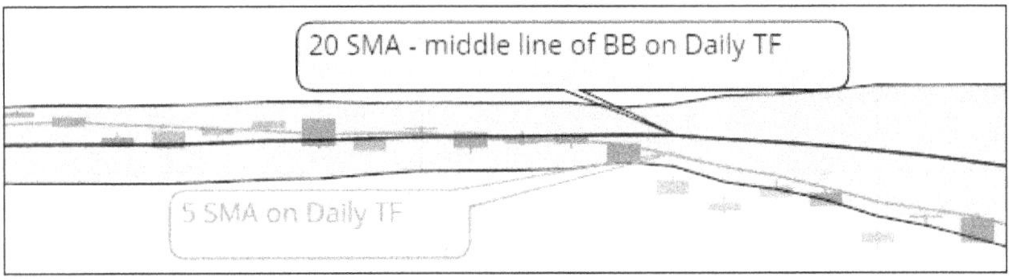

This approach can be effectively combined with key levels:

- **Long near lower Bollinger band (LBB)** when price closes above the 5 SMA (Low).
- **Long near 20 SMA** when price closes above the 20 SMA and remains above the 5 SMA (Low).

- **Short near upper Bollinger band (UBB)** when price closes below the 5 SMA (Low).
- **Short near 20 SMA** when price closes below the 20 SMA and remains below the 5 SMA (Low).

Trend confirmation improves when the **5 SMA (Low) and 20 SMA move in alignment**. If both are sloping upward, it indicates a strong uptrend, where **every dip can be viewed as a buying opportunity**. Conversely, if both slope downward, it reflects a downtrend, where **every rise can be treated as a selling opportunity**.

MOVING AVERAGES ARE MULTI-TOOL

Moving averages hold immense significance in understanding price behaviour, as they help smooth out volatility and present a clearer view of the underlying trend. At their core lies the concept of **mean reversion**—prices tend to oscillate around their average over time. When prices deviate excessively from key moving averages, there is often a natural tendency to revert back, making these levels crucial reference points for traders and investors alike.

Different moving averages such as the 20, 50, 100, 200, and even 400-period averages represent varying time horizons of market participants. Shorter averages reflect immediate sentiment and momentum, while longer ones capture broader, long-term trends. The interaction between these averages—their convergence and expansion—provides a powerful macro view of the market.

When multiple **moving averages converge**, it often indicates consolidation and a potential buildup for a significant move. Conversely, their expansion signals strength in trend, showing that price is moving decisively in one direction with alignment across timeframes, especially when observed on higher time frames.

Additionally, moving averages act as **dynamic zones of support and resistance**. Prices frequently react around these levels—finding support in uptrends and resistance in downtrends. Breaks and sustained movements beyond key averages often signal shifts in trend, helping traders identify potential reversals or continuations.

Moving averages observed on higher time frames such as daily, weekly, and monthly charts offer far more conclusive and reliable insights compared to lower time frames. As the time frame increases, the noise of short-term volatility reduces, and the signals derived from moving averages gain greater significance. Support and resistance levels formed around these averages tend to be stronger, as they reflect the collective positioning of a broader base of market participants. Similarly, crossovers between key moving averages on higher time frames often indicate more durable trend shifts, rather than short-lived fluctuations. The convergence and expansion of these averages on higher time frames provide a powerful macro perspective—convergence signalling potential buildup and expansion confirming sustained momentum. In essence, the higher the time frame, the stronger the conviction one can place on the behaviour and signals exhibited by moving averages.

In essence, moving averages are not merely indicators but foundational tools in price reading and price action analysis. They provide structure, context, and clarity—making them indispensable for anyone seeking to interpret market behaviour with discipline and precision.

Chapter – 6

Volume Weighted Average Price

Important Price Action

VWAP (Volume Weighted Average Price) and **AVWAP (Anchored Volume Weighted Average Price)** are price-based indicators that represent the average price at which an asset has traded, weighted by volume. While both derive from the concept of average price, their application and significance differ based on timeframe and anchoring.

VWAP is primarily an **intraday indicator**, recalculated from the start of each trading session. It reflects the fair value of price for that particular day and is widely used by traders to assess whether price is trading at a premium (above VWAP) or discount (below VWAP). As a result, VWAP acts as a dynamic support and resistance level during the day and plays a crucial role in intraday decision-making. It is important to note that VWAP is relevant only on the daily timeframe and lower, and does not extend to weekly or monthly charts.

AVWAP, on the other hand, is a more versatile and powerful tool, as it is anchored to a specific event, date, or price point—such as a major high, low, or significant market event. This allows AVWAP to be used across multiple timeframes, ranging from monthly and weekly charts down to intraday (e.g., 10-minute) charts. Because it captures the average price from a meaningful reference point, AVWAP is highly effective for both trading and long-term investment analysis, helping identify zones of accumulation, distribution, and trend continuation.

In practical application, VWAP and AVWAP together provide strong confluence. When both indicators generate similar buy or sell signals during intraday trading, it significantly enhances the reliability of the setup and increases confidence in trade execution. This alignment indicates that both the session-based average (VWAP) and the broader anchored average (AVWAP) are supporting the same directional bias, making it a high-probability trading opportunity.

USAGE OF VWAP

VWAP is designed primarily for **intraday trading** and is applicable on the daily timeframe and lower—it does not extend to weekly or monthly charts. Also, VWAP does not appear on indices (e.g.: Nifty) but can be plotted on its Futures' shorter timeframes (like Nifty Futures hourly timeframe and below).

VWAP in Intraday Trading:

VWAP is a powerful reference for identifying intraday bias, it should **not be used in isolation**. Its effectiveness improves significantly when combined with other factors such as static support and resistance levels (like trendline or pivot points), AVWAP, and price action patterns like Open High (OH) or Open Low (OL). With sufficient practice and proper confluence, VWAP-based setups can contribute to consistent trading performance.

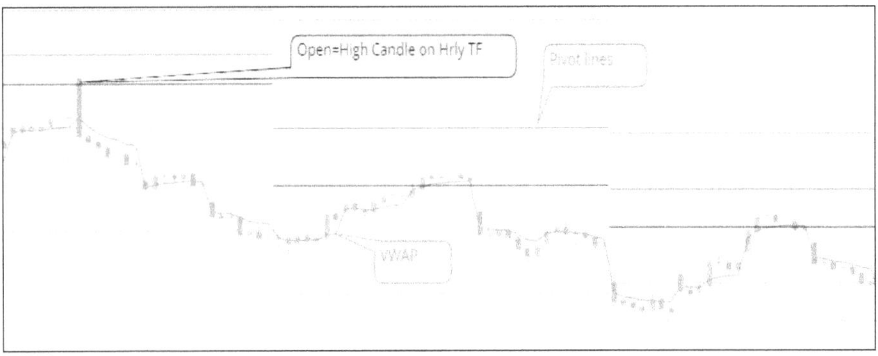

As a general intraday rule, when price is trading below VWAP, long positions should be avoided, and when price is trading above VWAP, short positions should generally be avoided—except in specific pattern-based exceptions. For better clarity and reliability, VWAP-based analysis is most effective when observed on **30-minute or 1-hour timeframes**, rather than very lower timeframes where noise is higher.

Intraday Trading Setup With VWAP:

VWAP-based intraday trades should not be executed on a daily basis; instead, they should be taken selectively when clear directional bias and supporting conditions are present. High-probability VWAP trades typically emerge in trending intraday markets.

i. When both **price and VWAP are trending downward during intraday**, it reflects a bearish environment. In such conditions, short positions can be initiated near VWAP, as it tends to act as dynamic resistance. The setup becomes even stronger if supported by price action patterns such as Open High (OH).

ii. Conversely, when both **price and VWAP are trending upward**, it indicates a bullish intraday trend. In this scenario, long positions can be initiated near VWAP, which acts as dynamic support. The probability of success improves further when aligned with bullish patterns such as Open Low (OL).

Entry near VWAP for intraday trade and SL:

During the trading day, especially after the initial volatility of the market open, price and VWAP tend to converge again—typically post noon. Therefore, it is often prudent to wait until this convergence occurs before considering an intraday trade. Once price and VWAP come closer, it provides a more favourable entry zone. Initiating trades near VWAP in such conditions allows for tighter stop losses placed close to the entry, thereby minimizing potential risk while maintaining a favourable risk-reward setup.

Use ITM to avoid VWAP-based Stop-Loss hunting:

When trading options using VWAP as a reference, it is preferable to use deep in-the-money (ITM) options with monthly expiry. Deep ITM options tend to move more in line with the underlying price and exhibit less erratic behaviour near VWAP, thereby reducing the chances of stop-loss hunting.

In contrast, out-of-the-money (OTM) and weekly options are more volatile and often fluctuate above and below VWAP during intraday sessions. This behaviour can lead to frequent stop-loss triggers, even when the broader trade direction remains intact.

Interplay of VWAP and 20 SMA:

When, on any intraday timeframe, price gets trapped between VWAP and the 20 SMA—for instance, trading above VWAP but below the 20 SMA, or below VWAP but above the 20 SMA—and both levels are in close proximity, it typically indicates indecision and lack of clear direction. In such conditions, trades should be avoided, as the market is likely to remain choppy and prone to false moves.

A trade should only be considered once price decisively sustains above both VWAP and the 20 SMA (for long positions) or below both levels (for short positions), indicating a clearer directional bias.

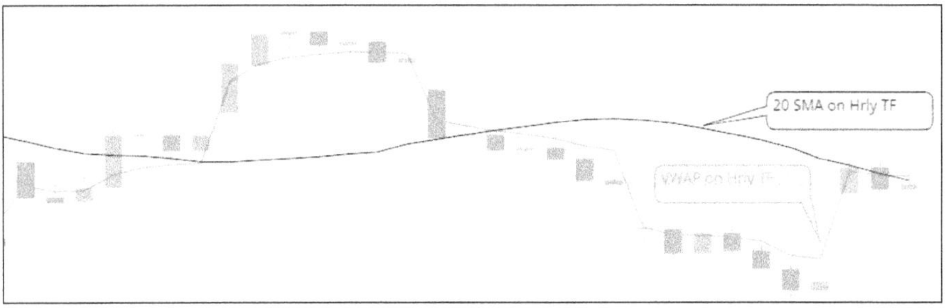

When VWAP and the 20 SMA converge, it is often observed that shorter-term averages (such as the 9 SMA High) also align with them in that range, creating a confluence zone. In such scenarios, greater importance should be given to the 20 SMA over VWAP, as it tends to be a more reliable indicator of trend and price behaviour.

Additionally, the relative positioning and crossover between VWAP and the 20 SMA on hourly timeframe can provide further directional cues for intraday trend. In a bullish intraday setup, VWAP typically crosses above the 20 SMA, indicating strengthening momentum. Conversely, when the 20 SMA crosses above VWAP, it signals a shift toward bearish inclination for intraday trades.

Reversal from 20 SMA:

If, during intraday trading on the 15-minute timeframe, price is trading below VWAP and begins to sustain or reverse from the 20 SMA, it is a signal to consider exiting or booking profits on existing short positions. The 20 SMA, in such cases, often acts as a strong dynamic support, indicating a potential pause or reversal in the downward move.

Furthermore, if price moves upward from the 20 SMA and later retraces, it is likely to again find support near the 20 SMA and bounce upward, reinforcing its reliability as a key level. Between VWAP and the 20 SMA on any given timeframe, greater importance should be given to the 20 SMA, as it generally proves to be a more dependable indicator of price behaviour and reversal zones.

Flat VWAP – indication of a range-bound trend:

A **flat VWAP during intraday**—i.e., when it neither slopes upward nor downward—indicates a lack of clear direction and suggests a range-bound market condition. On such days, VWAP-based directional trading should generally be avoided, as the market tends to remain indecisive and lacks sustained momentum.

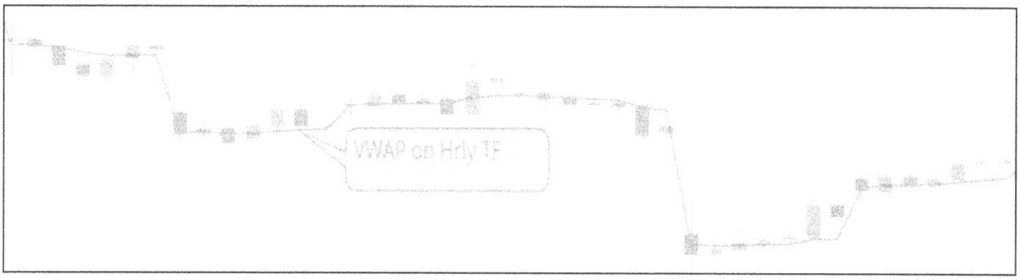

These conditions often represent a **"no-trade" or dilemma zone** for directional traders, particularly option buyers, as price is likely to oscillate within a narrow range. Instead, such environments are typically more favourable for Option sellers, who can benefit from time decay and lack of directional movement.

Exception to the VWAP Rule:

While VWAP generally acts as a guiding benchmark for intraday bias, there are specific situations and chart patterns where short positions may still be initiated even when price is trading above VWAP. These exceptions arise when strong reversal signals or structural weaknesses are evident despite price being above the average. Some of these situations are given below:

1. When the first 1-hour candle forms a strong bullish candle and closes above VWAP, but the subsequent 2nd and 3rd candles fail to break its high, it indicates weakening upward momentum. In such cases, a short trade can be initiated near the high of the first candle, with a stop loss placed on a closing basis above that level.

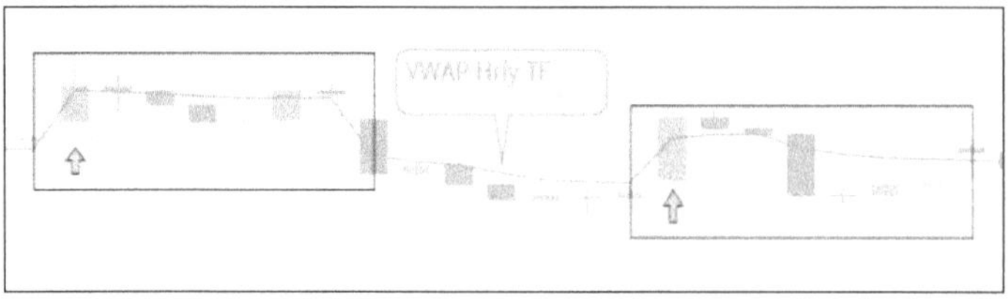

2. When trades are taken based on strong or major support/resistance levels, the position of price relative to VWAP becomes less significant. As long as the level is not breached convincingly (e.g., by the two-candle rule), the trade can be maintained irrespective of VWAP.
3. Golden entries based on Open High (OH) or Open Low (OL) patterns provide high-conviction setups where price action itself justifies the trade, even if VWAP conditions are not perfectly aligned.

These exceptions highlight the importance of price action and structural patterns alongside VWAP, rather than relying on VWAP in isolation. A few important Chart Patterns are discussed in detail under Chapter 12.

Trend Identification with VWAP & AVWAP:

Both AVWAP and VWAP can be used to assess market trend based on their slope and direction. When these averages are sloping upward at a steady angle (approximately 45 degrees), it indicates a strong uptrend. Conversely, when they are sloping downward, it reflects a downtrend. If either VWAP or AVWAP is relatively flat, it suggests a range-bound or consolidating market.

VWAP can indicate downward trend for positional trade:

When, over multiple sessions, both price and VWAP consistently trend downward, and price on the hourly timeframe continues to close below VWAP, it indicates a sustained bearish bias. This alignment can be considered a confirmation of a positional downtrend, where short positions may be initiated and held, until price begins to trade and sustain above VWAP on the hourly timeframe, signalling a potential shift in trend.

Trend identification through AVWAP for positional trade:

For a structured approach, AVWAP on the daily timeframe can be used to determine the broader market trend, while VWAP on the hourly timeframe can help identify the intraday trend. This combination allows traders to align short-term trades with the larger market direction, improving the probability of successful outcomes.

AVWAP and its usage is discussed in more detail below.

AVWAP AND ITS USAGE FOR INVESTMENT & TRADING

AVWAP is a powerful and flexible tool that allows a trader to measure the average price from a specific, meaningful point in time, chosen based on one's own analysis. Unlike VWAP, which resets daily, AVWAP is anchored manually to a crucial price point, enabling the trader to understand how price is behaving relative to that reference zone.

The effectiveness of AVWAP lies in selecting the right anchor point. Ideally, it should be placed at levels where market participants experienced extreme emotions—either maximum optimism (bullishness) or maximum fear (panic selling). These zones often correspond to major highs and lows, where significant accumulation or distribution by smart money takes place. As a refined approach, AVWAP is best anchored one candle prior to the identified high or low, as it better captures the beginning of the shift in sentiment.

Importantly, an AVWAP anchored at a major price high acts as a dynamic resistance, as it reflects the average price of participants who entered during peak optimism. Conversely, an AVWAP anchored at a major price low acts as a dynamic support, representing the average price of participants who accumulated during periods of fear. For instance, an AVWAP anchored at a major crisis low (such as the Lehman crisis) acted as a strong support level during later market corrections like the COVID crash—demonstrating how such levels continue to influence price behaviour over time.

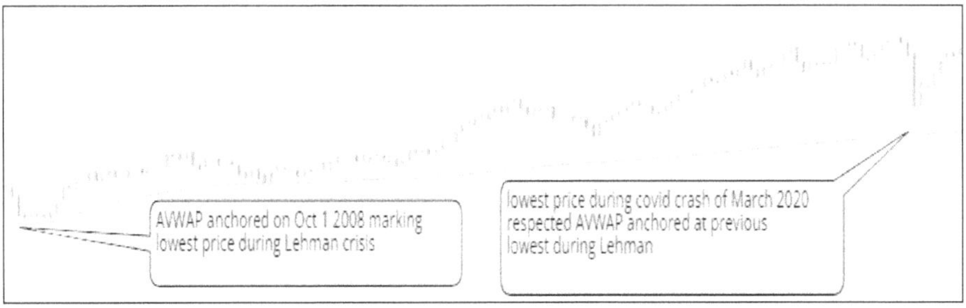

AVWAP must be anchored at the most recent high and low price points on a given Chart. For practical application, it is advisable to use multiple AVWAPs rather than relying on just one, as a single reference point may lead to incomplete analysis or traps. Typically, 2 to 3 well-placed AVWAPs are sufficient to create a reliable framework of dynamic support and resistance, while maintaining clarity on the chart.

When applied correctly, AVWAP helps identify high-probability zones for entry, exit, stop-loss placement, and position management across trading styles—whether in equities, futures, or options. It provides a clear view of where the majority of market participants are positioned, thereby helping traders decide which option to buy or sell, when to average positions, and when to exit.

AVWAP is equally effective across asset classes and market segments, including large-cap, mid-cap, and small-cap stocks, as well as indices. By tracking price relative to key anchored averages, traders and investors can align their decisions with the underlying flow of smart money and significantly enhance their trading precision.

Practical Placement of AVWAP – Identifying Key Support & Resistance Zones

AVWAP should ideally be anchored at zones of maximum optimism (hope) and maximum pessimism (fear). An AVWAP drawn from a major high typically acts as a dynamic resistance, while one anchored at a major low act as a dynamic support. For effective analysis, it is recommended to plot at least 2–3 AVWAPs—for example, two from significant lows (fear zones), one from a major high (hope zone), and optionally one from a relevant historical reference point (4–5 years back). AVWAP can be applied across timeframes, from the monthly chart down to the 10-minute timeframe, depending on the trading or investment horizon.

For instance, anchoring AVWAP on the most recent lowest point marks major "fear zone." This AVWAP often acts as a strong long-term support, and whenever price approaches such a level, it tends to become a high-probability investment zone (often referred to as a "golden area"). Historically, as discussed above, even during extreme events like the 2020 COVID crash, price corrected sharply but still respected this AVWAP anchored at previous lowest point (of Lehman crash), highlighting its strength.

For current times – we can place first AVWAP at the lowest price of March 2020 COVID bottom, representing a more recent fear-based accumulation zone of recent past. A second AVWAP may be anchored at a relevant intermediate point, such as a consolidation or structural phase (for example, around 2023 – Russia-Ukraine war times low), to capture medium-term price behaviour.

Finally, an AVWAP anchored at a recent major high (e.g., Nifty in January 2026 peak) serves as a dynamic resistance level, reflecting the average price of participants who entered during peak optimism. Price often reacts near such levels, making them important zones for profit booking or short opportunities.

By combining these AVWAP levels, traders and investors can build a multi-layered framework of support and resistance, enabling better decisions for entry, exit, averaging, and risk management across different time horizons.

In the Chart below we can see - AVWAP anchored at the lowest price point in the most recent past (was during Covid fall) will act as major support for any subsequent crash and likewise the AVWAP anchored at the highest point of recent past will act as the major resistance for the further upward trend. See Nifty's Chart below.

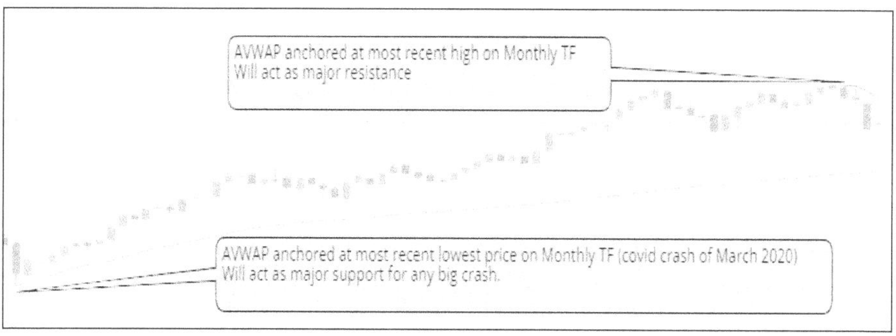

Using AVWAP on Indices & Stocks Charts:

AVWAP should be consistently applied on indices, as they reflect the broader market structure and provide a reliable directional framework. For investments in penny stocks, mid-cap, or small-cap stocks, AVWAP becomes even more valuable, as it helps in identifying potential multibagger opportunities by highlighting key accumulation and distribution zones.

One of the key advantages of AVWAP is its ability to filter out noise and reduce ambiguity created by standard technical indicators, offering clearer insight into true price positioning. Traders should first backtest applying AVWAP anchored at different significant levels and observe which levels are most consistently respected by a particular stock, option, or index. These respected zones often provide the most precise entry points and well-defined stop-loss levels.

For optimal placement, AVWAP should be anchored at major turning points—such as the highest point followed by a clear downward reversal (acting as resistance), and the lowest point followed by a meaningful reversal upward (acting as support). Proper use of AVWAP in this manner enables more structured and confident trading and investment decisions.

AVWAP works most effectively when combined with moving averages, as this confluence provides stronger confirmation of trend and key reaction zones. Trades based on AVWAP can be initiated on different timeframes depending on the holding period. For short-term positional trades (1–3 days), entries can be taken on the hourly timeframe, with the next pivot level acting as the stop loss. For slightly longer positional trades (around 6–7 days), the daily timeframe can be used, again with the next pivot level serving as the risk control point.

For investment purposes, AVWAP can be applied on the weekly timeframe, but the monthly timeframe offers the most reliable and meaningful signals, as it captures broader market sentiment and long-term accumulation zones.

In all cases, it is important to mark key static and dynamic support/resistance levels alongside AVWAP, as these zones often act as potential reversal or bounce areas. Using higher timeframes for AVWAP-based analysis generally results in more dependable signals and improves the overall quality of trading and investment decisions.

AVWAP on Monthly TF For Investments:

Whenever the market undergoes a meaningful correction and price averages itself near the Monthly AVWAP, it often presents a high-quality long-term investment opportunity. Such zones typically reflect deep value areas where strong hands accumulate, especially in large-cap stocks and sector leaders, which tend to outperform and lead the next phase of the market rally.

AVWAP when anchored at the max fear zone and viewed on a monthly Chart – offers insightful levels for great investment opportunities from best entry level perspective and best risk to reward perspective – which are relatively rare opportunities found once in several years (often 8–10 years), making them particularly significant for long-term investors. Historically, investments made near such levels have the potential to generate substantial returns, and in many cases, capital can multiply (2x–3x) within a reasonable time horizon, such as 150–200 trading sessions, as the market resumes its upward trend from these accumulation zones.

Trend Identification With AVWAP:

AVWAP can be effectively used to identify the broader market trend based on its slope and direction. When AVWAP is sloping upward at a steady angle (around 45 degrees), it indicates a clear uptrend, reflecting sustained buying strength. Conversely, when AVWAP is sloping downward, it signals a downtrend, indicating persistent selling pressure.

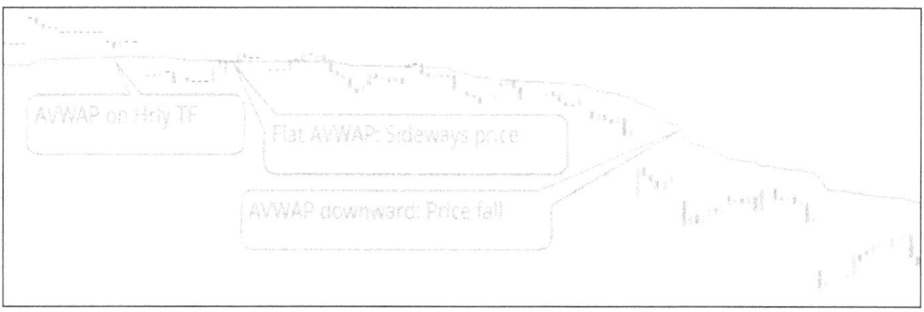

If AVWAP remains flat, it suggests that the market is range-bound, lacking clear direction. Using AVWAP on the daily timeframe helps in identifying the broader trend and aligning trades accordingly.

AVWAP Indicating Accumulation & Distribution:

A flat AVWAP typically coincides with a range-bound market, where price oscillates within a defined band. During such phases, Bollinger Bands on the daily timeframe often appear as a parallel channel, indicating low directional momentum. This structure usually represents a phase of accumulation or distribution by smart money.

The nature of this phase becomes clear upon breakout: if price breaks the range downward, it indicates that distribution was taking place; whereas if price breaks out upward, it suggests that accumulation was underway during the consolidation period.

AVWAP For Options Trading:

AVWAP can be effectively used for both option buying and selling, especially when applied to indices and their corresponding option chains. When AVWAP is anchored on a Futures' chart, the relevant options inherently reflect that structure from their inception ("born AVWAP"), allowing traders to analyse option price behaviour relative to meaningful average levels.

For intraday and short-term positional trades, AVWAP helps in trend identification. If AVWAP is sloping downward and the option's LTP is also declining, it indicates a bearish trend—favourable for option selling. Conversely, if AVWAP is sloping upward and LTP is rising, it indicates a bullish trend. For clearer trend assessment, it is advisable to analyse deep ITM options, as they closely track the underlying. Typically, when VIX is above 16, options with LTP above ₹1000 can be considered, and when VIX is lower, ITM options with LTP around ₹500–600 may suffice.

Role of AVWAP in Option selling

In options, AVWAP often acts as a strong dynamic resistance/support. When the LTP of an option approaches AVWAP and shows rejection or reverses from it, it presents a high-probability opportunity for option selling—especially if supported by price action patterns such as Open High (OH) near AVWAP. The deeper the ITM strike, the more reliable the signal.

If a trade is initiated near AVWAP but price crosses and sustains beyond it, the next reference should be the nearest pivot level. A confirmed breach and sustain beyond that pivot indicates invalidation, where losses should be booked. However, in most cases, if price has been trending consistently relative to AVWAP, it tends to respect nearby pivot levels and reverse.

For directional clarity:

- If deep ITM Call Options (CE) are trading below their AVWAP, it indicates a bearish trend in the underlying—favouring CE selling.
- If deep ITM Put Options (PE) are trading below their AVWAP, it indicates a bullish trend—favouring PE selling.

Once a short position is initiated and price begins to move favourably, and if a confirmed reversal setup forms above AVWAP and key pivot levels, traders may consider pyramiding positions with proper risk control.

It is also important to analyse the underlying index chart alongside the option chart. Key moves—such as momentum expansions (e.g., Bollinger Band expansion)—typically appear first on the relevant index / Futures' chart before reflecting in the option price. This helps in timely exits and better risk management.

Option buying using AVWAP

While AVWAP can also be used for option buying, it requires greater caution due to time decay and premium erosion. Generally, option selling using AVWAP is more consistent, but selective buying opportunities can still be identified.

For buying:

- Prefer far OTM options of monthly expiry (e.g., LTP below ₹200), as risk remains defined similar to a seller's stop loss.
- A buy setup emerges when price crosses above AVWAP, sustains above it, and consolidates near it (typically for 40–60 minutes on a 10-minute timeframe), indicating strength and acceptance above the level.
- Stop loss can be placed at the nearest support below AVWAP, or more conservatively at the third support level below AVWAP (to avoid stop-loss hunting in volatile conditions).

For better reliability, deep ITM options are preferred even for buying, as they exhibit less erratic movement and reduced stop-loss hunting near VWAP / AVWAP, compared to OTM or weekly options.

Overall, AVWAP provides a robust framework for option trading, particularly for identifying high-probability zones for selling, managing risk, and aligning trades with the underlying trend.

POWER OF VWAP & AVWAP

VWAP and AVWAP together form a powerful foundation for understanding price behaviour, trend, and market positioning. While VWAP provides a real-time intraday benchmark, helping traders identify fair value and short-term bias, AVWAP extends this concept across timeframes by anchoring price to key historical events and sentiment-driven turning points. Used in isolation, each indicator has its limitations—but when combined with price action, support/resistance, and moving averages, they offer a highly structured and reliable trading approach.

VWAP is best suited for intraday decision-making, guiding entries near dynamic support and resistance while helping avoid trades in indecisive or range-bound conditions. AVWAP, on the other hand, is a multi-timeframe tool that reveals deeper insights into accumulation, distribution, and long-term trend direction. It helps traders and investors align with smart money positioning for longer term investments, identify high-probability zones for entry and exit, and manage risk with greater precision.

A key takeaway is that **confluence is critical**. When VWAP and AVWAP align with each other and further coincide with major support/resistance levels or technical patterns, the probability of success increases significantly. Similarly, understanding when to avoid trades—such as during flat VWAP conditions or when price is trapped between key averages—is equally important in preserving capital.

Ultimately, consistent success with VWAP and AVWAP comes from practice, observation, and disciplined execution. By mastering their application across different market conditions and timeframes, traders can develop a robust, repeatable edge—whether for intraday trading, positional setups, or long-term investing.

Chapter – 7

Resistance & Support

The Stop-Overs

Support and resistance form the foundational pillars of price action, representing zones where buying and selling forces repeatedly interact. These levels are not random; they are largely created, respected, and sometimes decisively breached by smart money. Broadly, support and resistance can be understood in three forms:

i. First, **static levels**, which include clearly defined price zones such as pivots, CPR, or historical points where price previously reversed or consolidated.

ii. Second, **dynamic levels**, which evolve with price and are derived from indicators like VWAP, anchored VWAP, moving averages such as the 20 SMA, or volatility bands like Bollinger Bands.

iii. Lastly, **psychological levels**, often round-number zones like 17,000 or 18,000 in indices, where market participants tend to cluster their decisions. Together, these three types provide a structured framework to anticipate price behaviour and understand how market participants react at key levels.

Let us discuss each one of these types of resistance & support one by one.

STATIC RESISTANCE & SUPPORT

Static support and resistance refer to fixed price levels derived from historical market behaviour, where price has previously reversed, stalled, or consolidated. These levels remain constant over time and act as reference points for traders and investors to anticipate potential buying or selling interest. Common examples include previous swing highs and lows, pivot levels, and CPR zones. Since these levels are widely observed and often respected by market participants—especially institutional or smart money—they tend to influence price action repeatedly, making them a crucial element in Technical Analysis.

Static support and resistance based on CPR or pivot levels are relatively straightforward to use, as they can be easily added to the chart by selecting the respective indicator on the trading platform. In contrast, static support and resistance derived from previous swing highs and lows require manual identification and plotting, as they depend on interpreting past price movements directly from the chart.

Let us first discuss some of the major aspects about drawing the static resistance and support basis the previous swing high & low, respectively.

Resistance & Support Basis Previous High & Lows:

One of the most fundamental forms of static support and resistance is derived from previous swing highs and swing lows. A **swing high** represents a price level where the market previously faced selling pressure and reversed downward, while a **swing low** marks a zone where buying interest emerged, pushing price upward. These points act as natural reference levels because they reflect actual past reactions of market participants. Since traders and institutions closely watch these zones, price often tends to react when it revisits them, making swing highs and lows a simple yet powerful tool for identifying key resistance and support levels, respectively, on a chart.

Previous Resistance level

A **previous resistance level** represents a zone where the market was unable to move higher in the past, typically due to strong selling pressure—often referred to as a supply zone. Each time price approaches such a level, it tends to face rejection and move lower.

However, once price decisively breaks above a resistance level and sustains higher levels, the market structure begins to shift. If the price later reverses from a higher zone, that new zone becomes the next resistance, while the earlier resistance—now breached—transforms into support. In essence, a resistance level continues to act as resistance until it is broken; once breached, it often reverses its role and serves as a support level going forward.

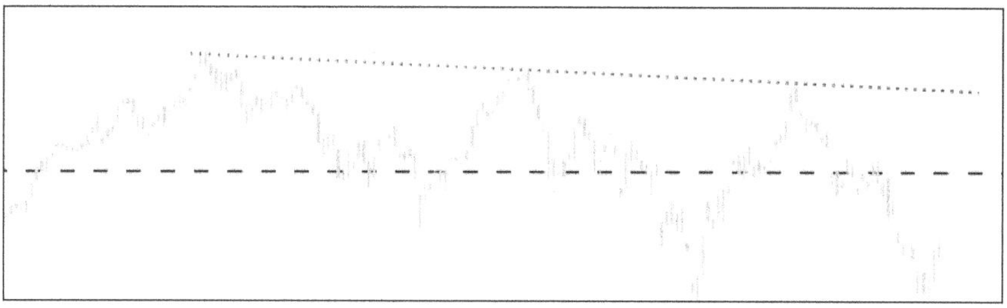

Previous Support level

Similarly, a **previous support level** represents a zone where the market was unable to decline further in the past, indicating the presence of strong buying interest or a demand zone. Each time price approaches such a level, it tends to find support and reverse upward.

However, once price decisively breaks below a support level and continues lower, the market structure shifts. If price later rebounds from a lower zone, that new zone becomes the next support, while the earlier support—now breached—turns into resistance. In other words, a support level continues to act as support until it is broken; once breached, it often reverses its role and acts as resistance.

Since price tends to respect previous support and resistance levels significantly, **it is essential to identify and mark these zones on the Chart** before planning or initiating any trade.

Plotting Resistance & Support level using trendline

Previous resistance and support (PR/PS) levels can be effectively identified using trendlines, typically requiring **at least two touchpoints formed by price** itself. It is important to understand that support and resistance are not precise lines but zones, often spanning a range of approximately 10–50 points.

A robust approach involves drawing one trendline connecting at least two candle closing points, and another along the wicks of at least two candles—thereby defining a clear **support or resistance zone.**

Trading previous Resistance & Support levels

Trading between support and resistance—buying near support and selling near resistance (and vice versa)—is generally considered a safer approach, as long as the levels hold. This is known as **range-bound trading**, which is often easier to execute compared to trending markets. However, during highly volatile conditions, such as periods of geopolitical or economic uncertainty, price may breach expected levels more frequently.

Stocks or indices that have been consolidating within a broad range over several weeks or months are particularly suitable for such strategies. Major support and resistance levels—especially those aligned with key indicators like the 20 SMA across multiple timeframes (monthly, weekly, or daily)—are often broken through:

- **gap-ups** or **gap-downs**; or
- even strong intraday momentum can lead to a decisive breakout or breakdown on the daily timeframe through a **single powerful bullish or bearish candle.**

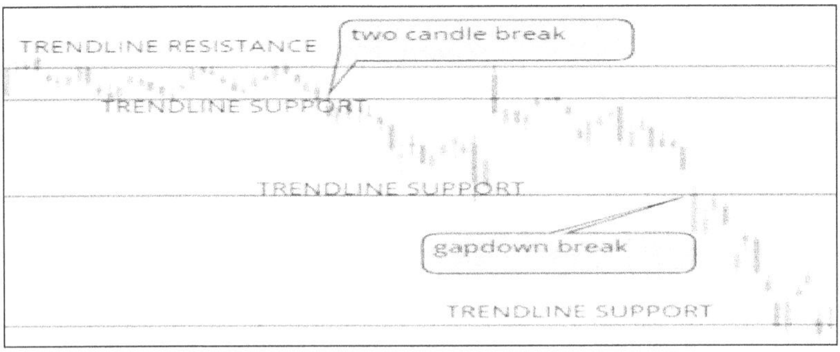

In an **uptrending market**, identifying resistance levels may be sufficient for trade planning. However, in a **downtrending market**, it becomes crucial to carefully identify multiple support zones—especially those where price has spent considerable time (typically 15–30 days or more) and has taken support repeatedly. The lowest such zone, where multiple lows have formed, can be used to establish a reliable support level in a falling market.

Let us know discuss the resistance & support levels basis the pivot levels plotted using the technical indicator.

Resistance & Support Basis Pivot levels:

Pivot levels provide a structured framework for identifying static support and resistance on any timeframe. The levels above the central pivot act as resistance—**R1**, **R2**, and **R3**—where R2 typically signals an overbought condition and R3 indicates an extreme or "super" overbought zone. Similarly, the levels below the central pivot act as support—**S1**, **S2**, and **S3**—where S2 reflects an oversold condition and S3 represents a deeply oversold zone.

Price generally tends to move **from one pivot level to another**, making these levels important reference points for both support/resistance and potential targets. The higher the timeframe, the stronger and more reliable these pivot-based levels tend to be.

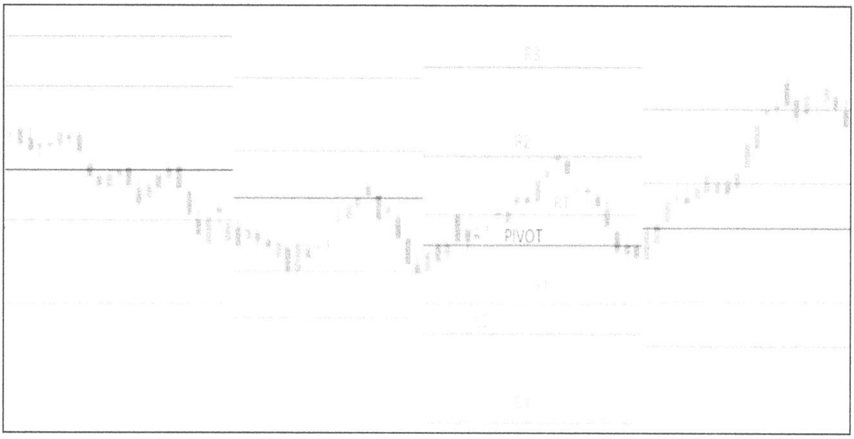

A key observation is that price should not linger or close repeatedly near a pivot level. For a meaningful move, price should cross a pivot decisively—either through a strong, **single big candle** or by following a **clear two-candle confirmation rule** (i.e. two candles clearly closing after crossing the relevant pivot line). If price fails to do so and instead starts consolidating around a pivot level, it often indicates a higher probability of reversal from that zone.

Trading Resistance & Support Levels:

When trading within a range defined by static support and resistance levels, the objective is to capitalize on price oscillations between these zones while respecting key confirmations and risk controls.

A **sell trade** is ideally initiated near a **major resistance** identified on the daily timeframe, with a stop loss placed on a closing basis above that resistance level. The entry is strengthened when price shows signs of reversal from the resistance zone and is supported by a sell signal (basis technical indicator) on the 1-hour timeframe. The target for such a trade is typically the next support level. A resistance continues to act as resistance until it is convincingly broken. A valid breakout is generally confirmed when two consecutive candles breach the level, with the second candle closing above the high of the first. If the second candle closes above the first candle's close but below its high, the breakout may be considered partially confirmed. Once resistance is decisively broken, it tends to act as support. In such cases, buying opportunities can be explored near this new support zone, provided there is a buy signal on the 1-hour timeframe, with stop loss placed below the new support or below the 5 SMA (low) on the daily timeframe, whichever is triggered first.

Similarly, a **buy trade** is initiated near a **major support** on the daily timeframe, with a stop loss on a closing basis below that support level. The setup is strengthened when price reverses upward from the support zone and is confirmed by a buy signal on the 1-hour timeframe. The target is typically the next resistance level. A support level remains valid until it is broken. A confirmed breakdown occurs when two consecutive candles breach the support, with the second candle closing below the low of the first. If the second candle closes below the first candle's close but above its low, the breakdown is only partially confirmed. Once broken, the previous support often acts as resistance. In such scenarios, short trades may be considered near this new resistance zone, with appropriate confirmation and stop loss above the level or above the 5 SMA (high) on the daily timeframe.

For **intraday trading**, the previous day's support and resistance levels are particularly important. If the **previous day's resistance** is not breached, price often reacts downward from that level. However, if it is broken, it tends to act as support. Likewise, the **previous day's support** acts as a key level—holding it may lead to a bounce, while a breakdown can turn it into resistance.

Intraday pivot levels also serve as important reference points. Trades initiated near support or resistance (based on signals from lower timeframes such as 10-minute charts) should generally be held unless the level is clearly breached with confirmation (e.g., two closing candles) and supported by indicator signals. In cases where a breakout or breakdown sustains for a reasonable duration (such as an hour), reverse trades can be considered to capture the momentum, using tools like VWAP, moving averages, or indicator confirmation, with stop loss based on the newly established level.

It is also commonly observed that if price tests a particular support or resistance level multiple times—typically four—there is a higher probability of a breakout or breakdown on the subsequent attempt, usually in the direction of repeated testing.

DYNAMIC RESISTANCE & SUPPORT

Dynamic support and resistance are derived from the average or median of price over a given period, rather than fixed historical levels. Unlike static levels, these zones continuously shift in response to ongoing price movements, making them adaptive in nature. Since they are based on evolving price data—such as moving averages, VWAP, or similar tools—dynamic support and resistance provide a real-time view of where buying or selling pressure may emerge, helping traders align with the current trend and market momentum.

Major dynamic Support and Resistance Levels

- **AVWAP & Moving Averages:**

  Tools such as AVWAP (anchored VWAP), VWAP and moving averages are key sources of dynamic support and resistance, as they are derived from the average price over a given period. Among these, AVWAP, the 20 SMA, 50 SMA, 200 EMA etc. are considered particularly strong levels—especially on higher timeframes like daily, weekly, and monthly charts. The higher the timeframe, the more reliable and influential these levels become. In practice, such strong dynamic levels are often breached only through decisive moves, typically via gap-ups / gap-downs or powerful momentum candles, reflecting significant participation from market players.

- **Bollinger Bands (upper & lower bands):**

  The upper and lower bands of Bollinger Bands (UBB and LBB) also act as dynamic support and resistance levels, as they are based on the statistical dispersion (and central tendency) of price. These levels often represent extreme zones, where price may face resistance (UBB) or find support (LBB). Dynamic levels derived from such median-based calculations tend to be highly responsive to volatility and can act as strong barriers, particularly on higher timeframes. Breaching these levels typically requires substantial momentum and volume, reinforcing their importance in identifying potential reversal or continuation zones.

DEMAND & SUPPLY ZONES

Demand and supply zones form an important category of support and resistance, rooted in the imbalance between buyers and sellers. A **demand zone** represents an area where buying interest is strong enough to halt a decline and push prices higher, thereby acting as a support zone. Conversely, a **supply zone** is an area where selling pressure dominates, preventing price from moving higher and causing it to reverse downward, thus acting as a resistance zone.

Unlike precise price levels, these zones are broader areas on the chart where institutional activity or large order flows are believed to have occurred. As a result, when price revisits these zones, it often reacts in a similar manner, either bouncing from demand or rejecting from supply.

How they are built:

These zones are typically formed during brief consolidation or basing phases, followed by a sharp and impulsive move in price. A **demand zone** is created when price pauses and then rallies strongly, indicating **accumulation**.

A **supply zone** forms when price consolidates and then drops sharply, indicating **distribution**.

The strength of the zone increases with the speed and magnitude of the subsequent move.

How they can be identified:

Demand and supply zones can be identified by spotting areas on the chart where price spent limited time before making a strong directional move. These are often characterized by small-bodied candles or tight consolidation followed by large bullish (demand) or bearish (supply) candles. The base of this move becomes the zone to watch for future price reactions.

Demand and supply zones can also be identified using technical indicators available on most trading platforms. Additionally, many traders create and share customized indicators—often open source—that automatically highlight these zones for easier analysis.

How they act as support and resistance:

When price revisits a demand zone, it often finds **support** as buyers step in again, causing a bounce. Similarly, when price returns to a supply zone, it tends to face **resistance** due to renewed selling pressure. These zones act as broader and often more reliable support and resistance areas compared to single price levels, as they reflect underlying market imbalances and unfilled orders.

These concepts are further discussed alongside other concepts in the relevant sections, where their identification and practical application in trading are discussed.

OVERBOUGHT & OVERSOLD ZONES

Overbought and oversold zones represent conditions where price has moved excessively in one direction relative to its recent behaviour. An **overbought** zone indicates that price has risen sharply and may be due for a pause or pullback, while an **oversold** zone reflects a steep decline where price may be ready to stabilize or rebound.

How they are built:

These zones are formed due to sustained momentum—either aggressive buying (leading to overbought conditions) or persistent selling (leading to oversold conditions). They often emerge when price deviates significantly from its average or equilibrium level over a given period.

How they can be identified:

Overbought and oversold conditions are typically identified using momentum and oscillating indicators such as RSI, Stochastic, or similar tools. For example, RSI values above a certain threshold (commonly 90 or above) may indicate overbought conditions, while values below a lower threshold (commonly 30) suggest oversold conditions. Visually, these zones may also coincide with price stretching far from key moving averages or volatility bands. You may learn more about this in Chapter 8 on Technical Indicators.

How they act as support and resistance:

Overbought zones often act as potential resistance areas, where upward momentum may likely gradually weaken and selling pressure can emerge. Conversely, oversold zones can act as support, where selling may likely exhaust and buying interest may step in. However, these are not exact price levels but rather **conditions that signal a higher probability of reversal or consolidation**.

How they differ from demand and supply zones:

While demand and supply zones are based on actual price areas where strong buying or selling occurred in the past, overbought and oversold zones are indicator-driven conditions derived from price momentum and relative positioning. Demand/supply zones are structural and price-based, whereas overbought/oversold zones are dynamic and derived from mathematical calculations of price behaviour.

How they can be used with indicators:

Overbought and oversold zones are most effectively used with technical indicators like RSI, Stochastic Oscillator, or Bollinger Bands. Traders often **combine them with price action—such as support/resistance or demand/supply zones—for better confirmation**. Additionally, customized indicators available on trading platforms can automatically highlight overbought and oversold conditions, helping traders quickly identify potential reversal or continuation opportunities.

MULTIPLE RESISTANCE & SUPPORT

When two or more types of support and resistance converge at the same price zone, it creates a significantly stronger and more reliable level. This phenomenon, often referred to as **confluence**, indicates that multiple market factors are aligned at a single point, increasing the probability of a meaningful price reaction. Such zones are closely watched by traders and institutions alike, making them highly tradable areas for both **reversal** and **breakout** strategies.

Dynamic levels like the upper and lower bands of Bollinger Bands (UBB/LBB) are inherently strong, as they are derived from the statistical behaviour (median and volatility) of price. When these levels align with other forms of support and resistance, their effectiveness is further amplified. The strength of such confluence zones increases with higher timeframes—making them particularly powerful on daily and weekly charts for positional trades, and on hourly charts for intraday setups.

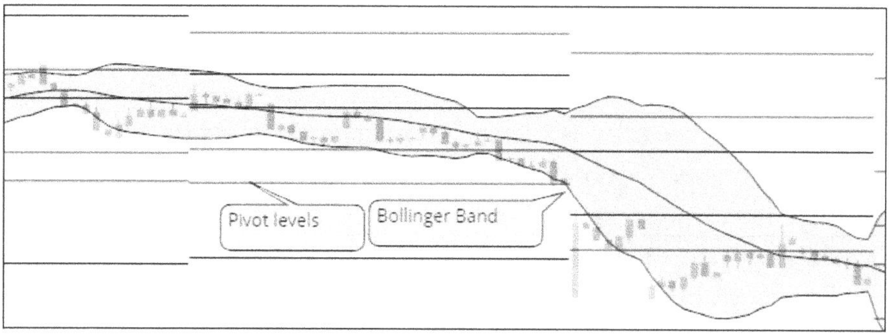

Common examples of strong confluence zones include the alignment of Bollinger Bands (UBB/LBB) with trendlines, pivot levels, or AVWAP; the overlap of key moving averages such as the 20 SMA with trendlines, pivots, or AVWAP; and the intersection of demand or supply zones with indicators like Bollinger Bands, moving averages, or pivot levels. When multiple such factors coincide, they form high-probability zones where price is more likely to react decisively, offering well-defined trading opportunities with favourable risk-reward setups.

Support and resistance levels derived from the median behaviour of price—such as those represented by the upper and lower bands of the Bollinger Bands (UBB/LBB)—are considered exceptionally strong. In many cases, these levels tend to be more reliable than other forms of dynamic or even static support and resistance.

The strength of such median-based levels lies in the fact that they incorporate underlying price distribution, volatility, and the cumulative impact of market participation. As a result, they often reflect zones where significant **accumulation** or **distribution** by institutional or "smart money" may have taken place, making them powerful areas where price is likely to react.

BREAKING OF RESISTANCE & SUPPORT

Support and resistance levels do not hold indefinitely; when price gathers sufficient momentum, these levels are eventually breached. Such breaches typically occur either through a **gap-up or gap-down opening** or via a **strong, wide-range momentum candle**, indicating decisive participation from market players. These moves often signal a shift in market structure and open up opportunities for continuation in the direction of the breakout or breakdown.

On lower timeframes, a breach may also be confirmed through a more structured approach known as the **two-candle rule**. In this method, the first candle crosses or breaches the support or resistance level, and the second candle confirms the move by closing beyond the extreme of the first candle—above the high in case of resistance breakout, or below the low in case of support breakdown. However, if the second candle closes beyond the close of the first candle but fails to cross its high (in breakout) or low (in breakdown), the move is considered only partially confirmed—often around 75%—leaving a degree of uncertainty and placing price in a potential "dilemma zone."

From a trading perspective, a breach of previous resistance (PR) or previous support (PS) can be used as an entry trigger. When resistance is convincingly broken, a long trade may be initiated, with a stop loss placed on a closing basis just below the breached resistance level. Similarly, when support is broken, a short trade can be initiated, with a stop loss on a closing basis just above the breached support. This approach allows traders to participate in emerging momentum while managing risk effectively around key structural levels.

Retesting of Resistance & Support:

Retesting is a common market behaviour where price revisits a previously established support or resistance level after reacting from it. Each time price approaches such a level and reverses, it offers a potential trading opportunity in the direction of the reversal—selling near resistance or buying near support. Typically, these retests can be traded with reasonable confidence for up to two or three occurrences, as the level continues to hold and demonstrate its validity.

However, caution is essential as the number of retests increases. When price approaches the same support or resistance level for the **fourth time**, the probability of a breakout or breakdown rises significantly. This is because repeated testing tends to weaken the level, gradually absorbing pending buy or sell orders at that zone. As a result, initiating reversal trades on the fourth retest is generally avoided.

Instead, traders should closely observe price behaviour during the fourth approach, as it often leads to a decisive move—either a strong breakout above resistance or a breakdown below support. Such moves are typically accompanied by increased momentum and can mark the beginning of a new trend or a meaningful shift in market structure.

Initiating Position of Resistance & Support:

Trades can be initiated based on one or more support and resistance zones identified on a given timeframe, with the highest probability setups emerging from **strong and well-established levels**. Ideally, traders look to initiate **short positions near major resistance** and **long positions near major support**, aligning with natural price behaviour within a range. However, it is essential to consider the broader market context before entering a trade. For instance, before initiating a **long trade near support** on a lower timeframe, one must check for any nearby resistance on higher timeframes (such as hourly, daily, or weekly), as this may limit upside potential.

Similarly, before initiating a **short trade near resistance**, it is important to assess whether a strong support exists on higher timeframes that could restrict downside movement. This multi-timeframe alignment helps improve trade quality and avoids entering positions against stronger opposing levels.

Caution Near Resistance & Support Before Position:

While support and resistance levels offer high-probability trading zones, it is equally important to exercise caution when price approaches these areas—especially under extreme market conditions. If the market is already in an **overbought or oversold state**, as indicated by tools such as RSI, higher timeframe trendlines, or broader market context (e.g., weekly timeframe), traders should avoid relying solely on signals from lower timeframes like 10-minute indicator setups. In such situations, short-term indicators may give misleading signals, and greater emphasis should be placed on **price action and overall market structure** rather than mechanical indicator triggers.

For **positional trades**, it is prudent to wait for confirmation on higher timeframes—preferably the hourly or, ideally, the daily chart—before initiating trades near major resistance or support levels. This ensures that the trade is aligned with stronger market signals and reduces the likelihood of false entries based on short-term noise.

Additionally, if price exhibits a **Bollinger Band expansion (BB blast)** near a major resistance or support level, it signals strong momentum. In such cases, initiating a reversal trade immediately can be risky. It is advisable to wait for signs of exhaustion or consolidation before considering a position—whether short near resistance or long near support.

Finally, traders must always remain prepared for the possibility that even strong support and resistance levels can be breached. Such breaches typically occur through **gap-up or gap-down openings** or via powerful momentum candles during intraday sessions. Recognizing this helps in maintaining disciplined risk management and avoiding overconfidence in any single level.

Initiating Intraday Position Near Resistance & Support:

Intraday trades are most effective when initiated around well-defined and high-probability levels. Broadly, entries can be considered at three key zones: **previous support/resistance (PR/PS)**, the **20 SMA on the hourly timeframe**, and **VWAP / AVWAP derived from the hourly context**. However, the entry should not be taken merely because price has reached these levels. It is important to wait for a **clear price reaction or reversal signal on a lower timeframe**, such as the 10-minute chart, to confirm that the level is being respected before entering the trade.

A useful intraday observation involves the behaviour of price around repeated retests. For instance, if price approaches a support level, rebounds toward VWAP, and then begins to decline again to retest the same support, it often signals weakening demand. In such cases, a **sell trade can be considered near VWAP**, anticipating that the second retest may lead to a breakdown and a sharper move downward. Conversely, if price tests resistance, pulls back toward VWAP, and then moves up again to retest the same resistance, it may indicate building strength. In such scenarios, a **buy trade near VWAP** can be considered, expecting a potential breakout and continuation upward.

Intraday trades can also be initiated around **pivot points and their associated support and resistance levels**, which often act as strong reference zones. When both pivot-based levels and VWAP are in close proximity, **greater weight should be given to pivot or support/resistance levels**, as price may temporarily move around VWAP and trigger stop losses before reacting at the stronger level. Ideally, trades should be initiated near these pivot or support/resistance zones, with a disciplined stop loss placed on a closing basis just beyond the level.

You can learn more about intraday trade setup and trading factors in Chapter 13 and about intraday chart patterns in Chapter 12.

WATCH THE RESISTANCE & SUPPORT

Thus, we note that Support and Resistance are among the most important and practical pillars of Technical Analysis because they represent the zones where market participants repeatedly react, hesitate, reverse, accumulate, distribute, or expand momentum. These levels may be static in nature, such as previous highs, lows, breakout zones, gap areas, or consolidation ranges; dynamic in nature, such as moving averages, VWAP, AVWAP, or trendlines; or psychological in nature, such as round numbers and emotionally significant price zones where market participants tend to react strongly. A sound understanding of these levels helps traders and investors identify where price may potentially pause, reverse, accelerate, or face rejection.

From a practical perspective, support zones often behave like a "trampoline" from where price absorbs selling pressure and attempts a bounce or reversal, while resistance zones frequently act as "show stoppers" where bullish momentum may slow down, face supply, or reverse downward. These zones therefore become extremely valuable for planning entries, exits, stop losses, profit booking, and risk management. Whether one is an intraday trader, swing trader, positional trader, or long-term investor, understanding how price behaves near key support and resistance levels can significantly improve trade quality and conviction.

Strong support and resistance zones often develop due to repeated market memory and institutional participation. Price tends to respect such zones because traders, investors, and institutions closely observe them and collectively react around these areas. This is why trades initiated near well-defined support or resistance zones are often considered stronger and more favourable trading plans, especially when confirmed by volume, price action, momentum, candlestick behaviour, Relative Strength, or broader market structure. In many situations, the best trading and investment opportunities emerge not in the middle of random price movement, but near significant support and resistance zones where risk can be better defined and probability becomes relatively more favourable.

Therefore, the ability to identify and interpret static, dynamic, and psychological support and resistance zones can provide a major practical edge in understanding market behaviour and planning disciplined market participation. Over time, close observation of how price reacts near these important levels can greatly enhance one's chart-reading ability, trade planning, patience, timing, and overall decision-making in the financial markets.

Chapter – 8

Technical Indicators

Pick the Tools, Use the Signals

Introduction to Technical Indicators:

Technical indicators are mathematical tools derived from **price, volume, and time**, designed to help traders interpret market behaviour and make informed decisions. They simplify complex price movements into **readable signals**, enabling traders to identify **trends, momentum, volatility, and potential reversal points**. Rather than relying on intuition, indicators provide a more **structured and objective framework** for analysing the market.

The significance of technical indicators lies in their ability to enhance decision-making through confirmation and confluence. No single indicator is sufficient on its own; however, when combined—such as **moving averages and VWAP / AVWAP for dynamic levels and pivot points and trendlines for key support / resistance**—they offer a clearer and more reliable market perspective. This layered approach helps traders filter out noise and focus on high-probability setups.

In practice, technical indicators are used to determine entry and exit points, stop-loss placement, and overall market bias. They guide traders in aligning with the prevailing trend, avoiding low-probability trades, and managing risk effectively. When applied with discipline and supported by price action, technical indicators become powerful tools for achieving consistency and precision in trading.

There are numerous technical indicators used across financial markets to study trend, momentum, volatility, volume, and market strength, such as Relative Strength Index (RSI), Moving Average Convergence Divergence (MACD), Bollinger Bands, stochastic oscillators, ADX, Ichimoku Cloud, ATR (Average True Range), Super trend, Donchian Channels, Keltner Channels, Fibonacci Retracement, Money Flow Index (MFI), OBV (On-Balance Volume), and several others. Each of these indicators has its own relevance, interpretation, strengths, and practical application, and it would certainly be useful for readers to gradually study and understand them over time. However, in this chapter, our focus will be on some of the most practical, reliable, and relatively less popular indicators and concepts which can provide powerful insights when used appropriately with price action, volume, and market structure. These tools can help traders and investors identify meaningful signals, improve probability assessment, and plan trades and investments with greater clarity, discipline, and conviction.

Let us discuss a few important and very reliable technical indicators below.

BOLLINGER BAND

Bollinger Bands are a powerful and versatile indicator that help in **identifying trends, key support and resistance levels, and market phases such as accumulation and distribution**. Owing to their adaptability, they serve as an excellent tool for **traders, investors, scalpers, as well as option buyers and sellers**.

Often regarded as an **"all-in-one" indicator**, Bollinger Bands provide valuable insights into volatility, price expansion, and contraction. Their effectiveness is further enhanced when used in combination with other systems or indicators, resulting in **more reliable and high-probability trading signals**. It is a ready-made indicator and can be selected from the trading terminal.

Bollinger Band Indicating Trend:

Bollinger Bands are highly effective in identifying the **direction and strength of a trend**. When **price moves upward and the bands themselves are curving and expanding upward**, it indicates a **strong uptrend**. Conversely, when both **price and the bands curve downward and move lower**, it signals a **downtrend**.

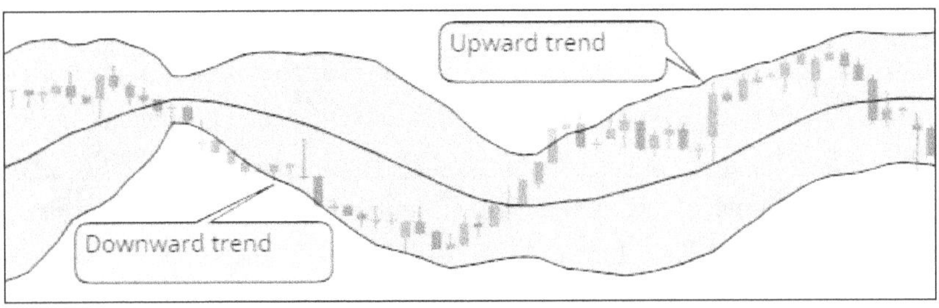

In a well-established uptrend, **pullbacks or dips toward the middle band or lower band often present buying opportunities**, as the overall direction remains bullish. Similarly, in a downtrend, **price rises or pullbacks toward the middle or upper band tend to offer selling opportunities**, as the broader trend remains bearish.

In simple terms, **"buy on dips in an uptrend and sell on rises in a downtrend"**, as indicated by the direction and curvature of the Bollinger Bands.

Bollinger Band Indicating Resistance & Support:

Bollinger Bands are highly effective in identifying **dynamic support and resistance (R/S) levels**. The **Upper Band (UBB) and Lower Band (LBB)** are derived from the dispersion of price around its average, while the **mid-line represents the 20-period moving average (20 SMA)** of the chosen timeframe (hourly, daily, weekly, monthly, etc.). Since these bands are based on price behaviour and volatility, they often act as **strong and reliable R/S zones**, especially on higher timeframes.

The **UBB typically acts as resistance**, while the **LBB acts as support**, particularly on higher timeframes such as Daily, Weekly, or Monthly charts, where price does not easily sustain beyond these levels. When **Bollinger Band levels align with trendline-based or static support/resistance**, the strength of that level increases significantly, making it a high-probability reaction zone.

On higher timeframes like the **Weekly chart**, the UBB and LBB act **as major resistance and support levels, respectively. Sustained breakouts beyond these levels are relatively rare. Therefore, short trades can be considered near the UBB (major resistance) and long trades near the LBB (major support), provided there is confirmation from lower timeframe indicators. Stop loss in such trades should be placed beyond the extreme of the band (above UBB or below LBB).**

Similarly, on the **Daily timeframe**, the UBB and LBB serve as strong positional R/S levels. Trades can be initiated near these zones once reversal is confirmed on a lower timeframe (such as hourly charts). These levels also remain relevant for intraday trading when higher timeframe bands are near the current price.

It is important to note that price may occasionally **pierce the UBB or LBB**, but often this results in wicks rather than sustained moves. Hence, traders must focus on whether the price closes beyond the band, rather than reacting to intraday spikes.

The **middle line of the Bollinger Band (20 SMA)** acts as a **dynamic equilibrium level or "line of gravity"**, continually attracting price. It functions as both **support and resistance**, depending on market direction. When a significant gap develops between price and the 20 SMA, it indicates that the market is likely to **revert toward the average**, either through price correction (distribution) or time correction (accumulation). Therefore, it is generally advisable to **avoid entries when price is far from the 20 SMA** and wait for price to re-align with its average before taking a position.

From a trend perspective, if **price sustains above the 20 SMA on the Daily timeframe**, the market is considered **bullish**, whereas sustaining below it indicates a **bearish trend**. When both price and the 20 SMA move upward together, it confirms an uptrend; when both move downward, it confirms a downtrend. A **flat 20 SMA** suggests a **range-bound market**, often accompanied by narrowing Bollinger Bands.

A strong breakout from this range typically requires **high volume and momentum**. Once price makes a decisive **Bollinger Band "blast"** (breaking out of the band with strength), it often leads to a **new trending phase** in that direction.

The **20 SMA on the Daily timeframe also serves as a key exit zone**. For instance, if a trader is holding a long position and price approaches the 20 SMA from below, it may act as resistance and prompt an exit. However, if price **breaks above and sustains beyond the 20 SMA**, it may signal a shift in trend, allowing for fresh long positions.

In terms of price movement within the bands, when price **rises from the LBB**, it often moves toward the **middle band (20 SMA)**, which initially acts as resistance. Once price **breaks and sustains above the 20 SMA**, it tends to move toward the **UBB**. Conversely, when price **falls from the UBB**, it typically moves toward the **middle band**, which acts as support; a sustained breakdown below it can lead price toward the **LBB**.

Such transitions across the 20 SMA often occur through **gap-ups, gap-downs, or strong momentum candles**, which may not always provide ideal entry points. As a result, traders may need to **wait for the next opportunity away from the 20 SMA** to participate in the emerging trend effectively.

Bollinger Band Indicating Momentum:

A **Bollinger Band (BB) Blast** signifies a powerful breakout backed by **strong volume and momentum**. For price to **sustainably break above the Upper Band (UBB)** or **below the Lower Band (LBB)**, it must be supported by significant strength. Such moves are not random—they typically emerge after a **phase of low volatility and consolidation**.

A BB Blast is most likely to occur when the bands remain narrow for an extended period (approximately 15–30 candles on a given timeframe). The tighter the bands, the stronger the potential breakout. This phase often reflects **smart money accumulation or distribution**, preparing for a directional move. Once the breakout occurs, the bands expand sharply ("open up"), and price tends to trend strongly in the breakout direction.

The duration and impact of a BB Blast depend on the timeframe:

- On **Hourly TF**: Momentum may sustain for **2–3 days**
- On **Daily TF**: Momentum may continue for **7–28 days**
- On **Weekly TF**: The move can be **significant and long-lasting**

For confirmation on the **Daily timeframe**, if the **first candle breaks the UBB/LBB**, the **second candle should ideally open with a gap (gap-up/gap-down)** to validate the breakout. Weekly BB Blasts should be confirmed **only on the weekly close (Friday)**.

Trading the BB Blast:

Once a BB Blast is confirmed, **price typically rides along the UBB/LBB**, maintaining momentum. Traders can initiate **long/short positions around the 2nd or 3rd candle**, preferably when price retraces to about the **1/3rd level of the previous candle**, offering a better risk-reward setup. If supported by strong patterns like **OH/OL**, the setup becomes even more reliable.

In **intraday trading**, BB Blasts on **5-min, 10-min, or 15-min charts** can be effectively traded. On the **Daily TF**, if price sustains **above/below VWAP for about an hour**, it further strengthens the probability of a trending move.

Traders may consider **futures or even naked options** in such high-momentum environments (with prudent risk management, such as partial profit booking).

A practical exit approach is to **trail using the 5 SMA (low/high)**—stay in the trade as long as price respects it and exit once it is breached.

Exit Signals / Caution Zones:

It is advisable to exit the trade when:

- Price forms a **BB trap (completely outside the band)**
- Price **re-enters inside the band** after breaching the 5 SMA
- Reversal candles like **Doji / Hammer** form near UBB/LBB, followed by confirmation candles (e.g., OH/OL patterns)

Additionally, confirmation from **lower timeframe indicators** should be used to validate exits.

Important Rules:

- **Avoid buying when price is riding the LBB**
- **Avoid shorting when price is riding the UBB**
- In a BB Blast on LBB, if the **UBB starts curving downward**, it reinforces continued downside
- In a BB Blast on UBB, if the **LBB curves upward**, it supports continued upside

Pre-Blast Identification:

If the market remains **range-bound for 2–3 days** and Bollinger Bands become **extremely narrow (funnel/balloon mouth formation)**—especially on the **Hourly TF**—it signals an impending BB Blast. Traders can anticipate this and prepare for a **high-momentum breakout**.

A strategic approach is to **enter based on a BB Blast on a lower timeframe (e.g., 30-min TF)**, using **5 SMA-based stop-loss**, and manage positions using even lower TFs (e.g., 10-min for option buyers).

On **expiry days**, if a BB Blast occurs on the **Hourly TF**, it can lead to **exceptionally strong trending moves ("jackpot days")**. Traders can attempt to ride such trends until **1:30–2:00 PM**, and even beyond if the option has moved deep ITM, as it starts behaving like futures in the later part of expiry day.

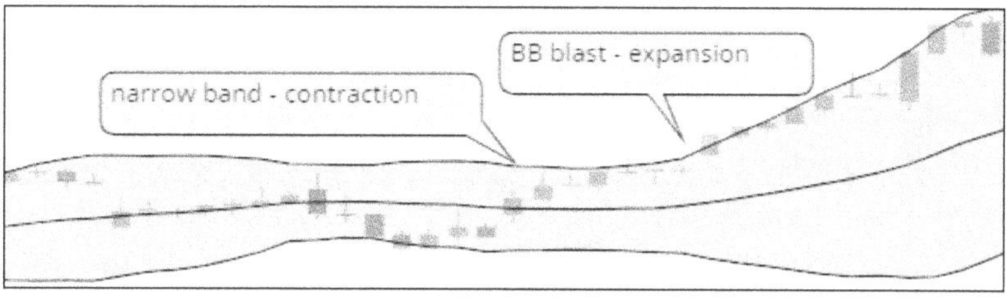

In essence, a **BB Blast marks the transition from consolidation to expansion**, offering some of the **highest-probability momentum trading opportunities**—provided it is traded with discipline and confirmation.

Confirmation of Bollinger Band (BB) Blast on Daily Timeframe:

A potential **BB Blast on the Daily timeframe** is identified when the **first candle breaks above the Upper Band (UBB)** or **below the Lower Band (LBB)**. However, this initial breakout alone is not sufficient—**confirmation is essential** to validate the move.

A BB Blast is considered **confirmed** when the **second candle opens with a gap-up (for bullish) or gap-down (for bearish)** and **sustains its position for at least 1–2 hours in intraday trading above/below VWAP** in the direction of the breakout. Additionally, the second candle should **close beyond the high (in a bullish case) or below the low (in a bearish case) of the first candle**, reinforcing the strength of the move.

Such confirmation indicates that the breakout is backed by **strong participation and momentum**, increasing the probability of a **sustained trending move** in the direction of the BB Blast.

False Bollinger Band (BB) Blast:

Not every BB Blast results in a sustained trending move. A **false BB Blast** occurs when the breakout lacks a strong foundation of **proper consolidation and volatility contraction**, and therefore fails to generate lasting momentum.

Such false signals typically arise in the following situations:

- When the prior range is **not sufficiently narrow**, but rather appears as a **wide channel that expands further near its breakout point**
- When the consolidation phase is **too short-lived**, resembling a **balloon with a very small mouth**, indicating inadequate buildup before the breakout

In these cases, although price may initially **break above the UBB or below the LBB**, the move tends to **lose strength within a few candles**. Subsequently, the bands begin to **curve back inward**, with the UBB (in an upside breakout) or LBB (in a downside breakout) **flattening or turning toward the price**, signalling exhaustion of momentum.

Such setups are classic **traps for momentum traders, investors, and scalpers**, as they create the illusion of a strong breakout but fail to sustain direction.

Key takeaway: A reliable BB Blast requires **tight consolidation over a meaningful period**. Without this, any breakout should be treated with caution, as it is more likely to **fizzle out rather than evolve into a sustained trend**.

Failed Bollinger Band (BB) Blast:

A BB Blast does not always evolve into a sustained trend. At times, after an initial breakout and brief movement along the **UBB/LBB**, the setup begins to lose momentum—indicating a **failed BB Blast**. Recognizing early signs of failure is critical to **protect profits and avoid reversals.**

A BB Blast may be considered **failing or failed** if any of the following conditions emerge:

1. Price Closes Outside the Band with Reversal Signs

If price moves completely outside the UBB/LBB (either fully detached or only partially touching the band), it signals potential exhaustion. This becomes more significant if the candle forms reversal patterns such as *Doji, Hammer, Inverted Hammer, or Spinning Top*. In such cases, traders should watch **the next candle closely**.

Also, if it:

- Forms an **OH/OL-type pattern**, or
- **Breaches the 5 SMA**, or

- **Closes below the low (near UBB) / above the high (near LBB)** of the reversal candle

It is advisable to **exit the trade**, as the blast is likely failing.

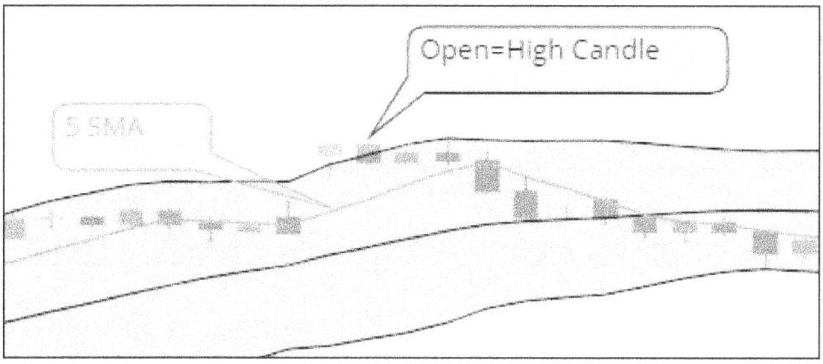

2. Price Re-enters the Band After Breakout

If price, after initially riding the band, **comes** back inside the Bollinger Bands and closes within them, it indicates weakening momentum. This is especially important if accompanied by reversal candles.

If the 2nd or 3rd candle continues to form within the band, it confirms that price is no longer trending along the band.

Exit signals in such scenarios include:

- Formation of **OH/OL patterns**
- **Breach of 5 SMA (low/high depending on TF)**
- Breakdown of the **reversal candle structure near UBB/LBB**

In such cases, it is prudent to exit by the 3rd or at most the 4th candle, as continuation becomes unlikely.

3. Rejection at Key Levels (Pivot / AVWAP / Major R-S)

While price is moving along the band, if it approaches a significant level such as:

- **Pivot points**
- **AVWAP levels**
- **Strong static or dynamic support/resistance,**

and **fails to break through**, followed by reversal-type formations (as described above), it signals **loss of momentum**.

In such situations, traders should remain cautious and look for timely exits, as the probability of a failed BB Blast increases.

A successful BB Blast requires continuity along the band with strong momentum. The moment price starts showing exhaustion, reversion inside the band, or rejection at key levels, it is a warning that the trend may not sustain. Early identification of these signs helps in locking profits and avoiding sharp reversals.

Bollinger Band Indicating Accumulation & Distribution:

When price remains confined within the Bollinger Bands for an extended period (typically 3–6 months or more), it reflects a **phase of consolidation**, during which the market is either undergoing **accumulation** (strategic slow buying by smart money) or **distribution** (strategic slow selling by smart money).

During such phases, the bands often **contract and move sideways**, indicating reduced volatility and a lack of clear direction. However, this quiet phase is usually a **prelude to a significant move**.

- If price eventually breaks out above the Upper Band (UBB) and sustains, it suggests that the prior phase was one of **accumulation**. Demand begins to dominate, leading to the **start of an uptrend**.
- Conversely, if price breaks down below the Lower Band (LBB) and sustains, it indicates that the prior phase involved **distribution**. Supply takes control, resulting in the **start of a downtrend**.

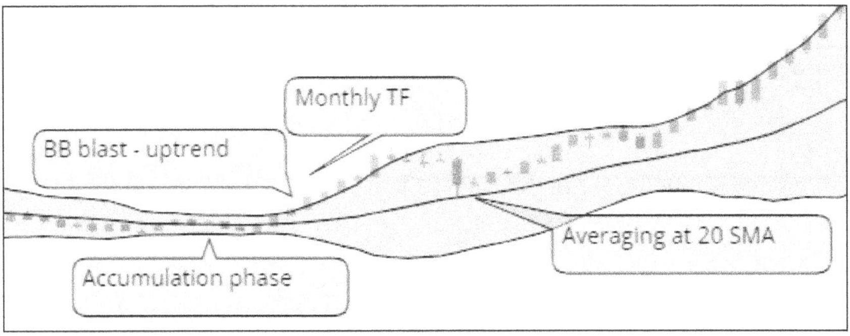

Key takeaway: Prolonged range-bound movement within Bollinger Bands should not be ignored—it often represents smart money positioning. The eventual breakout or breakdown from this range typically defines the next major directional move in the market.

CENTRAL PIVOT RANGE & PIVOT LEVELS

Central Pivot Range (CPR):

It is a ready-made indicator and can be selected from the trading terminal. The width of the CPR is a powerful indicator of expected market behaviour across timeframes.

- A **narrow CPR** suggests a high probability of trending or volatile movement
- A **wide CPR** indicates a likely range-bound or sideways trend

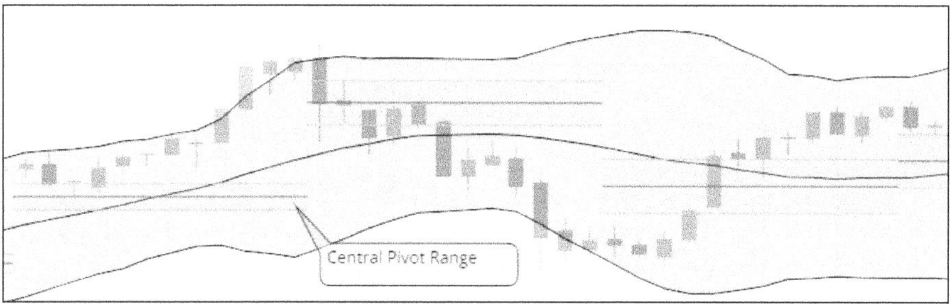

CPR can be interpreted across multiple timeframes to gauge momentum at different horizons:

- **Monthly (M TF):** Provides insight into the **expected momentum for the year ahead**
- **Weekly (W TF):** Reflects **quarterly momentum trends** within the year
- **Daily (D TF):** Indicates the **likely momentum for the ongoing month**
- **Hourly (H TF):** Helps assess **weekly momentum**, further broken down into days
- **10-15 Min TF:** Offers guidance on **intraday momentum for the current trading session**

Pivot Levels:

Pivot Points act as **key static support and resistance levels**, helping traders identify **market direction, entry zones, and targets** across timeframes.

- The **central line of the CPR** is the **main Pivot (P)**, which serves as the focal point of the market. It indicates whether the market is leaning bullish or bearish.
- Pivot levels above the main Pivot—**R1, R2, and R3**—act as **resistance levels**:
  - **R2** indicates an **overbought zone**
  - **R3** represents a **highly overbought (extreme) zone**
- Similarly, pivot levels below the main Pivot—**S1, S2, and S3**—act as **support levels**:
  - **S2** indicates an **oversold zone**
  - **S3** represents a **highly oversold (extreme) zone**

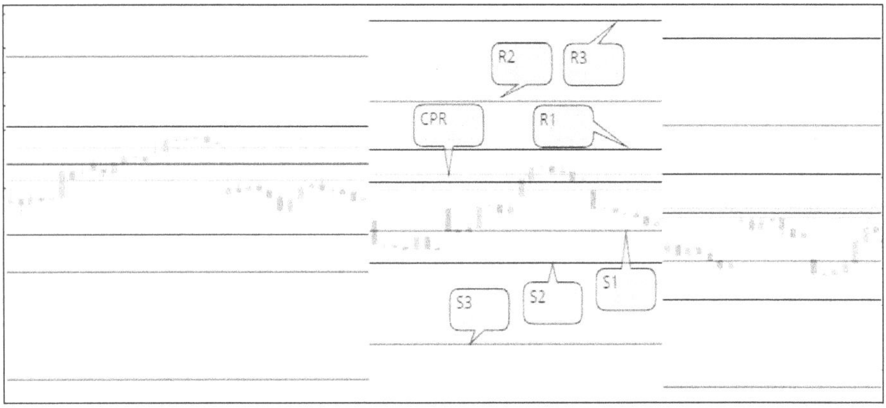

Price typically **moves from one pivot level to another**, making these levels useful for **target identification** in addition to traditional support/resistance.

For experienced traders, **Pivot Points combined with VWAP** can be sufficient to trade effectively based purely on **price action**, provided there is adequate confirmation.

Timeframe usage of Pivot Levels:

- **10-min TF: Intraday trading**

- **Hourly & Daily TF: Positional trading**
- **Weekly & Monthly TF:** Investment perspective

Behaviour around Pivot Levels:

Price should ideally not linger near a pivot level. A valid move occurs when price crosses a pivot decisively, either via a strong momentum candle or by the two-candle confirmation rule. If price instead starts consolidating near a pivot, it often indicates a possible reversal from that level.

Overbought / Oversold Zones of Pivot Levels:

Reaching **R2/R3 (overbought)** or **S2/S3 (oversold)** does **not automatically signal reversal.** Markets can continue trending beyond these levels.

- In strong uptrends, price may **move higher up from R1 → R2 → R3 and beyond** before reversing
- In strong downtrends, price may **fall from S1 → S2 → S3 and lower** before finding support

Hence, reversal trades should be taken only with additional confirmation (e.g., RSI extremes, reversal patterns, or indicator support).

Daily TF Pivot (Monthly View):

Pivot levels on the **Daily timeframe** provide a **monthly directional bias.**

- If price opens and sustains below the pivot, the bias remains bearish (sell on rise), unless it closes above the pivot convincingly.
- Once price crosses above and sustains over the pivot, it signals a shift toward bullishness.

This analysis should be validated using other tools like HM system, Fractals, and Bollinger Bands before initiating trades.

Monthly TF Pivot (Investment Perspective):

For longer-term investments, price often moves from the **central pivot toward R1 and R2.**

  - **R2** is a practical level for **profit booking**
  - **R3** is less frequently achieved in a single move and should be treated as an extended target

Key Insight: Pivot Points provide a structured framework for market movement, helping traders align entries, exits, and targets—but they are most effective when used in conjunction with other technical tools and confirmations.

HM SYSTEM: CUSTOMIZED INDICATOR

The **HM System** is a customized technical indicator developed by Mr. N K Singh of NK Stocktalk. It is widely known and popularly referred to as the "*hilega milega" system* among traders.

The HM System is created on the logic that the price movement is driven by the **flow of volume**—either being absorbed or distributed—which in turn determines the **momentum of price**. This momentum ultimately shapes the **strength or weakness of the trend**. The HM System is designed to capture and integrate these key elements—**volume, momentum, and price strength**—to provide a clearer indication of **market direction**, thereby aiding in informed buy or sell decisions.

The **HM System** is constructed using a combination of indicators: **RSI (9 period)** with overbought & oversold markers both at 50, **EMA (3 period applied on RSI 9)**, and **WMA (21 period applied on RSI 9)**, which together help in identifying shifts in momentum and trend strength with greater clarity. Once this combination is plotted – it can be used on all timeframes to identify strength and initiate trading / investment positions.

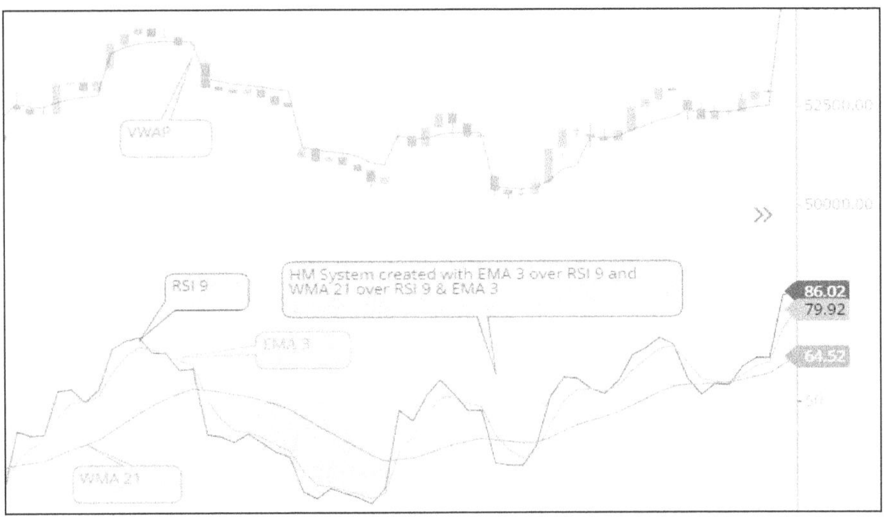

HM System – Buy & Sell Signal:

A **buy signal** is generated when RSI (9) is above 50 and RSI (9) is above WMA (21). Conversely, a **sell signal** is indicated when **RSI (9) is below 50 and also below WMA (21)**. Signals derived from higher timeframes are more reliable. For instance, a sell indication on the **Hourly timeframe** may suggest the onset of a downtrend; however, stronger confirmation from higher timeframes—such as a **3-hour or Daily timeframe buy/sell signal**—provides greater conviction for trend validation.

HM System Indicating Cessation of Trend or Reversal:

In any given timeframe, when RSI (9) crosses above WMA (21), it indicates that the downward momentum is likely to pause, though a confirmed **uptrend** begins only when RSI (9) crosses above 50 while remaining above WMA (21). Similarly, when WMA (21) crosses above RSI (9), it suggests that the **upward momentum is weakening**, and a confirmed **downtrend** begins once RSI (9) crosses below 50 with WMA (21) above it.

HM System Indicating Trend Continuation:

When both RSI (9) and WMA (21) are below 50, and EMA (3) is above RSI (9) with a clear gap, the market is likely to continue its downtrend. This fall tends to pause when RSI (9) and EMA (3) converge. A potential bullish reversal begins when RSI (9) crosses above EMA (3), and is further confirmed when RSI (9) crosses above WMA (21) and then above 50.

Conversely, when both RSI (9) and WMA (21) are above 50, and RSI (9) is above EMA (3) with a clear gap, the market is in a sustained uptrend. The rise weakens when **RSI and EMA converge**. A potential bearish reversal starts when **EMA (3) crosses above RSI (9)**, and is confirmed when RSI (9) falls below WMA (21) and then below 50.

HM System Indicating Momentum After Failed Reversal:

In a downtrend (RSI and WMA below 50), if RSI (9) crosses above EMA (3) but fails to cross WMA (21) and subsequently falls back below EMA (3), it indicates a failed reversal attempt. In such cases, the downward momentum strengthens, often leading to a sharper decline. This behaviour highlights that incomplete reversals tend to accelerate the prevailing trend, making it crucial to wait for full confirmation before acting.

HM System For Investment Decisions:

For investment perspective, the aforesaid information about HM System indication is equally applicable. Further, early signals like RSI crossing EMA (3) on higher timeframes (e.g., Monthly / Weekly) may indicate bottom or top formation, though they carry higher risk of false signals.

A **multibagger trend** is often indicated when **RSI (9) sustains above 70 on Monthly or Weekly timeframes**, reflecting strong and sustained bullish momentum. However, when RSI (9) approaches or exceeds 86 on these higher timeframes, the market typically enters an **extremely overbought zone**, making it prudent to **consider exiting or booking profits** as the probability of correction increases. Likewise, when RSI (9) in HM System approaches or drops below 27 on higher timeframes, the market typically enters an **extremely oversold zone** – from where it is likely to take a bounce – either temporary or a sustained reversal.

The effectiveness of the **HM System** improves significantly when used in conjunction with **Bollinger Bands (BB)**. Situations where HM signals may appear ambiguous or inconclusive can often be clarified through BB behaviour, such as volatility expansion, band positioning, or price interaction with bands. **Using both together enhances decision-making and reduces uncertainty**.

In terms of overall effectiveness and reliability, **Bollinger Bands** are considered the most comprehensive indicator, followed by **AVWAP** for dynamic support/resistance and trend identification, and then the **HM System** for momentum and directional confirmation. When these indicators are used in combination, they provide a robust and well-rounded trading framework.

FRACTAL CHAOS BAND

The **Fractal Chaos Band** is a volatility-based indicator derived from **fractal highs and lows**, which dynamically plots an **upper and lower band** around price. It helps traders identify **market structure, trend direction, and breakout zones** by highlighting areas where price has historically reversed or consolidated.

Unlike static levels, this band adapts to price action, making it useful for understanding whether the market is **trending or rangebound**. It is a ready-made indicator and can be selected from the trading terminal.

Fractal Chaos Indicating Support & Resistance:

The Fractal Chaos Band acts as a **dynamic support and resistance (R/S) framework** on any given timeframe. When applied on higher timeframes such as the **Weekly chart**, it provides a **broad perspective of market direction**—whether the market is trending upward, downward, or moving sideways within a range. It also helps define the **outer boundaries of price movement**, offering a structured range within which the market operates.

Fractal Chaos Indicating Breakout - Breakdown:

A **bullish breakout** is confirmed when price closes above the upper band and sustains with at least two consecutive closes outside the band. Before initiating a long trade, it is important to assess nearby resistance factors such as AVWAP, Bollinger Bands, 20 SMA, Pivot levels, trendlines, or supply zones, which may hinder further upside. Once price establishes itself above the band and continues trending, the market is considered bullish until price re-enters the band. During such phases, short trades should generally be avoided, unless clear weakness is observed (e.g., price moving below VWAP).

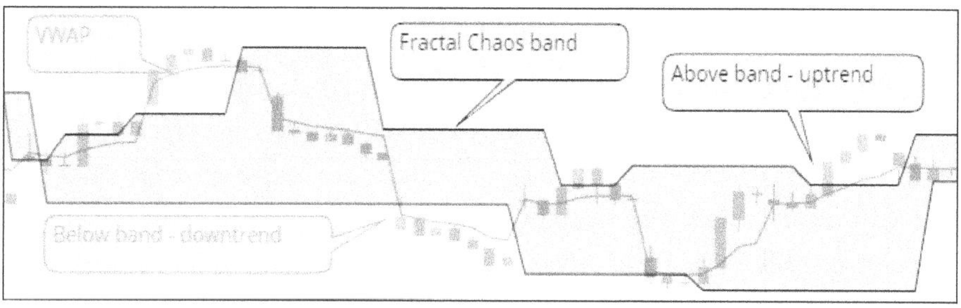

A **bearish breakdown** is confirmed when price closes below the lower band with at least two sustained closes outside it. Prior to initiating short trades, traders should evaluate nearby support levels such as AVWAP, Bollinger Bands, 20 SMA, Pivot levels, trendline supports, or demand zones. Once price trends below the band, the market is considered bearish until it re-enters the band.

In such conditions, long trades should be avoided, unless price begins to regain strength (e.g., sustaining above VWAP).

Fractal Chaos for Investment:

On the **Monthly timeframe**, the Fractal Chaos Band becomes a powerful tool for **long-term investment decisions**. A sustained breakout above the upper band can signal the beginning of a **strong bullish phase**, where long positions may be initiated and held until price re-enters the band. However, re-entry into the band does not necessarily indicate an immediate short opportunity.

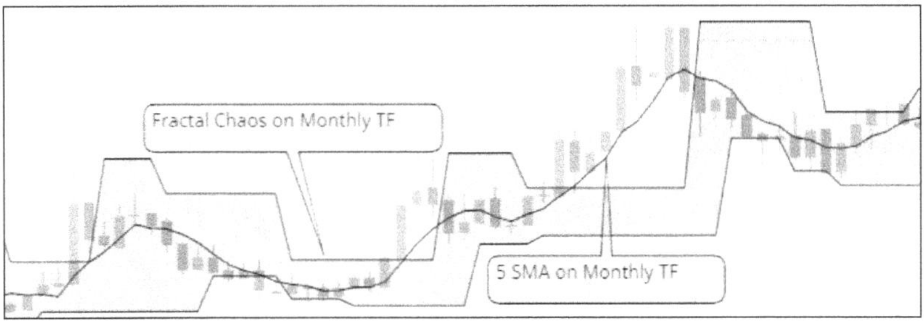

For bearish positioning on higher timeframes, additional confirmations—such as **price failing to sustain above key moving averages (e.g., 5 SMA low)**—should be considered before taking a short view.

EHLER FISHER TRANSFORM

The **Ehler Fisher Transform** is a momentum-based technical indicator designed to **identify trend direction, turning points, and extreme price conditions** with high sensitivity. By transforming price data into a normalized scale, it helps highlight **clear bullish and bearish signals**, making it particularly effective for **intraday as well as positional trading**. It is a ready-made indicator and can be selected from the trading terminal.

EF Transform Indicating Trend:

The zero line in the Ehler Fisher Transform acts as a **key reference level**. When the **indicator line is above the zero line**, it signifies a **bullish bias** on that timeframe; when it is **below the zero line**, it indicates a **bearish bias**. On higher timeframes such as **Daily, Weekly, or Monthly**, the position of the EF line relative to the zero line provides a strong indication of the **overall market trend**, making it highly useful for investment decisions.

EF Transform Confirming Continued Trend:

When the EF line is **above the zero line and rising with a strong upward slope (around 45 degrees)**, it reflects sustained bullish momentum, allowing traders to **ride the uptrend**, ideally entering near the zero line on pullbacks.

Similarly, when the EF line is **below the zero line and sloping downward**, it indicates a strong bearish trend, where traders can look to **ride the downtrend**, again preferably entering near the zero line.

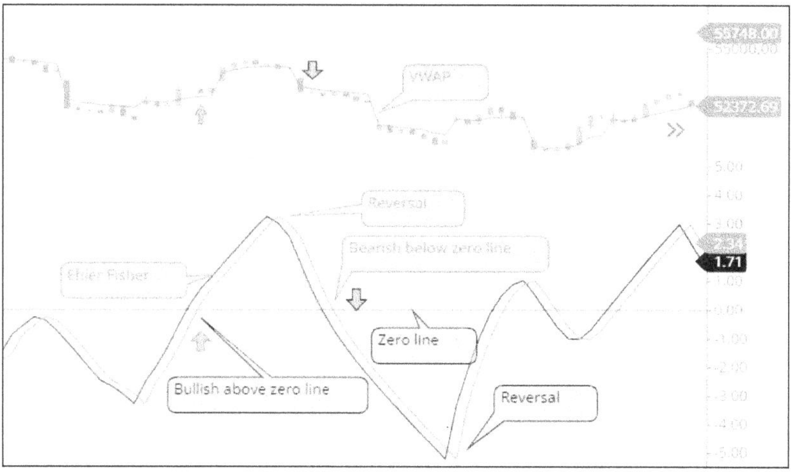

EF Transform For Trading & Investment:

The Ehler Fisher Transform is highly versatile across timeframes. It is **particularly effective on lower timeframes such as 10-minute charts for intraday trading**, while for **positional or investment decisions**, it is best applied on **Daily or higher timeframes** to capture broader market trends.

EF Transform Indicating Overbought & Oversold Levels:

The EF indicator also helps identify extreme market conditions. Readings around **+4.5 indicate overbought levels**, while values near **+6.8 suggest extreme overbought conditions**, where a trend reversal becomes more likely. Conversely, readings around **–4.5 indicate oversold levels**, and near

–6.8 indicate extreme oversold conditions, signalling a potential upward reversal.

EF Transform Indicating Trend Reversal:

Adding a **WMA (21) overlay on the EF indicator** enhances early trend reversal and helps filter out ambiguous signals. When **WMA (21) crosses below the EF line**—even if EF is still above the zero line—it broadly signals that a **potential bearish shift** may be developing. This allows traders to anticipate a sell setup **well before EF itself crosses below zero**, especially when supported by price action or chart patterns. In intraday trading, such a crossover serves as a **clear cue to exit long (buy) positions**.

Conversely, when **WMA (21) crosses above the EF line**—even if EF remains below the zero line—it indicates the likelihood of an **emerging bullish move**. This early signal helps in identifying buy opportunities ahead of a full EF crossover above zero, particularly when confirmed by supporting price structures. In intraday scenarios, this crossover acts as a **signal to exit short (sell) positions**.

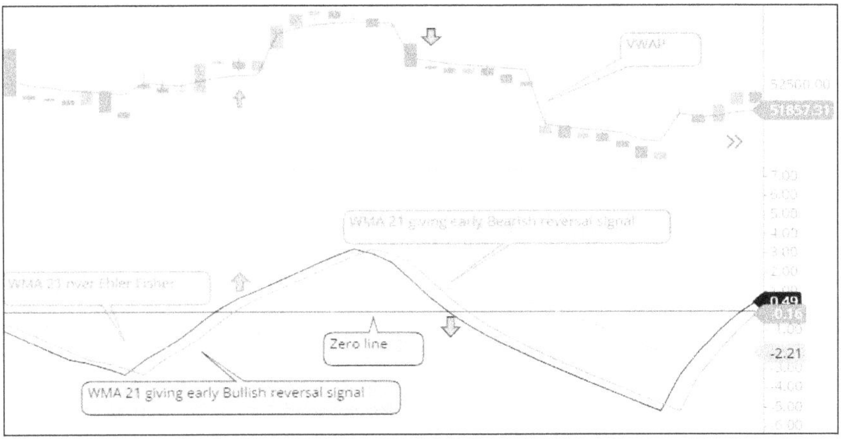

Overall, combining WMA (21) with EF not only provides early trend indications but also helps resolve minor uncertainties in other systems (such as HM), enabling more timely and confident trading decisions.

Overall, the Ehler Fisher Transform is a powerful tool for capturing momentum shifts and identifying high-probability trend continuation or reversal zones, especially when used in conjunction with other indicators like VWAP, AVWAP, WMA 21 or Bollinger Bands.

VOLUME PROFILE

The **Volume Profile** is a powerful analytical tool that displays the **distribution of traded volume across different price levels** over a specific period. Unlike traditional volume indicators that plot volume against time, Volume Profile reveals **where the most trading activity has occurred**, thereby highlighting key areas of **value, demand, and supply**. These levels often act as **strong support and resistance zones**, making the indicator highly valuable for both intraday traders and positional investors.

One of the key advantages of Volume Profile is its ability to identify **fair value zones and imbalance areas**. Price tends to spend more time in high-volume zones (indicating acceptance), while it moves quickly through low-volume areas (indicating rejection). This helps traders understand whether the market is **accumulating, distributing, or trending**, and accordingly plan entries, exits, and stop-loss levels with greater precision.

Volume Profile indicating Point of Control:

The **Point of Control (POC)** is the most critical level in the Volume Profile, representing the **price level with the highest traded volume** on a given timeframe. It signifies the area of **maximum market participation and strong acceptance**, often acting as a key **support or resistance level**.

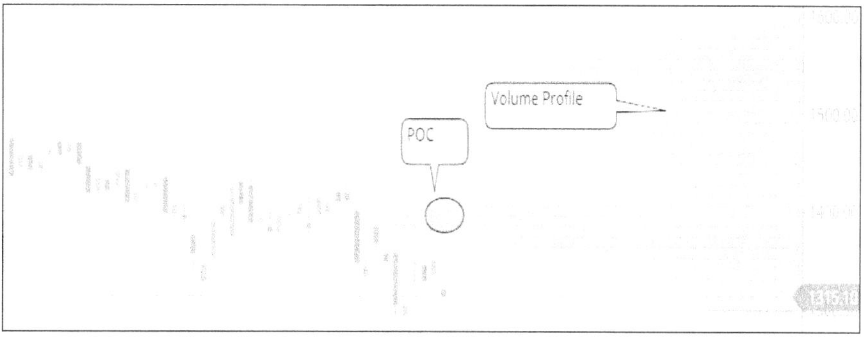

For practical application, traders may consider two POC levels—the highest volume node (primary POC) and the second-highest volume node—to define a zone of strong demand or supply. From investment perspective, when **price breaks above the highest POC** and sustains, it indicates strength, and a long position can be initiated, with the stop-loss placed just below the second POC.

This approach allows traders to align with areas of strong institutional interest while maintaining a well-defined risk framework.

High Volume vs Low Volume Areas in Volume Profile:

Volume Profile clearly distinguishes between **High Volume Nodes (HVNs)** and **Low Volume Nodes (LVNs)**.

- **HVNs** represent areas where significant trading activity has taken place, indicating strong acceptance of price. These zones often act as support or resistance because the market has previously agreed on value there.
- **LVNs**, on the other hand, represent price levels where little trading has occurred, indicating rejection or inefficiency. Price tends to move quickly through these areas, often leading to sharp moves or breakouts.

This distinction helps traders understand whether the market is in a phase of balance (consolidation) or imbalance (trend or breakout).

Demand–Supply Dynamics Through Volume Profile:

Volume Profile offers a clearer lens into demand and supply dynamics. Areas with high volume suggest a balance between buyers and sellers, while low-volume areas indicate an imbalance where one side dominated.

When price moves away from a high-volume area, it often signals that a new imbalance is developing, leading to directional movement. Conversely, when price returns to a high-volume zone, it may slow down or consolidate as the market reassesses value.

Role in Breakouts and Reversals:

Volume Profile is particularly useful in identifying breakout and reversal opportunities. A breakout that occurs from a low-volume area into another low-volume zone often accelerates quickly due to the lack of resistance. Conversely, when price approaches a high-volume area, it may face resistance or support, leading to consolidation or reversal.

This makes Volume Profile a powerful tool for anticipating where price is likely to pause, reverse, or move rapidly.

Institutional Perspective and Market Structure:

From an institutional standpoint, Volume Profile reflects where large players have accumulated or distributed positions. Institutions prefer to transact in areas of high liquidity, which are often visible as high-volume nodes.

By identifying these zones, traders can align themselves with institutional activity and better understand the underlying structure of the market.

Understanding Volume Profile Shapes:

Volume Profile is not just about levels like the Point of Control (POC); it also forms distinct shapes that reflect how the market is distributing volume across prices.

These shapes provide insight into whether the market is trending, balancing, accumulating, or distributing. Among the most commonly observed patterns are **P-shape, b-shape, and D-shape profiles**, each carrying a different market message.

P-Shape Profile: Short Covering and Bullish Bias

A P-shaped profile typically forms after a downtrend or during a reversal phase. It is characterized by a **bulge of volume at the upper end** of the price range, with a relatively thin lower section. This indicates that after an initial move up, price consolidates at higher levels with increasing acceptance. The shape often reflects **short covering**, where traders who had sold earlier are forced to buy back positions, pushing prices higher. The POC in this case shifts upward, signalling a **potential bullish bias** and the possibility of further upside if supported by continued participation.

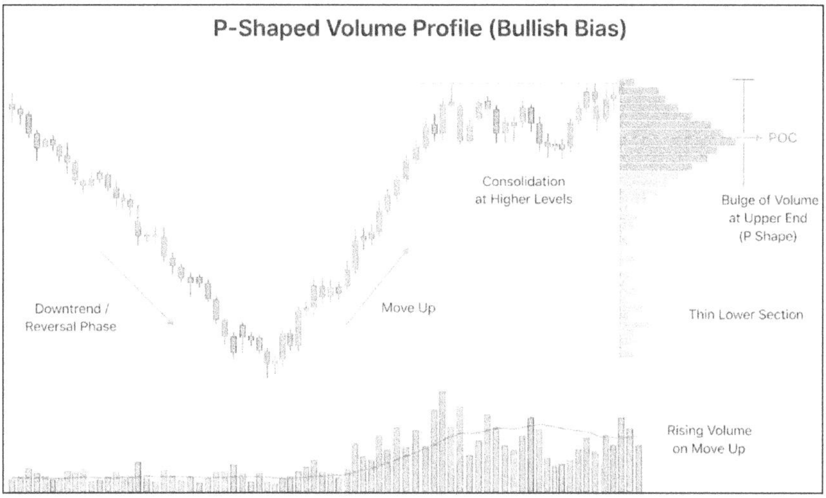

b-Shape Profile: Long Liquidation and Bearish Bias

The b-shaped profile is essentially the opposite of the P-shape. It shows a **bulge of volume at the lower end** of the range, indicating that price has moved down and is now consolidating at lower levels. This pattern often represents **long liquidation**, where traders who were previously holding long positions are exiting, adding to selling pressure.

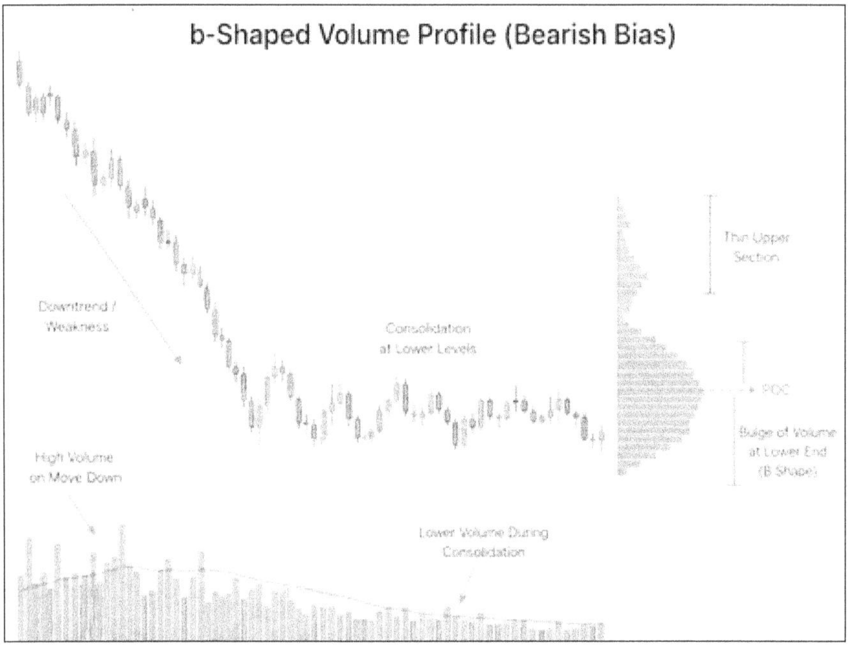

The POC tends to form near the lower region, suggesting **acceptance at lower prices** and a bearish undertone. This structure may indicate continued weakness unless strong buying emerges.

D-Shape Profile: Balanced Market and Fair Value

The D-shaped profile is a **symmetrical, bell-shaped distribution**, where volume is evenly spread around the POC. This represents a **balanced market condition**, where buyers and sellers are in agreement about price. The POC lies near the centre, acting as a fair value zone.

In such conditions, price tends to rotate within the value area rather than trend strongly. D-shaped profiles are typically seen during consolidation phases and often precede **breakouts**, once the balance is disturbed.

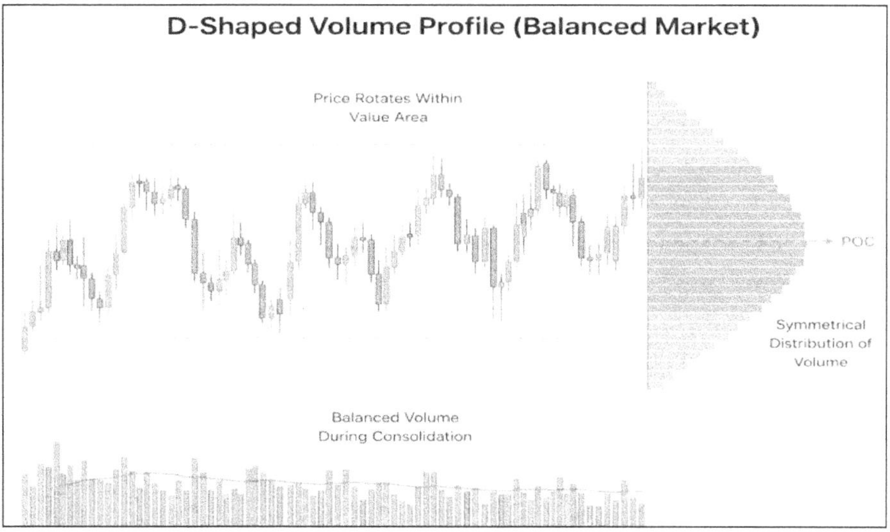

Thin and Elongated Profiles: Trending Markets

In strongly trending markets, the Volume Profile may appear **elongated or skewed**, with volume distributed across a wide price range and a less prominent central bulge. The POC may shift gradually in the direction of the trend.

These profiles indicate **imbalance**, where either demand or supply is dominating. Price tends to move quickly through low-volume areas and spends less time consolidating, reflecting strong directional conviction.

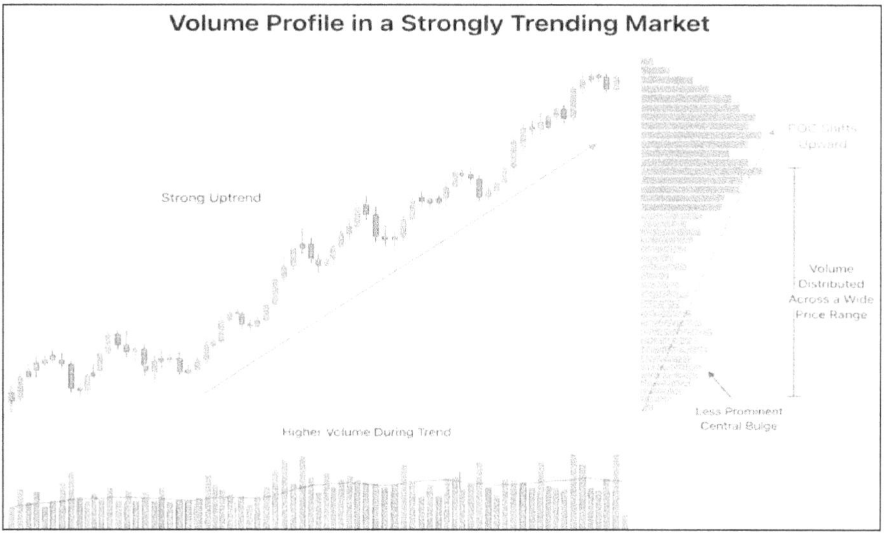

Significance of POC in Volume Profile Patterns:

Across all these shapes, the **Point of Control (POC)** plays a crucial role. It represents the price level with the highest traded volume and acts as a key reference point for market acceptance. In P- and b-shaped profiles, the location of the POC helps identify whether the market is accepting higher or lower prices. In D-shaped profiles, it serves as the centre of balance. Observing how price behaves around the POC—whether it holds, rejects, or shifts—provides valuable clues about future direction.

Practical Significance of Volume Profile:

Volume Profile shapes offer a visual representation of market intent. Whether it is accumulation, distribution, balance, or trend, each pattern reflects how participants are positioning themselves.

For traders, Volume Profile provides actionable insights into entry, exit, and risk management. It helps in identifying key levels where price is likely to react, allowing for more precise trade planning. For investors, it offers a broader understanding of value zones, helping in making informed decisions about accumulation and long-term positioning. Unlike traditional indicators, Volume Profile is grounded in actual traded activity, making it a highly reliable tool.

In essence, Volume Profile acts as a map of market behaviour, showing where the market has found value, where it has rejected price, and where it is likely to move next. By combining Volume Profile with price action and other technical tools, traders and investors can gain a deeper, more structured understanding of market dynamics, leading to more informed and confident decision-making.

Overall, Volume Profile, when combined with other tools like VWAP, AVWAP, or moving averages, provides a deeper insight into market structure and participant behaviour, significantly enhancing trading decisions.

RELATIVE STRENGTH

Relative Strength (RS) is one of the most powerful practical concepts in technical analysis and portfolio management because it helps identify whether a stock, sector, commodity, or instrument is performing better or worse compared to the broader market or a benchmark index.

In simple terms, RS measures the *comparative strength* of one instrument against another. A stock may be rising, but if the overall market is rising much faster, then that stock may actually be weak in relative terms. Likewise, even if a stock is falling slightly during a broad market crash, it may still be exhibiting strong relative strength because it is resisting the fall better than the market.

This concept is extremely significant because smart money and institutional participants generally prefer stocks that are already outperforming the market. Strong relative strength often indicates hidden accumulation, institutional participation, superior momentum, or leadership quality within a sector. Therefore, RS becomes a highly valuable tool for identifying potential market leaders before they make major price expansions.

Understanding Alpha and Beta in Relation to Relative Strength:

Relative Strength is closely connected with the concepts of **alpha** and **beta**.

Alpha – Excess Return or Outperformance

Alpha refers to the additional return generated by a stock or portfolio over and above the benchmark market return. It reflects the ability of a stock, strategy, or portfolio to outperform the broader market.

For example:

- If the market gives a 10% return
- But a stock rises 18%
- Then the additional 8% outperformance represents alpha.

Thus, alpha is essentially the practical outcome of strong relative strength over time. Stocks consistently showing strong RS generally tend to generate positive alpha.

Beta – Sensitivity or Volatility Relative to the Market

Beta measures how aggressively a stock moves compared to the broader market. A beta value around 1 implies that the stock generally moves in line with the market. A beta above 1 indicates that the stock is more volatile and tends to move more aggressively than the market, while a beta below 1 suggests comparatively lower volatility and more stable movement.

For example:

- A beta of 1.5 means the stock may rise 15% when the market rises 10%, but may also fall more sharply during market corrections.
- A beta of 0.7 suggests the stock is relatively defensive and less volatile.

Thus:

- Alpha measures performance quality
- Beta measures movement intensity or volatility
- Relative Strength helps identify leadership and comparative performance

A strong stock ideally exhibits **positive alpha with manageable beta**.

Relative Strength Is Not Same As RSI:

It is very important to understand that Relative Strength (RS) is completely different from the Relative Strength Index (RSI), even though their names may sound similar.

Relative Strength (RS) is a comparative performance measure that compares a stock or instrument against a benchmark index or another instrument to determine whether it is outperforming or underperforming the broader market, whereas RSI is a momentum oscillator that measures the internal momentum, speed, and strength of price movement within the same stock itself over a specific time period.

In simple terms, RS answers the question: "Is this stock stronger or weaker than the market?", while RSI answers the question: "Is this stock internally overbought, oversold, strong, or weak at the moment?"

Thus, RS is used primarily for identifying market leadership, alpha generation, and comparative strength, whereas RSI is mainly used for identifying momentum conditions, reversals, and overbought or oversold zones within the stock's own price structure.

Calculation & Charting of Relative Strength:

The simplest formula for Relative Strength is:

$$RS = \frac{\text{Price of Stock}}{\text{Price of Benchmark Index}}$$

> For example:
>
> $$RS = \frac{\text{Reliance Price}}{\text{Nifty Price}}$$
>
> If:
>
> - Reliance = 3000
> - Nifty = 25000
>
> Then:
>
> $$RS = \frac{3000}{25000} = 0.12$$

This value by itself is less important than its *trend over time.*

- If the RS value keeps rising → stock is outperforming the market
- If RS value falls → stock is underperforming

Thus, traders usually observe the **direction of the RS line** rather than the absolute number, and hence plot it over price Chart to track.

Relative Strength Charting Over Time

Relative Strength becomes significantly more meaningful when tracked over a period of time rather than at a single point. The RS line is generally plotted from:

- A significant market bottom
- A major breakout point
- Beginning of a trend

- Last 20, 50, 100, or 200 trading sessions
- Any discretionary starting point relevant to the analysis

The formula for normalized RS over a selected time period may be expressed as:

$$RS_t = \frac{(Stock\ Price_t / Stock\ Price_0)}{(Index\ Price_t / Index\ Price_0)}$$

Where:

- $Price_0$ = starting point price
- $Price_t$ = current price

This method compares percentage performance rather than absolute price.

For example:

- Stock rises from 100 → 150 = +50%
- Index rises from 20000 → 22000 = +10%

Then normalized RS becomes:

$$RS = \frac{1.50}{1.10} = 1.36$$

This clearly indicates strong outperformance.

A trader or investor need not necessarily calculate Relative Strength (RS) manually or feel bothered with which kind of formula to apply, because today most modern trading platforms already provide several pre-built and customizable RS indicators. In fact, many reliable RS indicators are freely available and can be directly plotted on price charts for comparative analysis against benchmark indices such as the NIFTY 50 or sectoral indices.

By using a dependable RS indicator, traders and investors can visually track whether a stock is outperforming or underperforming the broader market over a selected time period. When RS continues to rise along with strong price action and volume participation, it often indicates increasing strength, momentum, institutional participation, and potential alpha generation. Conversely, when the RS line starts flattening or declining despite price moving higher, it may indicate weakening momentum, reduction in relative strength, possible distribution, or an early warning signal for profit booking and cautious exit planning.

Thus, RS indicators can significantly enhance technical analysis by helping market participants identify leadership stocks, track momentum sustainability, and make more informed trading and investment decisions over time.

Practical Insight from RS:

When the **RS line rises:**

- The stock is outperforming the market
- Institutional participation may be increasing
- Momentum and leadership are improving
- Probability of sustained trend increases

When the **RS line declines**:

- The stock is lagging the market
- Demand is weakening
- Capital may be shifting elsewhere
- Momentum is deteriorating

Combining RS with Price Action and Volume:

Relative Strength alone should not be used in isolation. Its effectiveness increases significantly when combined with:

- Price action
- Volume analysis
- Trend structure
- Breakouts

- Moving averages
- AVWAP
- Demand-supply zones

Strong RS + Strong Volume

When a stock:

- Outperforms the market
- Gives volume breakout
- Shows bullish candles
- Sustains above key moving averages

then it often reflects active accumulation by smart money.

Such stocks frequently become:

- Momentum leaders
- Swing trade candidates
- Positional winners
- Sector outperformers

Strong RS During Weak Market

One of the most powerful observations in practical trading is:

"The stocks that refuse to fall during market weakness often become future leaders."

If the market is correcting sharply but a stock:

- Consolidates tightly
- Holds support strongly
- Shows lower decline
- Maintains strong RS

then it reflects hidden strength and institutional confidence.

Relative Strength and Momentum

RS also helps identify:

- Whether momentum is genuine or weak
- Whether price movement is sustainable
- Whether a breakout has leadership quality

A breakout without RS improvement may fail quickly. However, a breakout accompanied by:

- Rising RS
- Volume expansion
- Strong price action
- Sectoral strength

often has a higher probability of continuation.

Therefore, Relative Strength is one of the clearest methods to identify where institutional money is flowing and which stocks are emerging as market leaders. A stock exhibiting strong RS, healthy volume participation, strong price structure, and positive momentum often provide higher probability trading and investing opportunities. When combined with concepts such as alpha, beta, price action, moving averages, AVWAP, and volume analysis, Relative Strength becomes an exceptionally powerful framework for identifying quality opportunities with superior conviction and clarity.

CHOOSE YOUR WEAPONS

Thus, Technical indicators are extremely valuable tools in Technical Analysis because they help simplify and visualize complex market behaviour relating to trend, momentum, strength, volatility, volume participation, overbought or oversold conditions, and market sentiment. Indicators such as moving averages, VWAP / AVWAP, RSI, MACD, Bollinger Bands, volume indicators, Relative Strength, stochastic oscillators, ADX, and several others help traders and investors understand the broader structure and behaviour of the market with greater clarity and objectivity. While no single indicator can predict the market with certainty, their practical significance lies in helping market participants improve probabilities, identify high-conviction setups, and avoid emotionally driven decision-making.

The true strength of technical indicators emerges when they are studied in association with one another and in conjunction with price action, volume behaviour, support and resistance zones, trend structure, and broader market context. When multiple factors begin converging toward a similar conclusion — such as momentum strengthening along with volume expansion and price sustaining above moving averages or VWAP — the quality and reliability of the signal often improve significantly. This process of convergence and confirmation helps traders and investors develop stronger conviction, better timing, and more disciplined trade planning across varying market conditions.

Over time, continuous observation of charts and indicators gradually trains the eyes and mind to identify important signals, changing momentum, trend transitions, fake breakouts, reversals, accumulation, and distribution phases with better accuracy and confidence. Eventually, experienced market participants often realize that simplicity tends to work better than excessive complexity. Relying on too many indicators may create confusion, conflicting signals, and delayed decisions. In many situations, lesser but well-understood indicators used with discipline, consistency, and strong price-action understanding may produce better practical results over time. Ultimately, indicators should be treated as guiding tools and supporting frameworks rather than standalone decision-makers, while price action and market structure continue to remain the core foundation of Technical Analysis.

Chapter – 9

Trend Identification

Continuing Trend and Reversal

Trend identification is the foundation of successful trading and investing. In simple terms, a trend represents the **direction in which price is moving over a period of time**—whether upward (bullish), downward (bearish), or sideways (range-bound). Understanding the prevailing trend is critical because markets tend to **move in phases**, and aligning trades with the dominant direction significantly improves the probability of success.

The significance of trend identification lies in its ability to provide **clarity and context**. It helps traders decide whether to **buy, sell, or stay aside**, and more importantly, prevents taking trades against the broader market direction. A clear understanding of trend also aids in **timing entries and exits**, managing risk, and avoiding false signals generated by short-term noise.

In the foregoing discussions, we have explored several **practical and reliable methods to identify trends**. These include analysing **price action through support and resistance**, observing the behaviour of **moving averages (such as 20 SMA, 50 SMA, and 200 EMA)**, and understanding the slope and positioning of **VWAP and AVWAP**. Tools like **Bollinger Bands**, pivot levels, and dynamic averages further enhance our ability to read whether the market is trending or consolidating.

Each of these approaches provides a different perspective—some capture **short-term momentum (VWAP, lower timeframes)**, while others reveal the **broader structure and long-term direction (AVWAP, higher timeframes, major moving averages)**. When used together, they create a **comprehensive framework** for identifying and confirming the current trend.

Ultimately, trend identification is not about predicting the market but about **reading what the market is already indicating**. By combining multiple tools and aligning them across timeframes, traders can develop a disciplined and structured approach to follow the trend—because in the market, **the trend is not just your friend, it is your edge**.

DIFFERENT METHODS

Let us look at some of the most significant ways by which the current trend can be identified with clarity.

Trend Identification using BB, 5 & 20 SMA:

When **Bollinger Bands (BB), 5 SMA (Low), and 20 SMA** on the daily timeframe are all **curving upward**, and price is consistently moving higher (with the bands expanding upward), the market is considered to be in a **strong uptrend**. In such conditions, the preferred approach is to **buy on dips**, as pullbacks are typically temporary within the broader upward move.

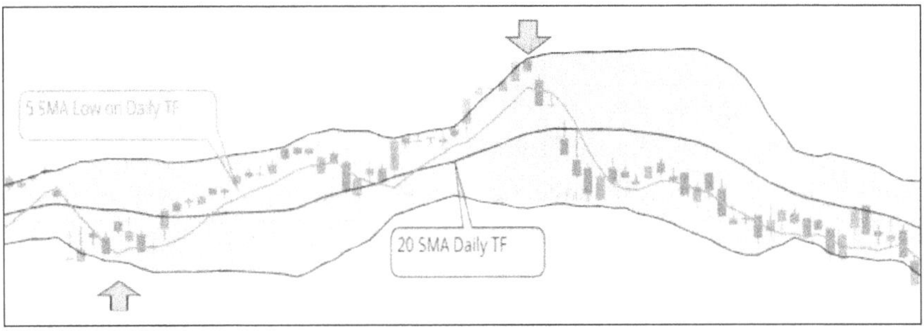

When **BB, 5 SMA (Low), and 20 SMA** are all **curving downward**, and price is trending lower (with the bands expanding downward), the market is in a **downtrend**. In this scenario, the strategy should be to **sell on rises**, as upward movements are generally corrective in nature.

When **BB and 20 SMA are relatively flat**, and price oscillates within a defined range (with **Bollinger Bands contracting or narrowing**), the market is **range-bound**. Such conditions indicate low momentum and indecision, making it an **ideal environment for option sellers**, as price is likely to remain within a confined zone.

Trend Identification using VWAP & AVWAP:

Slope-Based Trend Identification:

The direction and slope of **VWAP and AVWAP** provide a clear indication of market trend. When these averages are **sloping upward (around a 45-degree angle)**, it reflects a **bullish trend**, indicating sustained buying strength. Conversely, when they are **sloping downward**, it signals a **bearish trend**, driven by consistent selling pressure. If VWAP or AVWAP appears **flat**, the market is considered **range-bound**, lacking clear direction.

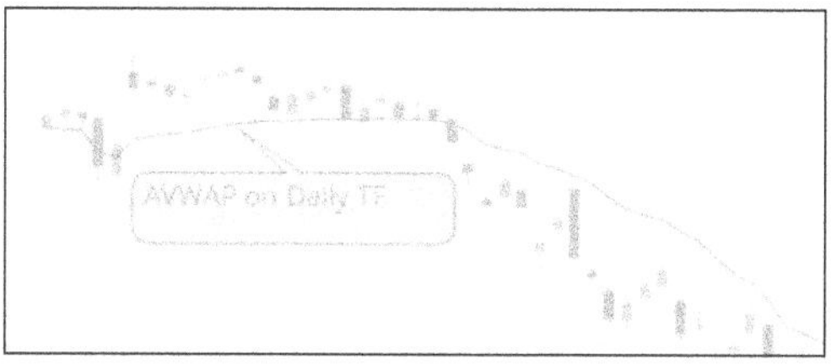

For practical application, **AVWAP on the daily timeframe** is best suited to identify the **broader market trend**, while **VWAP on the hourly timeframe** helps in assessing **intraday direction and bias.**

Born AVWAP on Options Chart:

Another effective method to gauge trend is by analysing deep ITM Call (CE) and Put (PE) options in relation to their born AVWAP (i.e., AVWAP from the inception of the option contract). We have to analyse the chart of deep ITMs of the underlying for which we like to conclude the trend.

If deep ITM CE options of the given underlying are trading below or sustaining below their born AVWAP (i.e. anchored on its born date which is the first candle on daily TF), it indicates a bearish trend in the underlying—favouring call option selling (CE shorting).

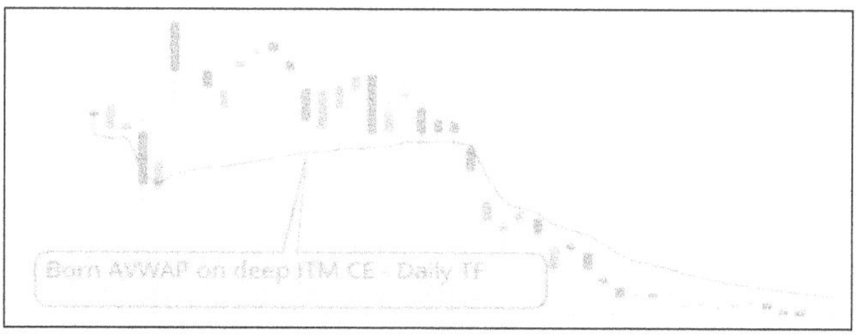

Conversely, if the deep ITM PE options of such underlying are trading below or sustaining below the born AVWAP of the deep ITM PE (i.e. anchored on its born date which is the first candle on daily TF), it reflects a bullish trend—favouring put option selling (PE shorting).

Overall, AVWAP serves as a highly effective tool for option sellers, as it helps identify strong directional bias and provides reliable zones for initiating trades with better probability and risk control.

Trend Identification drawing Trendlines:

Trendlines are drawn from left to right by connecting at least two significant touchpoints, either forming horizontal levels or sloping channels (upward or downward). While trendlines are useful for visualizing price structure, their standalone reliability is relatively limited (around 30%) and should ideally be combined with indicators like Bollinger Bands and moving averages for stronger confirmation.

When price moves between two horizontal trendlines—one acting as resistance (upper boundary) and the other as support (lower boundary) and continues to respect these levels without closing beyond them, the market is considered range-bound. This is especially true when the range is narrow and price oscillates within it. However, if a strong candle closes beyond either boundary, or if there are two consecutive candle closes outside the range, it indicates a breakout or breakdown, suggesting a shift from consolidation to a trending phase.

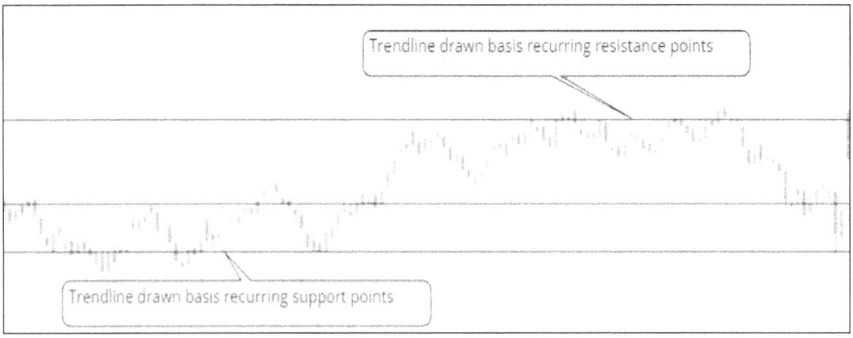

Uptrend Identification:

When price moves consistently upward within a rising channel, formed by connecting at least two higher lows, the market is in an uptrend with strong momentum. Alternatively, if price progresses in a cyclical manner—forming higher highs and higher lows, it still reflects an uptrend, though with relatively moderate momentum.

Downtrend Identification:

When price moves consistently downward within a falling channel, formed by connecting at least two lower highs, the market is in a downtrend with strong momentum. Similarly, if price follows a cyclical pattern—forming lower highs and lower lows, it indicates a downtrend, albeit with less aggressive momentum.

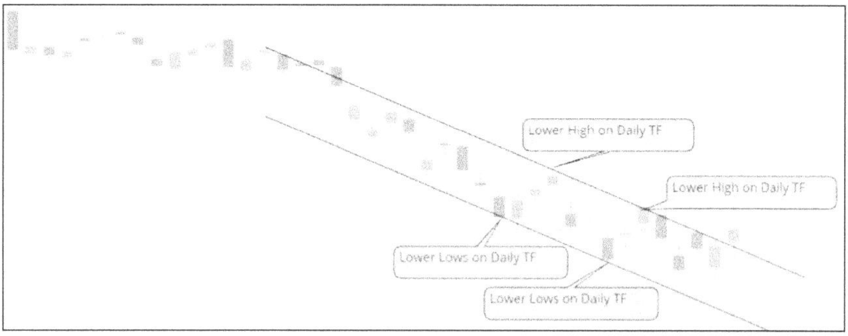

In essence, trendlines help in identifying market structure and boundaries, but their effectiveness improves significantly when used in conjunction with other technical tools for confirmation.

Trend Identification using line chart:

Trend Identification Using Line Chart (Daily Timeframe) A line chart on the daily timeframe offers a simplified view of price by focusing on closing levels, helping to clearly identify the broader trend. When the line is curving and progressing upward, it indicates an uptrend, reflecting sustained strength in price.

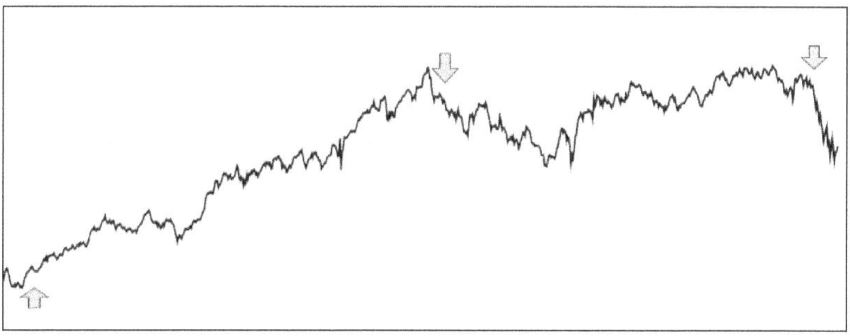

Conversely, when the line is curving downward and declining, it signals a downtrend, indicating persistent weakness. This method is particularly useful for filtering out noise and understanding the overall market direction.

Trend Identification using Heikin-Ashi Candle chart:

The Heikin-Ashi (HA) chart smoothens price action and helps in identifying trends with greater clarity. On the daily timeframe, if green HA candles consistently appear one after another, with each candle closing above and respecting the 5 SMA (low), it indicates a strong uptrend. Similarly, if red HA candles appear consecutively, with each candle closing below and respecting the 5 SMA (low), it reflects a downtrend.

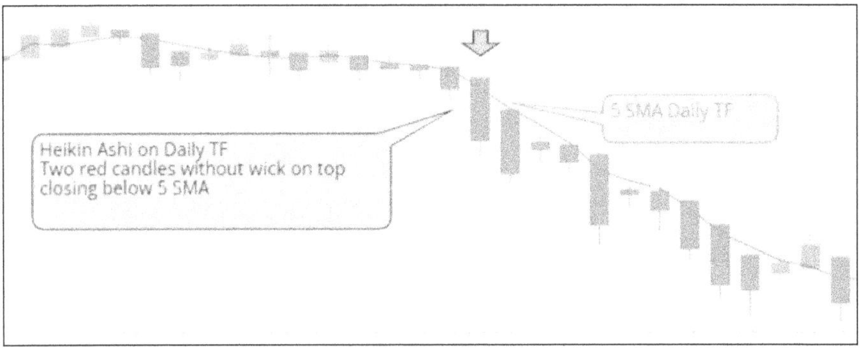

Trend Reversal Using Heikin-Ashi (HA) Chart

HA charts also provide early signals of potential trend reversal. In a falling market, if the HA chart begins to show two consecutive green candles without lower wicks, followed by a green candle that closes above the 5 SMA (low), it suggests a possible reversal from downtrend to uptrend. Conversely, in a rising market, if the chart forms two consecutive red candles without upper wicks, followed by a red candle that closes below the 5 SMA (low), it indicates a potential reversal from uptrend to downtrend.

Overall, Heikin-Ashi charts are effective in identifying trend strength, continuity, and early reversal signals, especially when used alongside moving averages.

TREND REVERSAL

Introduction to Trend Reversal and Its Identification

A trend reversal marks a shift in the prevailing market direction, where an existing uptrend turns into a downtrend or a downtrend transition into an uptrend. Identifying such reversals at the right time is crucial, as it allows traders to protect profits, limit losses, and position themselves early in a new directional move. Unlike continuation phases, reversals are often accompanied by changes in momentum, sentiment, and participation, making their identification both challenging and highly rewarding.

The significance of recognizing a trend reversal lies in avoiding the common mistake of trading with an exhausted trend. Many traders enter late into a move, only to face sharp reversals. A structured approach to reversal identification helps in exiting existing positions timely and initiating fresh trades in the new direction with better risk-reward.

In the foregoing discussions, several practical methods have been explored to identify potential reversals. These include observing price behaviour around key support and resistance levels, especially when previously respected zones are breached and retested. The interaction of price with moving averages (such as 20 SMA, 50 SMA, and 200 EMA)—particularly crossovers, slope changes, and sustained closes above or below—also provides strong reversal signals.

Additionally, tools like VWAP and AVWAP help detect shifts in trend through changes in slope, price acceptance above or below these averages, and reactions at key anchored levels. Indicators such as Bollinger Bands (including band contraction, expansion, and "band blasts"), along with Heikin-Ashi candle patterns, further assist in spotting early signs of reversal through changes in structure and momentum.

No single method is sufficient on its own; rather, confluence of multiple signals provides higher conviction. By combining price action with dynamic and static indicators across timeframes, traders can develop a disciplined framework to identify, confirm, and act upon trend reversals effectively, thereby improving overall trading performance.

Reversal Setups and Practical Trading Guidelines

- *Reversal After Breach of Resistance:*

  If price breaks above a resistance level but fails to sustain and starts reversing downward, it often signals weakness and a potential sharp decline. Ideally, after a breakout, price should continue to hold and move higher. Failure to do so indicates a false breakout, which frequently leads to a strong move in the opposite direction.

- *Reversal with Breakout/Breakdown:*

  Breakouts and breakdowns are commonly accompanied by gap-ups or gap-downs. Trades can be initiated in the direction of the breakout/ breakdown, with stop loss placed near the breached level—for example, a long trade above previous resistance (PR) with SL as one close below PR, and a short trade below previous support (PS) with SL as one close above PS.

  If a gap sustains for at least 30 minutes for intraday position, it provides initial confirmation, while sustaining for about 1 hour offers a much stronger conviction of continuation.

- *Reversal on the 4th Retest of R/S:*

  Price often respects support and resistance levels for the first few retests. Trades can be taken on reversals from R/S up to the third retest. However, when price approaches the same level for the fourth time, the probability of a breakout or breakdown increases significantly. Hence, it is advisable to avoid reversal trades on the 4th retest and instead wait for a potential trend reversal or breakout confirmation.

- *Mid-Week Reversal Tendency:*

  If the market has been trending strongly in one direction throughout the week, there is a high probability (often observed) of a reversal around Wednesday or Thursday.

  For instance, in a strong uptrend, if price starts sustaining below VWAP, it may indicate the beginning of a reversal; similarly, in a downtrend, sustaining above VWAP may signal a bounce. If no reversal occurs on Wednesday, the probability increases further for Thursday, especially in the second half of the session, which can offer high-reward trading opportunities due to low option premiums.

- *Intraday Entry at Reversal Zones:*

  Intraday trades should ideally be initiated at key reaction zones, namely:

  1. Previous Resistance/Support (PR/PS)
  2. 20 SMA on the hourly timeframe
  3. VWAP/AVWAP on the hourly timeframe

  Entries should only be taken when price reverses from these levels, confirmed on a lower timeframe (such as 10-minute charts). This ensures better timing, tighter stop-loss, and improved risk-reward.

TREND IS YOUR FRIEND

Trend is one of the most fundamental and powerful concepts in Technical Analysis because price generally tends to move in a particular direction for a period of time before reversing or consolidating. Identifying the prevailing trend — whether bullish, bearish, or sideways — is therefore one of the first and most important steps before planning any trade or investment. A strong understanding of trend structure helps traders and investors align themselves with market direction rather than trading against the broader flow of momentum and sentiment.

The identification of trend becomes even more significant when studied on higher time frames such as daily, weekly, or monthly charts. Higher time frame trends generally carry greater reliability, stronger conviction, and deeper institutional participation compared to smaller time frames. Although price may fluctuate or correct temporarily on lower time frames, eventually price tends to respect and follow the broader trend exhibited on the higher time frame. This is why experienced market participants often say that "the higher time frame controls the broader direction of price."

Equally important is the ability to identify early signs of trend reversal. Changes in price structure, momentum weakness, breakdown of support or moving averages, volume behaviour, Relative Strength deterioration, or reversal price action can often indicate that the prevailing trend may be weakening or reversing. For investors, recognizing a major trend reversal can help protect capital by signalling timely exit or reduction of exposure. For traders, however, a reversal itself may become a fresh trading opportunity, where one can align with the new emerging trend and participate in the reversal move.

Therefore, one of the core principles of practical Technical Analysis is to first understand and gauge the prevailing trend and then position oneself accordingly. Following the trend generally improves probabilities, reduces emotional conflict, and enhances decision quality. As the popular market saying goes — "Trend is your friend until it bends." Hence, learning to identify trends, track their continuation, and recognize their reversal remains one of the most valuable and practical skills for both traders and investors alike.

Chapter – 10

Market Behaviour

Core Dynamics

This chapter brings together three foundational pillars of market understanding—**accumulation–distribution, demand–supply, and overbought–oversold conditions**—which together define the core structure and dynamics of price movement. These concepts go beyond surface-level chart patterns and indicators; they help us understand *why* the market behaves the way it does. Accumulation and distribution reveal the intent and positioning of smart money over time, demand and supply highlight the exact zones where buying and selling forces are most active, and overbought–oversold conditions indicate when price has stretched too far from its equilibrium.

Studying these aspects is crucial because they form the **cause behind price action**, not just the effect. They help a trader or investor identify where price is likely to react, whether a trend is being built or exhausted, and whether the current move has strength or is nearing a turning point. Together, they provide a deeper lens to interpret market behaviour—allowing one to align with the underlying forces of the market rather than reacting blindly to price movements.

In essence, these concepts act as the bridge between raw price data and meaningful decision-making. A strong grasp of accumulation–distribution, demand–supply, and overbought–oversold conditions equip market participants with the ability to read structure, anticipate shifts, and participate with greater confidence and clarity.

As we explore these in detail, you will begin to see how they interconnect and collectively form the backbone of technical analysis.

ACCUMULATION & DISTRIBUTION

Accumulation and distribution are foundational concepts in market *behaviour* that reflect the actions of **smart money**—institutional participants who operate with large capital and long-term intent.

Accumulation refers to a phase where strong hands gradually build positions at relatively lower price levels without causing a sharp rise in price. In contrast, **distribution** is the phase where these participants gradually offload their holdings at higher levels, again without triggering an immediate sharp decline. These phases are critical because they often precede major trends—accumulation typically leads to a **markup (uptrend)**, while distribution is followed by a **markdown (downtrend)**.

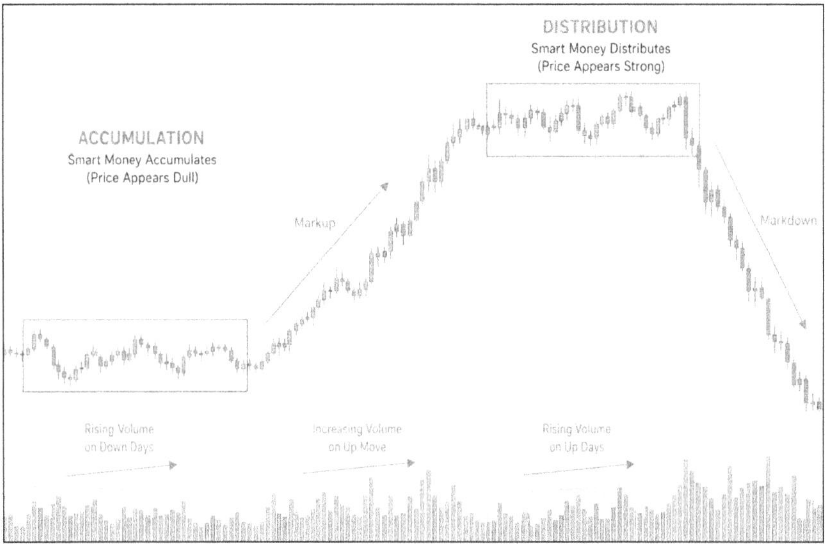

Significance of Accumulation-Distribution:

Understanding accumulation and distribution helps a trader or investor align with the dominant market participants rather than getting trapped on the wrong side of the move.

During accumulation, price may appear dull, range-bound, or slow-moving, which often discourages retail participation. However, beneath this quiet phase, **strong hands are positioning themselves** for a future rally.

Similarly, during distribution, prices may still be rising or moving sideways near highs, giving a **false sense of strength**, while in reality, large players are exiting their positions.

Recognizing these phases allows one to enter early in trends and exit before reversals, which is a key edge in both trading and investing.

Identifying Accumulation-Distribution:

Both phases are usually characterized by **range-bound price action** over a period of time.

In accumulation, **price tends to form a base near support levels** with multiple tests of similar lows, indicating buying interest. Volume behaviour is crucial—there may be increased volume on up-moves and relatively lower volume on down-moves, suggesting silent buying.

In distribution, **price often forms a range near resistance** with repeated failures to move higher, and volume may increase on down-moves, indicating selling pressure.

False breakouts (**bull traps** in distribution and **bear traps** in accumulation) are also common features of these phases.

Several tools can help decode these phases effectively:

- **Volume analysis** is the most important—observing volume spikes, dry-ups, and their relation to price movement gives strong clues.
- **Volume profile** helps identify high-volume nodes (areas of heavy trading), which often coincide with accumulation or distribution zones.
- **Price structure and support-resistance levels** provide context—accumulation typically happens near strong support, while distribution occurs near resistance.
- Additionally, **candlestick patterns** such as long wicks, indecision candles, and repeated rejections within a range further confirm the presence of these phases.

Accumulation and distribution can be effectively interpreted using **Bollinger Bands** and the behaviour of **major moving averages**, because both reflect volatility, price compression, and participation—key characteristics of these phases. These are discussed below.

Accumulation using Bollinger Bands (BB)

During accumulation, price typically moves in a tight range near support, and volatility reduces. This is clearly visible when Bollinger Bands contract (become narrow), indicating low volatility and lack of aggressive movement. Price oscillates between the upper and lower band without any sustained breakout.

Often, you may observe:

- Repeated touches of the lower band but no strong breakdown
- Small-bodied candles and reduced volatility
- Occasional false breakdowns (bear traps) followed by quick recovery inside the bands

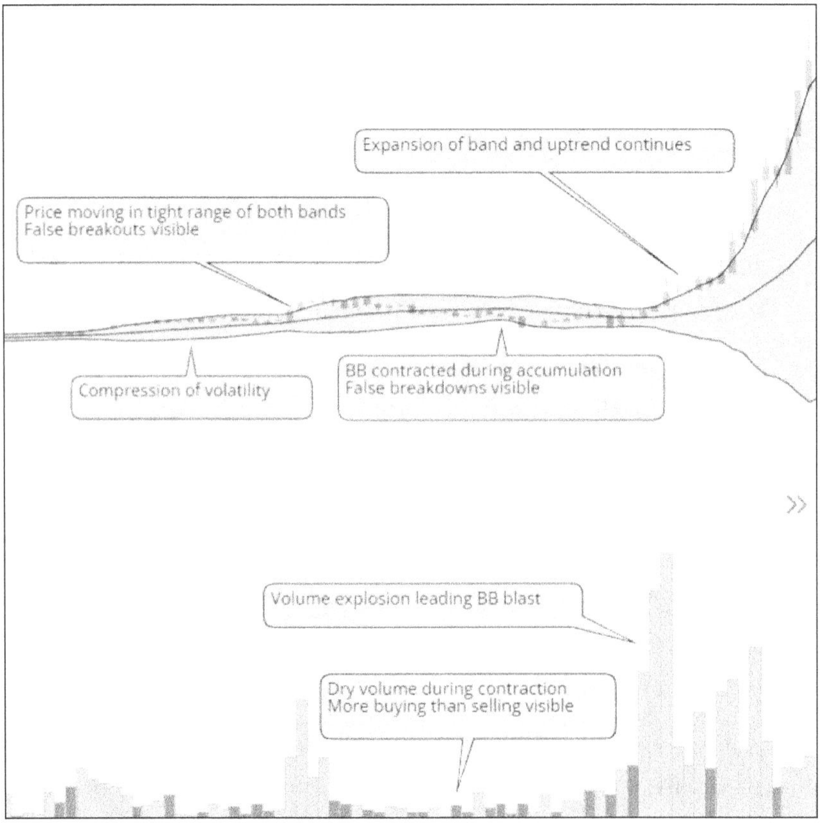

This contraction phase suggests that smart money is quietly absorbing supply, preparing for a future expansion (upmove). A subsequent BB expansion with price closing above the upper band often signals the end of accumulation and start of markup.

Distribution using Bollinger Bands (BB)

In distribution, price again moves in a range but near resistance levels. Bollinger Bands may remain narrow or start showing slight expansion due to volatility spikes.

Typical signs include:

- Price repeatedly touching the upper band but failing to sustain higher
- Increased volatility with long wicks (rejections at higher levels)
- False breakouts above the upper band (bull traps) followed by reversal

Here, smart money is distributing (selling) into strength, even though price appears strong. A decisive move below the lower band with expansion confirms the transition into markdown (downtrend).

Accumulation through Moving Average Convergence

When accumulation is taking place, **major moving averages (like 20 SMA, 50 SMA, 200 EMA)** tend to **converge and flatten**, coming very close to each other.

This indicates:

- Lack of clear trend
- Price equilibrium between buyers and sellers
- Reduced momentum

Price keeps crossing above and below these averages without direction. This clustering of averages reflects balance and absorption, which is typical of accumulation before a breakout.

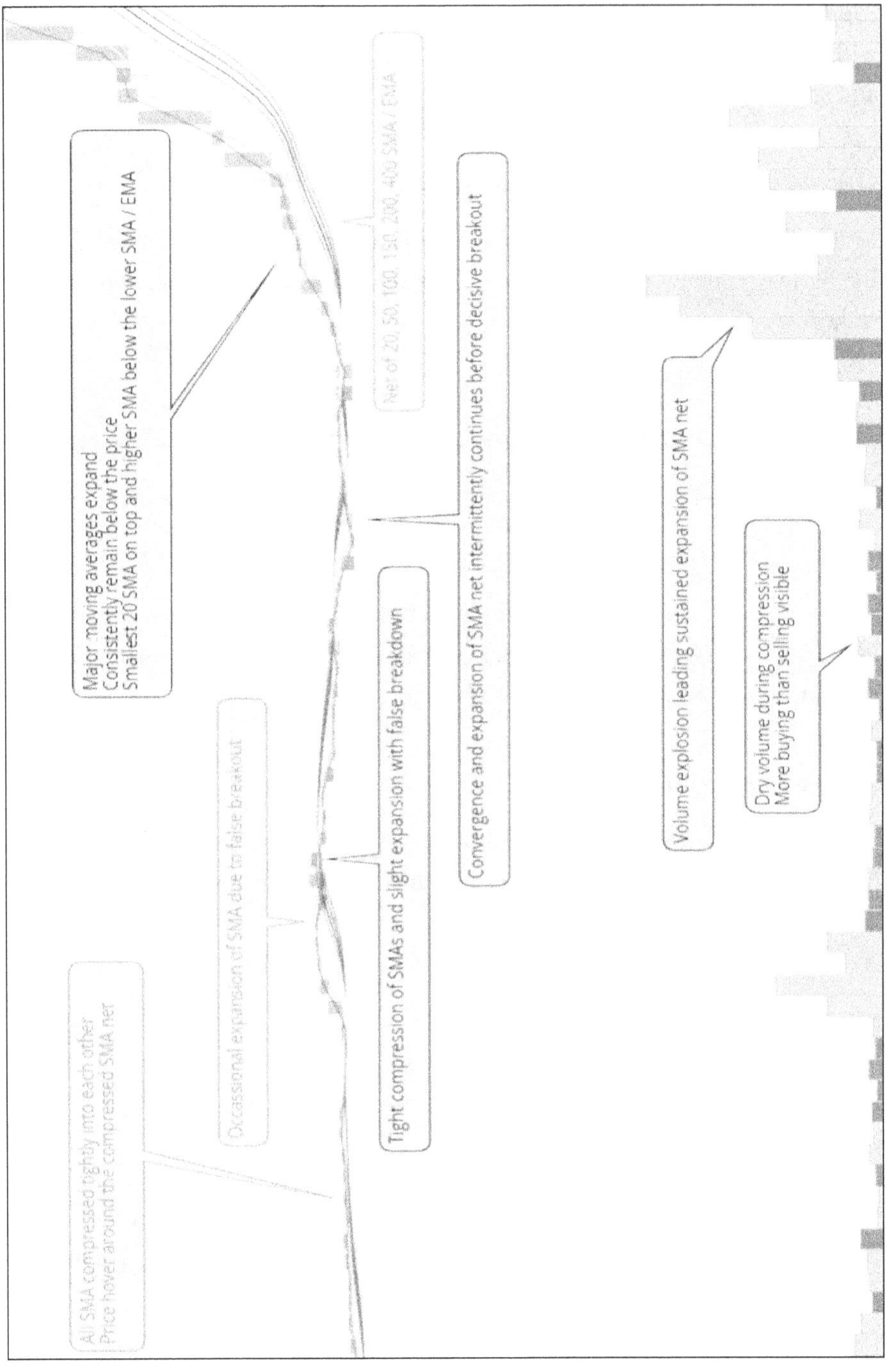
All SMA compressed tightly into each other
Price hover around the compressed SMA net
Occassional expansion of SMA due to false breakout
Tight compression of SMAs and slight expansion with false breakdown
Major moving averages expand
Consistently remain below the price
Smallest 20 SMA on top and higher SMA below the lower SMA / EMA
Convergence and expansion of SMA net intermittently continues before decisive breakout
Net of 20, 50, 100, 150, 200, 400 SMA / EMA
Volume explosion leading sustained expansion of SMA net
Dry volume during compression
More buying than selling visible

Distribution through Moving Average Convergence

Similarly, in distribution, moving averages again **converge and flatten**, but this time near higher price levels. You may observe:

- Price struggling to stay above moving averages
- Frequent crossovers without follow-through
- Slight downward tilt beginning to form

This shows that uptrend momentum is weakening, and supply is gradually overpowering demand. Once price decisively breaks below these clustered averages, it often leads to a stronger downmove.

Accumulation-Distribution Vs Demand-Supply:

Accumulation–distribution and demand–supply are closely related but not identical concepts. Both describe buying and selling activity, but from slightly different perspectives:

- **Common Ground:** Both reflect the actions of market participants and explain why price moves. Accumulation happens in demand zones, and distribution often occurs in supply zones.
- **Key Difference:** Demand and supply are more **localized concepts**—specific price zones where buying or selling occurs. Accumulation and distribution are **phases over time**, describing a broader process where smart money builds or exits positions gradually.

In simple terms, demand and supply are "where" price reacts, while accumulation and distribution are "how" and "over what period" those actions unfold.

Let us now understand the demand-supply metric and its dynamics.

DEMAND & SUPPLY

Demand and supply are the fundamental forces that drive all price movement in financial markets. **Demand** represents buying interest—zones where buyers are willing to step in aggressively—while **supply** represents selling pressure—zones where sellers dominate. Whenever demand exceeds supply, price tends to rise;

when supply exceeds demand, price falls. In simple terms, every move on the chart is a visible outcome of this continuous battle between buyers and sellers.

Thus, price movement in the market is fundamentally driven by the forces of demand and supply. When an asset is scarce—i.e., supply is limited—demand tends to exceed availability, resulting in a rise in price and the formation of an uptrend. Over time, such sustained buying pressure can lead to an overbought condition. Conversely, when an asset is abundantly available—i.e., supply exceeds demand—prices tend to decline, leading to a downtrend, which may eventually culminate in an oversold condition after a prolonged fall.

In practical terms, lower selling pressure (i.e., fewer sellers) combined with strong buying interest leads to upward price movement, while excessive selling (higher supply) with weak demand results in price decline. These imbalances in demand and supply are reflected through volume and price action, shaping the overall trend and momentum of the market.

A **demand zone** generally acts as a support area, where buying interest may emerge, potentially leading to a price reversal or upward movement. Similarly, a **supply zone** acts as a resistance area, where selling pressure may dominate, often causing price to reverse downward.

Demand-Supply Dynamics:

At first glance, it may seem that demand and supply should always remain balanced—because for every buyer there must be a seller and vice versa. However, what determines the trend is not the *number* of buyers and sellers, but their **aggressiveness and willingness to transact at different prices**.

In an uptrend, buyers are more aggressive—they are willing to **pay higher prices** to acquire the asset, while sellers are either reluctant or demand even higher prices to sell. This continuous willingness of buyers to lift offers pushes price upward, creating rising demand in terms of price levels.

Conversely, in a downtrend, sellers become more aggressive—they are willing to **accept lower prices** to exit their positions, while buyers step back or bid lower. This causes price to decline as supply overwhelms demand at each successive level. Thus, even though transactions remain matched, it is the urgency and price acceptance of participants that shifts the balance, causing price to trend upward or downward.

Demand and supply are dynamic and continuously evolving. A strong demand zone can weaken if repeatedly tested, and similarly, supply zones can get exhausted over time. When price breaks through a supply zone with strength, it indicates that demand has absorbed the available supply—often leading to further upside. Likewise, a breakdown below a demand zone shows that supply has overtaken demand. This interaction creates the familiar concepts of **support and resistance**, along with role reversal where old resistance becomes new support and vice versa.

Trading Demand-Supply Zones:

Understanding demand and supply gives a trader or investor a direct view into *where price is likely to react.* Markets often move from one demand zone to a supply zone and vice versa, creating swings. Strong **demand zones** typically lead to sharp upward moves (impulsive rallies), while strong **supply zones** lead to quick declines.

These zones also reflect the footprints of institutional activity, making them highly relevant for identifying high-probability entry and exit points. Market behaviour around these zones—such as strong rejection, consolidation, or breakout—provides insight into whether demand or supply is gaining control.

From a trading perspective, if a long position is initiated following a breakout from a demand zone, a prudent stop-loss would be placed below the low of the most recent candle. Likewise, for short trades initiated after a breakdown from a supply zone, the stop-loss can be placed above the high of the recent candle. However, it is important to remain cautious—false breakouts and stop-loss hunting are common around these zones. Price may temporarily breach a demand or supply zone to trap traders before reversing in the opposite direction. Hence, confirmation through price action and supporting indicators is essential before committing to a trade.

Identifying Demand-Supply Zones:

Demand and supply zones are typically identified by observing areas where price has made **strong, impulsive moves**.

- A **demand zone** is usually the base from which price rallies sharply (a "base + rally" structure).
- A **supply zone** is the area from which price drops sharply (a "base + drop" structure).

Key signs include:

- Strong momentum candles leaving the zone
- Little time spent at the level (quick rejection)
- High volume or sudden expansion in volatility
- Fresh zones (not tested multiple times) tend to be stronger

Tools Helpful in Identifying Demand and Supply

Several tools can assist in identifying and validating these zones:

- **Price action and structure** (most important): identifying impulsive moves and base formations
- **Support and resistance levels**: static representation of demand/supply zones
- **Bollinger Bands**: help identify contraction (base) and expansion (impulse) phases
- **Moving averages and AVWAP**: indicate dynamic areas where demand/supply may emerge
- **Volume and volume profile**: highlight zones of heavy participation and interest
- **Candlestick patterns**: rejection wicks, engulfing candles, and strong bodies indicate active demand or supply

These tools together help visualize where demand and supply are active and how price is reacting to them. Besides, there are customized technical indicator depicting demand and supply zones – which may be used for identification of these zones – from where the price is finding rejection.

By mastering demand and supply, a trader / investor learns to read the cause behind price movement, align with institutional activity, and identify high-probability trading opportunities with better precision and confidence. Demand & supply zones are a sub-set within a broader accumulation or distribution phases.

OVERBOUGHT & OVERSOLD

While demand and supply can be viewed as localized expressions within the broader phases of accumulation and distribution, their significance extends further when price begins to move decisively beyond these zones. Once price breaks out of a demand or supply zone with strength, the underlying imbalance can intensify, often pushing the market into **overbought or oversold territories**. These are conditions where price moves excessively away from its average or fair value due to heightened buying or selling pressure. Therefore, to fully understand market behaviour in its larger context, it becomes essential to study the concept of overbought and oversold zones—because they help us assess whether a move is sustainable, stretched, or approaching a potential pause or reversal.

Overbought and oversold are key concepts in technical analysis that describe extreme price conditions in a market. An **overbought condition** occurs when price has risen sharply over a period and may be due for a pause, correction, or reversal. Conversely, an **oversold condition** arises when price has fallen significantly and may be nearing a potential bounce or recovery. These conditions do not necessarily indicate immediate reversals but rather signal that the current trend may be overstretched.

The significance of identifying overbought and oversold zones lies in risk management and timing decisions. Traders and investors use these signals to avoid entering trades at unfavourable levels, plan profit booking, or look for early signs of trend exhaustion. However, it is important to understand that in strong trending markets, prices can remain overbought or oversold for extended periods, and hence these signals should always be used in conjunction with other indicators and price action.

Overbought and oversold conditions are generally identified using indicators such as RSI (Relative Strength Index) within the HM System framework. Typically, RSI (9) helps gauge whether an instrument is trading at extreme levels. Additionally, metrics like SRT values can further support the assessment of market extremes, aiding in decisions related to exiting existing positions or initiating fresh investments.

It is important to note that these concepts may not be reliable in instruments exhibiting abnormal price behaviour, such as penny stocks, indices, currencies, **or** stocks locked in continuous upper/lower circuits, where price movement is driven more by external constraints than natural demand-supply dynamics.

Overbought Condition:

An overbought condition arises when an instrument has been aggressively bought by a large number of participants, leading to high demand and relatively lower supply, which in turn drives prices upward into a strong uptrend. Such conditions are often fuelled by broad market participation, particularly from retail traders, along with institutional activity. However, this excessive buying eventually leads to a stage where the price becomes stretched beyond its sustainable levels.

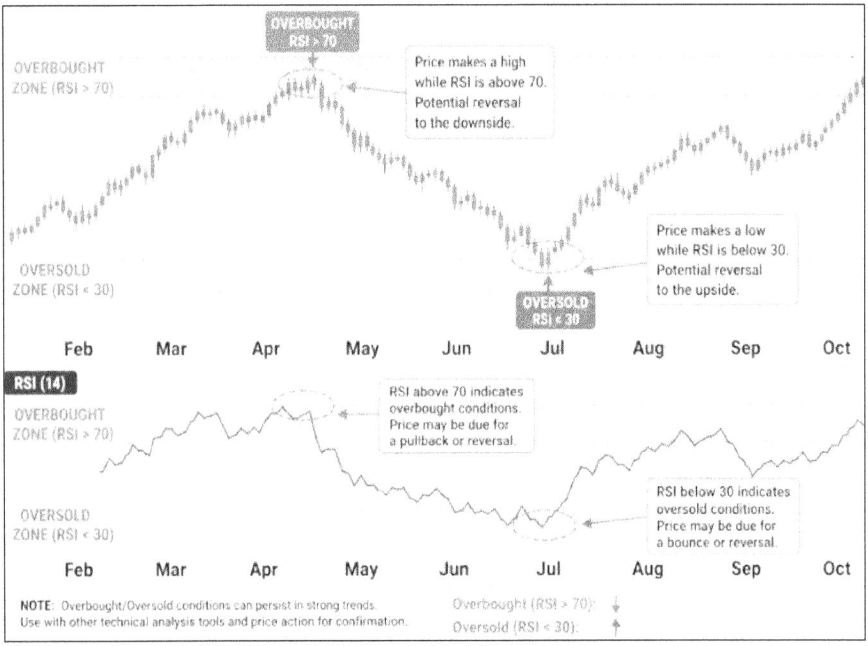

It is important to refine the common understanding of overbought conditions for Stock prices. When RSI (9) on higher timeframes such as Weekly or Monthly is above 70, it does not necessarily indicate immediate overbought levels—in fact, it often reflects strong bullish momentum, where the stock may continue to perform and even multiply over the next 12–15 months. Extremely overbought conditions typically emerge when RSI (9) reaches extreme levels, such as **above 85 on Weekly / Monthly timeframes**, or when RSI (9) reaches extreme level of above 90 on the Daily timeframe. At such levels, the probability of correction or reversal increases significantly, often within the next few weeks.

Overbought and oversold conditions can also be traced in the standard RSI (14).

Overbought conditions are generally easier to trade from a contrarian perspective. Once momentum starts weakening and confirmation is received from technical indicators like HM System on the Daily timeframe, traders can consider initiating short positions. Additionally, broader market corrections—such as declines in benchmark indices—tend to pull down individual stocks, especially those already in overbought zones. Hence, identifying overbought conditions helps in timely profit booking and planning short trades with better risk-reward.

Oversold Condition:

An oversold condition occurs when an instrument is heavily sold by market participants, resulting in low demand and excess supply, which drives prices downward into a sustained downtrend. Unlike overbought conditions, oversold phases are typically driven by broad-based selling across all participants—including retailers, FIIs, DIIs, and even promoters—often triggered by fear, panic, or prolonged negative sentiment.

When a market becomes deeply oversold, RSI (9) on higher timeframes such as Monthly may flatten and continue to hover below the 30 level on the HM System, indicating persistent weakness. In such conditions, many retail investors tend to get trapped, either due to delayed exits or continuous averaging at lower levels. As a result, the stock may remain under pressure for an extended period, sometimes even for several years, until weaker hands gradually exit and stronger institutional participation (smart money) begins to build positions.

It is generally more challenging to trade oversold conditions from the long side, as price may continue to drift lower or remain stagnant for long durations. However, a potential opportunity arises when RSI (9) on the Weekly timeframe approaches extremely low levels (around 15) and the price begins to show signs of curvature and upward reversal after a prolonged base formation. In such cases, once supported by a confirmed buy signal on the Daily timeframe in the HM System, a long position may be considered.

Stocks with lower retail concentration and stronger institutional presence tend to recover and trend upward more smoothly, often moving in a steady 45-degree trajectory. Thus, identifying true oversold conditions is not just about price levels, but also about market participation and accumulation by informed players, which ultimately drives sustainable upside momentum.

Identifying Overbought & Oversold Condition:

A refined way to assess overbought and oversold conditions is by mapping strength-based support and resistance zones using RSI (9) within the HM System. On the upper side (RSI above 50), drawing a trendline using at least two significant peaks helps define a strength-based resistance zone; using the two highest such trendlines provides a broader resistance band. Similarly, on the lower side (RSI below 50), connecting at least two major troughs helps identify a strength-based support zone, with the lowest two trendlines forming a reliable support band.

When price approaches this strength-based resistance zone, it is prudent to exit long positions near the upper boundary and prepare for a potential short trade upon confirmation of reversal. Conversely, when price nears the strength-based support zone, traders should consider exiting short positions near the lower boundary and prepare for long opportunities on reversal.

RSI divergence further strengthens this analysis. If price continues to rise while RSI begins to decline, it signals weakening strength despite higher prices, indicating a likely overbought reversal. Likewise, if price falls but RSI starts rising, it suggests diminishing selling pressure, pointing toward an oversold reversal. The presence of strong price action signals such as OH/OL formations at these zones significantly increases the reliability of trade entries. In essence, overbought zones act as resistance, while oversold zones act as support.

Investment Zones in Historical Oversold Conditions:

Historical observations of the Nifty index highlight how extreme RSI levels on higher timeframes define major market bottoms. On the Monthly timeframe, RSI (14) dropping below ~42 has coincided with extreme bearish phases such as the 2008 financial crisis and the 2020 COVID crash.

Similarly, RSI (9) on the HM System dropped to extreme lows on Daily TF—around 28 (2008), 30 (2016), and 25 (2020)—marking deep oversold conditions. As a broader example, the image below shows RSI (9) based overbought and oversold range for Nifty Index on Monthly timeframe.

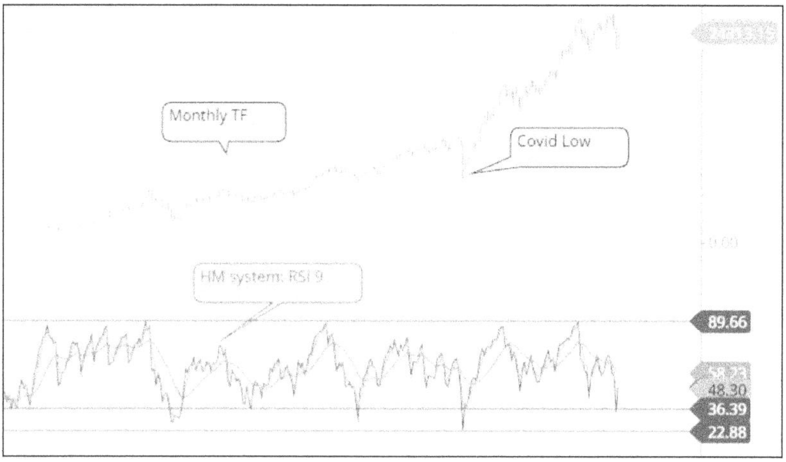

Such levels often represent exceptional long-term buying opportunities, especially for investors. However, since oversold conditions can persist, investments should be made gradually in tranches and preferably on pullbacks, rather than attempting to time the exact bottom. These zones also tend to align with strong SRT readings and, more importantly, with major AVWAP support levels anchored at historical panic points (e.g., the 2008 Lehman crisis and the March 2020 COVID crash). These anchored levels often act as powerful long-term support zones, offering high-probability investment areas.

On the Daily timeframe, when RSI (14) falls below 30, it not only indicates an oversold condition but also reflects extreme bearish momentum. In such cases, prices can continue to decline significantly despite appearing "cheap." Therefore, initiating long trades prematurely in such conditions can be risky. A more prudent approach is to wait for a meaningful pullback, where RSI **reclaims** and sustains above the 30 level, indicating a potential shift in momentum before considering long positions.

Similarly, in extreme overbought conditions (e.g., RSI reaching 90–95 on the Daily timeframe), once the price begins to reverse downward, the market typically does not resume the uptrend immediately. Such reversals often mark the beginning of a broader corrective phase, making it an opportune time to exit longs and evaluate short opportunities based on confirmation signals.

Overall, combining **RSI-based strength zones, divergence analysis, and confirmation through price action and AVWAP levels** provides a comprehensive framework to identify, and trade **overbought and oversold conditions with greater precision and confidence.**

SRT Calculation for Overbought & Oversold Condition:

The **SRT (Spot-to-Range Trend) value** is a useful metric to assess the broader market's overbought and oversold conditions. It is calculated using the Nifty 50 by dividing its current spot price by its 124-day simple moving average (SMA). The use of the 124 SMA reflects approximately half a trading year (about 250 sessions annually), making it a reliable benchmark for medium-term market valuation and sentiment.

Formula:

$$SRT = \frac{\text{Current Spot Price of Nifty}}{\text{124-day SMA of Nifty}}$$

Example (Illustrative)

- Current Nifty Spot Price = 22,500
- 124-day SMA = 21,000

$$SRT = \frac{22{,}500}{21{,}000} = 1.071$$

From an overbought perspective, an SRT value of around **1.35** marks the beginning of stretched valuations, where caution is warranted. As the value rises further—towards **1.45 and beyond**—it signals increasing market euphoria. An SRT of **1.5** represents an extreme overbought zone, often coinciding with excessive optimism and aggressive participation. At such levels, it is prudent to avoid fresh investments and progressively book profits. In fact, partial profit booking can begin once SRT crosses 1.35, with complete exit advisable if the value reverses downward after reaching elevated levels.

On the other hand, **oversold conditions** begin to emerge when the SRT declines to around **0.9**, indicating undervaluation and weakening sentiment. As the value drops further—towards **0.8 or 0.7**—the market enters deeper oversold territory. An SRT of **0.6** represents an extreme oversold zone, typically observed during periods of widespread panic and capitulation. Such levels historically present exceptional long-term investment opportunities, often appearing once in several years. A disciplined approach involves gradual accumulation (e.g., SIP mode) as SRT approaches and moves below 0.9, with patience to hold positions as the market stabilizes and reverses upward.

In essence, the SRT framework helps investors align their actions with market cycles—**reducing exposure during euphoric peaks and accumulating during fearful lows**—thereby improving long-term returns while managing risk effectively.

KNOW THE MARKET

As said earlier, accumulation, distribution, demand-supply dynamics, and overbought-oversold conditions form some of the most important foundational pillars of market structure and behaviour in Technical Analysis. These concepts help market participants understand what may be unfolding beneath the visible price movement — whether institutions are quietly accumulating positions, distributing holdings, aggressively demanding higher prices, or creating supply pressure near important zones. In many situations, major market trends and reversals originate from these underlying phases long before they become obvious to the broader market.

A sound understanding of these concepts helps traders and investors develop deeper insight into momentum sustainability, trend exhaustion, possible reversals, and areas where price may strongly react. Accumulation phases often precede powerful bullish moves, while distribution phases may quietly signal weakening momentum before broader declines emerge. Similarly, demand and supply zones help identify areas where buyers or sellers may dominate, while overbought and oversold conditions provide important clues regarding stretched price behaviour, emotional excess, and possible mean reversion or cooling-off phases.

The practical value of these concepts increases significantly when they are studied together in association with price action, volume behaviour, moving averages, VWAP / AVWAP, Relative Strength, momentum indicators, candlestick patterns, and broader trend structure. Over time, repeated observation of charts gradually trains the eyes and mind to identify these setups and behavioural patterns with better clarity and confidence. Eventually, traders and investors begin to understand not only what price is doing, but also why it may be behaving in a particular manner.

Like all important aspects of Technical Analysis, mastery of accumulation-distribution behaviour, demand-supply dynamics, and overbought-oversold structures comes through observation, patience, discipline, and practical market experience. The more one studies these concepts in live market conditions and historical charts, the stronger one's ability becomes to identify high-probability setups, avoid emotional decisions, manage risk better, and align with the underlying market structure. These concepts therefore become invaluable tools in building deeper market understanding and improving overall trading and investing decision-making over time.

Chapter – 11

Market Corrections

Play the Bear

Market corrections are a natural and healthy part of every financial market cycle. No market moves in a straight line indefinitely—periods of sustained rise are often followed by phases of pullback, consolidation, or decline. These corrections help the market absorb excessive optimism, remove weak hands, rebalance valuations, and prepare for the next major directional move.

A correction should not always be viewed negatively. In many cases, it serves as a necessary pause within a broader trend, allowing prices to realign with averages, technical levels, valuation comfort, and fresh demand–supply dynamics. For traders, corrections offer both caution signals and fresh opportunities—either to protect profits, enter at better levels, or identify the continuation or reversal of trend.

Broadly, market corrections may be classified into the following two types:

- **Price-wise Correction**
- **Time-wise correction**

PRICE-WISE MARKET CORRECTION

A price-wise correction occurs when the market experiences a sharp and sudden fall, causing prices to quickly retrace from elevated levels and move back toward a key average or support zone—such as the **200 EMA on the Daily time frame**, **50 EMA on the Weekly time frame**, or **5 SMA on the Monthly time frame**.

Such corrections are usually swift and emotionally driven, often creating panic among market participants (e.g. war time news or US tariff imposition news etc). However, they generally last for a shorter duration and tend to recover relatively quickly once the excess price expansion is absorbed. The recovery pattern in such cases is often **V-shaped** or sometimes **W-shaped**, indicating a strong resumption of the broader trend after the correction.

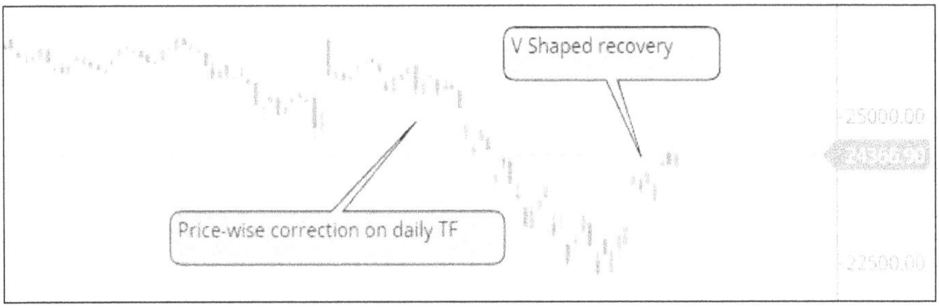

TIME-WISE MARKET CORRECTION

A time-wise correction occurs when the market does not witness a sharp fall in price, but instead enters a prolonged phase of sideways movement, consolidation, or slow drift. In this type of correction, rather than price moving sharply downward, **time itself becomes the corrective factor**, allowing moving averages and broader indicators to catch up with the price.

This type of correction is generally less panic-driven and more gradual in nature. It may continue for days, weeks, or even months, depending on the time frame under consideration. During this phase, the market often trades within a defined range, absorbing previous gains and preparing for its next decisive move.

As mentioned above, time-wise correction unfolds primarily through the passage of time rather than an immediate sharp decline in price. On the Monthly time frame (M TF), once indices or stocks reach overbought zones or approach significant levels such as maximum-hope AVWAP, the market often begins a gradual process of mean reversion. When a substantial gap develops between price and its key averages—particularly the **20 SMA on M TF—a correction becomes likely**, as price and averages tend to converge over time.

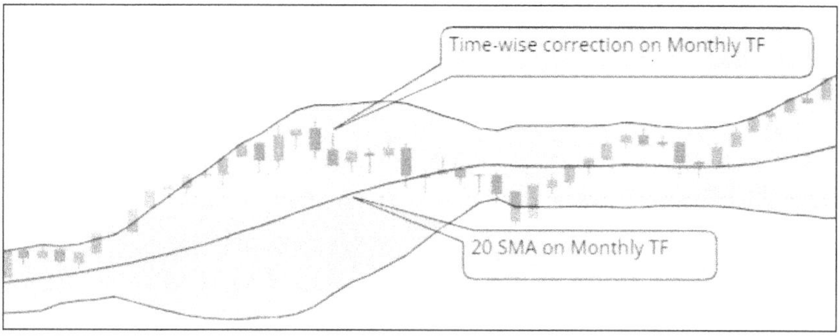

This phase is often triggered when price moves back inside the Bollinger Band after previously travelling along the upper band, combined with extreme overbought conditions indicated by tools such as SRT values or RSI levels (for instance, RSI 9 exceeding 86 on M TF in the HM System). Such conditions signal that the market is entering an averaging phase, wherein either price drifts downward toward the 20 SMA, or the moving average gradually rises toward price while the market oscillates within a broad range. This process—often influenced by macro triggers such as geopolitical events, recession fears, or global uncertainties—marks the beginning of a time-wise correction. Key averaging levels on the Monthly time frame include the 20 SMA initially, followed by deeper support levels such as the lowest AVWAP (e.g., levels formed during extreme panic phases like the COVID-19 market fall).

During a time-wise correction, the market typically exhibits a pattern of gradual decline interspersed with prolonged consolidation phases. Price may make lower lows, stabilize within a range, and then drift further downward before again consolidating. Over time, this results in the convergence of price with major averages such as the 20 SMA or AVWAP on the Monthly time frame. As the market stabilizes within a defined range for an extended period, Bollinger Bands on the Daily and Weekly time frames tend to narrow, indicating reduced volatility and preparation for a future expansion. Once this consolidation matures and price aligns with its key averages, the market eventually attempts a breakout from this range. A sustained breakout—often accompanied by a Bollinger Band expansion (BB blast) on higher time frames—signals the resumption of the broader upward trend.

Typically, a time-wise correction may last anywhere between **six months to one year or more**. During this phase, benchmark indices such as Nifty 50 or

Bank Nifty may drift gradually lower, while broader markets—especially mid-cap and small-cap stocks—can experience significant drawdowns, sometimes declining by as much as 40–50%.

To confirm the end of a time-wise correction and the beginning of a fresh bullish phase, higher time frame signals are crucial. The HM System on the Monthly time frame should indicate a buy signal (i.e., RSI 9 crossing above WMA 21), accompanied by price closing above the highest recent Monthly closing level from where the correction originally began. Until such confirmation occurs, the market is likely to remain within a broad range, defined by a major resistance (previous peak closing level) and a strong support zone formed by repeated price convergence with key averages.

This range-bound phase offers tradable opportunities. Traders can operate within this range by taking contrarian positions near extremes—selling near resistance and buying near support—until a decisive breakout occurs. However, once the market closes above the prior major resistance on the Monthly time frame, it signals the completion of the time-wise correction and the start of a new bullish cycle.

It is also observed that during such phases, most stocks participate in the correction cycle, although certain micro-cap or SME stocks may behave independently due to localized demand–supply dynamics.

From an investment perspective, **the 20 SMA on the Monthly time frame serves as a strong accumulation zone**, while the **lowest AVWAP levels—formed during periods of extreme panic—represent the most attractive long-term buying opportunities**. These zones often provide the foundation for the next major uptrend once the correction phase concludes.

CORRECTION GIVES OPPORTUNITIES

In conclusion, market corrections are an inherent and essential part of any financial market cycle, broadly manifesting either as sharp **price-wise corrections** or gradual **time-wise corrections**. While price-wise corrections are swift, panic-driven declines that quickly bring prices back to equilibrium levels, time-wise corrections unfold more subtly—allowing markets to consolidate, absorb excesses, and realign valuations over an extended period. Both forms serve the same underlying purpose: restoring balance between price, value, and market sentiment.

External triggers often determine the nature of the correction. Sudden geopolitical developments—such as wars, global conflicts, policy shocks, or unexpected crises—tend to induce **price-wise corrections**, characterized by rapid sell-offs and equally sharp recoveries. In contrast, **time-wise corrections** are typically driven by deeper structural or macroeconomic factors, such as economic slowdowns, liquidity tightening, valuation excesses, or cyclical resets. These phases reflect a more organic adjustment process, where markets move sideways to downward over months, allowing averages like the 20, 50, 100, 150, 200 SMAs or AVWAP to converge with price.

For traders and investors, the key lies not in predicting corrections but in understanding their nature and adapting strategy accordingly. Price-wise corrections often present short-term opportunities due to their sharp reversals, whereas time-wise corrections demand patience, disciplined accumulation, and range-based trading approaches. Recognizing whether the market is undergoing a panic-driven decline or a structural consolidation can significantly enhance decision-making, risk management, and capital allocation.

Ultimately, corrections—whether driven by fear or fundamentals—are not disruptions but preparatory phases for the next market move. A well-informed participant views them not with apprehension, but as opportunities: to protect capital during extremes, and to deploy it strategically when markets reset and new trends begin to emerge.

Chapter – 12

Chart Patterns

For Long & Short, Intraday & Positional

Chart patterns form the foundation of price action analysis and are among the most effective tools available to a trader. They are not random shapes on a chart, but a direct reflection of how price and volume interact over time—capturing the underlying battle between demand and supply. Every pattern represents a story of accumulation, distribution, breakout, or reversal, and therefore provides early insight into the likely direction of the market.

In practical trading, chart patterns should always be given precedence over indicators. Indicators are inherently lagging in nature—they are derived from price and simply replicate past movements with a delay. While they can help in supporting or re-validating a view, they cannot replace the immediacy and clarity that patterns offer. Patterns emerge from real-time price behaviour, whereas indicators follow it.

A disciplined trader, therefore, focuses first on identifying clean and convincing chart patterns, and then uses indicators only as a secondary layer of confirmation. This approach ensures that decisions are based on the most direct and reliable market signals, improving both timing and conviction in trades.

There are several well-known chart patterns such as **Cup & Handle, Double Top, Double Bottom, Triple Top, Triple Bottom, Head & Shoulders, Inverse Head & Shoulders, Flags, and Triangles**. However, in this chapter, we will focus on some **less common yet highly effective and unique patterns** that can be extremely useful for intraday, positional trading, as well as investing—when understood with precision and developed into a skill.

Further, multiple support and resistance levels often combine together to form identifiable price patterns, which provide valuable insights into market structure and trader psychology. These patterns emerge as price repeatedly reacts within certain boundaries, reflecting the ongoing battle between demand and supply. One common example is a **parallel channel**, where price oscillates between upward or downward sloping support and resistance lines, indicating a controlled trending market.

Similarly, price may form patterns such as **ascending triangles**, where resistance remains relatively flat while support gradually rises, signalling increasing buying pressure; or **descending triangles**, where support remains fixed while resistance slopes downward, reflecting growing selling pressure. **Rectangles or range-bound zones** indicate consolidation between horizontal support and resistance, often preceding a breakout. Patterns like **wedges**, **flags**, and **pennants** also develop through the interaction of multiple support and resistance levels, frequently acting as continuation or reversal structures.

These chart pattern formations become even more significant when observed on higher time frames and when accompanied by volume confirmation, moving averages, or broader trend alignment. Understanding such patterns helps traders anticipate potential breakouts, reversals, or continuation moves, thereby enhancing the overall interpretation of price action.

In this Chapter we explore some of the most unique but not-so-popular, high probability chart patterns – very helpful for profitable trading and investing.

Let us now delve into a selection of these remarkable chart patterns that can be effectively used for intraday trading, positional setups, as well as long-term stock investments.

OPEN-HIGH AND OPEN-LOW PATTERNS

OH (Open = High) and OL (Open = Low) candle formations are powerful price action signals that act as strong resistance and support levels, respectively. In an OH formation, the high of the candle becomes a key resistance level, and price often tends to revisit that level before facing rejection and moving downward. Similarly, in an OL formation, the low of the candle acts as a strong support level, from where price is likely to bounce upward upon retest.

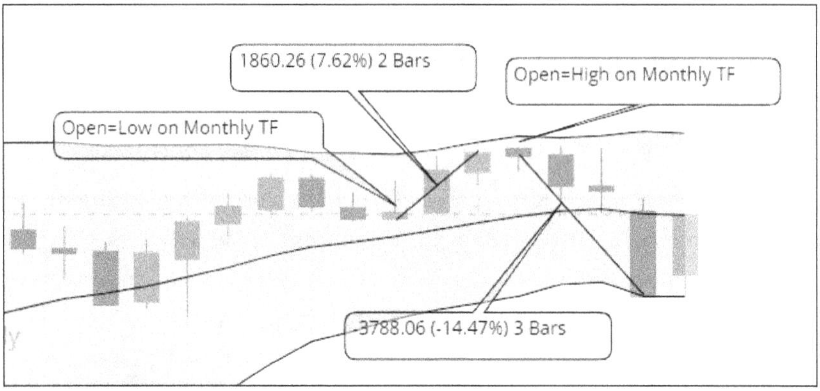

When multiple OH formations occur in a falling market, the most recent OH becomes the immediate resistance, while earlier OH levels act as secondary resistance zones. The same principle applies to OL formations in a rising market. These formations gain higher reliability when observed across both spot and futures charts (for example, in indices like Nifty), as alignment across instruments strengthens the level's significance. It is important to note that OH/OL formations need not occur only in the first candle—they are equally effective when formed at any point during the session.

From a trading perspective, OH/OL formations on the Daily timeframe are useful for positional trades, while those on lower timeframes like 10-minute charts are suitable for intraday and scalping opportunities. On the Hourly timeframe, their effect can extend into the next trading session, especially if the closing structure supports continuation (such as a close below the prior candle's low for bearish setups). Overall, these formations provide clear, actionable levels for entry, stop-loss placement, and target identification when used with proper context and discipline.

OH and OL in Intraday:

When an OH/OL formation appears in the very first candle on market opening (10-minute timeframe), it provides an early and actionable intraday setup. However, this signal should not be traded in isolation. A trade decision should be taken only after considering key confluences such as VWAP, nearby support/ resistance levels, and overall market context.

The ideal entry is taken on the second candle, preferably near VWAP, once price confirms direction—i.e., breaking below the low of the OH candle for a short trade or moving above the high of the OL candle for a long trade. This setup must be further validated by the HM System on the 5-minute timeframe: a sell signal (WMA 21 > RSI 9) for OH-based shorts, and a buy signal (RSI 9 > WMA 21) for OL-based longs. This multi-layer confirmation significantly enhances the probability of a successful trade.

Stop-loss should be placed on a closing basis beyond the high (for OH) or low (for OL) of the first candle. Targets can be set at previous or next support/resistance levels, pivot points, or dynamic levels such as AVWAP or the 20 SMA on the 10-minute timeframe. Additionally, it is important to cross-check the setup on higher timeframes (Hourly and Daily). If a static support/resistance level aligns with a dynamic level (like VWAP, AVWAP, or moving averages), it creates a strong confluence zone, from where price is highly likely to react or reverse.

Second Candle Confirmation:

For an OH/OL setup to evolve into a strong trending move, confirmation from the subsequent candles is essential. If the first opening candle forms an OH (Open = High), and the second or third candle decisively breaches the low of that first candle while sustaining below VWAP for intraday setup, it indicates strong selling pressure and a high probability of a sustained downtrend. This follow-through confirms that the initial OH was not just a rejection, but the beginning of a directional move.

Similarly, if the first opening candle forms an OL (Open = Low), and the second or third candle breaks above the high of the first candle and sustains above VWAP in intraday, it signals strong buying interest and the likelihood of an uptrend. In both cases, the key lies in the continuation and acceptance of price beyond the OH/OL range, supported by VWAP alignment.

Trades initiated on such confirmed setups should be managed actively, with profits booked at the next significant support/resistance levels or upon early signs of reversal, ensuring disciplined execution and protection of gains.

OH / OL with HM System Confirmation:

When an OH/OL formation appears on the 10-minute timeframe, it should not be traded in isolation. For higher reliability, the setup must be confirmed by the HM System (customized technical indicator) on a lower timeframe, such as the 5-minute chart. A long trade based on an OL formation should be considered only when the HM System indicates a buy signal (i.e., RSI 9 crossing above WMA 21), while a short trade based on an OH formation should be taken only when the HM System confirms a sell signal (i.e., WMA 21 above RSI 9).

This multi-timeframe alignment ensures that the price action signal (OH/OL) is supported by underlying momentum, thereby increasing the probability of a successful trade.

Strong OH / OL Setup for Intraday:

An OH/OL formation on the 10-minute timeframe becomes significantly stronger when it is simultaneously formed in both the Spot and Futures charts. Such alignment indicates a high-conviction move driven by broader market participation, often resulting in a clear trending day—downtrend in the case of OH and uptrend in the case of OL. However, if the formation appears in only one (either Spot or Futures), the trend is likely to be weaker, choppier, and may even lead to intraday traps. Hence, preference should always be given to setups where both Spot and Futures confirm the same OH/OL structure.

Trading OH / OL via Options in Intraday:

When a strong OH/OL setup is confirmed across both Spot and Futures on the 10-minute timeframe, traders can further refine entries by identifying similar OH/OL formations in options on the same timeframe. An OL formation in options can be used for initiating option buying trades, while an OH formation can be used for option selling strategies. This alignment across underlying and derivative instruments strengthens the trade conviction.

However, before executing option trades, it is important to assess intraday volatility conditions (such as VIX behaviour) to decide whether option buying, option selling, or futures trading is more appropriate. For such setups, stop-loss should be strictly based on the breach of the high of the OH or the low of the OL on the Futures chart, rather than relying on VWAP-based stop-loss, as OH/OL formations tend to play out more cleanly with price structure-based risk management.

OH/OL with Bollinger Band Trap – A High-Probability Setup:

An OH/OL formation becomes significantly stronger when it aligns with a Bollinger Band (BB) Trap. If the first candle on the 10-minute (or any) timeframe forms an OH/OL and simultaneously reflects a BB Trap condition, and the second or third candle quickly closes and sustains above/below VWAP in the direction of the trade, it signals a high-probability intraday opportunity.

This setup should be further confirmed by the HM System. For a long trade (OL-based), a buy signal is validated when RSI 9 crosses above WMA 21 (or at least above EMA 3). For a short trade (OH-based), a sell signal is confirmed when WMA 21 is above RSI 9 (or at least EMA 3 is above RSI 9). When trading such setups on higher timeframes like Hourly or Daily, the HM confirmation can be taken on the same timeframe as the pattern.

Such OH/OL + BB Trap combinations are known for cleaner moves with minimal stop-loss hunting, making them particularly effective for intraday trading. The first target can be set at the 9 SMA high/low or the 20 SMA on the 10-minute timeframe, followed by the upper/lower Bollinger Band (UBB/LBB) as the second target. Stop-loss should be strictly placed on a closing basis beyond the high of the OH or the low of the OL, while VWAP-based stop-loss should be avoided in this setup due to its tendency to cause unnecessary exits.

OH/OL – Jackpot Intraday Trade Setup:

An OH/OL formation on the Hourly timeframe can lead to exceptionally strong intraday opportunities when supported by clear trend alignment. If both price and VWAP are sloping consistently in the same direction (downward for OH, upward for OL) on the Hourly as well as the 10-minute timeframe, it indicates strong directional momentum. When the very next candle after the OH/OL formation decisively sustains and closes below the low of the OH candle (for shorts) or above the high of the OL candle (for longs), it confirms continuation and can result in a "jackpot" intraday move.

The ideal entry in such setups is near VWAP on a pullback, allowing for a better risk-reward structure. Stop-loss should be placed on a closing basis (on the 10-minute timeframe) beyond the high of the OH or the low of the OL. This ensures that the trade is protected while allowing the trend to play out without premature exits.

Additionally, if the final Hourly candle of the trading session confirms continuation—i.e., it closes above the previous candle's close in case of an OL setup, or below the previous candle's close in case of an OH setup—then BTST

(Buy Today Sell Tomorrow) or STBT (Sell Today Buy Tomorrow) trades can be considered. In the absence of such confirmation, it is prudent to avoid carrying forward the position.

Entry Strategies in OH/OL Formation (Intraday):

First Golden Entry (Highest Probability):

In an OH/OL setup on the Hourly timeframe, the most favourable entry—referred to as the *golden entry*—is taken near the extreme of the formation: near the high in case of OH and near the low in case of OL. However, this entry should only be executed when price shows a clear reversal from these levels on the 10-minute timeframe. This ensures that the level is being respected and not broken impulsively. The stop-loss should be placed on a closing basis (10-minute timeframe) beyond the high of the OH or the low of the OL, as applicable.

Second Golden Entry (VWAP Pullback):

Another high-quality entry arises when, after the initial OH/OL formation, price retraces back toward VWAP during the day and then resumes its original direction. In case of an OH setup, a short entry can be taken when price approaches VWAP and shows signs of reversal downward on the 10-minute timeframe. Similarly, in an OL setup, a long entry is taken when price revisits VWAP and bounces upward. The stop-loss in this case should be placed at the day's high (for OH) or day's low (for OL), based on a closing breach on the 10-minute timeframe.

Secondary Entry (Breakout Confirmation):

A slightly more aggressive but still reliable entry is taken on the second candle itself. In an OH formation, a short trade can be initiated near VWAP when the second candle shows a breakdown below the low of the first candle. Conversely, in an OL setup, a long trade can be taken when the second candle breaks above the high of the first candle. The stop-loss remains consistent—placed on a closing basis beyond the high of the OH or the low of the OL on the 10-minute timeframe.

These structured entry approaches help traders participate in OH/OL setups with clarity, discipline, and improved risk-reward positioning.

Trading basis OL Formation on 10-Minute Timeframe (Intraday):

When the first candle on the 10-minute timeframe forms an OL (Open = Low) and closes above VWAP, it indicates initial buying strength. However, confirmation is essential. Ideally, the second candle should close above both the close of the first candle and VWAP. If this happens, a long trade can be initiated near VWAP, aligning with bullish momentum.

If the second candle fails to sustain strength and instead reverses to close below VWAP, it signals weakness. In such a case, a short trade may be considered near VWAP, as an immediate reversal below VWAP after an OL setup reflects lack of buying follow-through. However, for this short trade to gain conviction, price must eventually close below the low of the first OL candle. If already in a short position, the stop-loss should be a closing basis above VWAP. Once price breaks the OL low, the trade can be trailed, keeping in mind nearby support levels such as previous day support, pivot levels, or dynamic supports like the 20 SMA or Bollinger Bands on higher timeframes. Profits should be booked just above these support zones.

If price again reverses upward and reclaims VWAP, a long trade can be reconsidered near VWAP. However, confirmation requires a decisive close above the day's high (formed by the first OL candle or any subsequent candle). For such long trades, stop-loss should be a closing basis below VWAP. If the breakout sustains, the trade can be carried forward toward higher resistance levels, such as previous day resistance, pivot points, or dynamic resistance levels (like the 20 SMA or Bollinger Bands on higher timeframes). Profits should be booked near these resistance zones.

To manage risk more effectively, especially when the OH/OL candle range is wide, a **1/3rd candle stop-loss** can be used. This involves placing the stop-loss at one-third beyond the OH/OL candle range (on a closing basis), which helps reduce risk and avoid unnecessary stop-loss hunting around VWAP.

Breach of OH/OL – Reversal vs. Continuation:

A decisive breach of key OH/OL levels often signals a strong directional move. If the high of an OH candle is broken on the upside, or the low of an OL candle is breached on the downside, the market is likely to trend powerfully in that direction. Such breakouts typically occur with a single strong candle (on a closing basis), reflecting clear momentum and participation.

However, if price approaches the high of an OH or the low of an OL and begins to **sustain or stall** around these levels—without a convincing breakout—it indicates rejection and a higher probability of reversal. This situation presents a high-quality *golden entry* opportunity for intraday trading: initiate a short near the high of an OH, or a long near the low of an OL, with appropriate confirmation and risk management.

In essence, a clean breach signals continuation, while sustained hesitation near the level often signals reversal—both offering structured trading opportunities when read correctly.

Trapping / Reversal in OH/OL Formation:

OH/OL formations are directional signals, but they are not always conclusive. They indicate a *potential* trend, not a guaranteed one. Hence, traders must remain alert for possible traps and reversals. It is important to closely monitor price action on the 10-minute timeframe and take confirmation from supporting indicators like the HM System and Ehler Fisher (EF). Additionally, alignment with higher timeframes such as Hourly and Daily should always be considered before committing to a trade.

We discuss below a few situations indicating likely reversal in trend inspite of OH / OL formation.

Large OH/OL Candle on 10-Minute TF:

If an OH/OL formation appears as an unusually large candle on the 10-minute timeframe, it is advisable to avoid trading it, as such setups often lead to traps due to extended price movement already being exhausted. However, large OH/OL candles on the Hourly timeframe can still be valid and tradable. After an OH formation followed by a decline, the first logical target is typically the 20 SMA, nearby support, or pivot levels—where price may pause or reverse. Also, if 2–3 small candles start forming at a particular level during the move, it often signals exhaustion and a possible reversal.

OH/OL on Hourly TF – 3-Candle / 5-Candle Rule:

If the first candle on the Hourly timeframe forms an OH and closes below VWAP, followed by a cluster of 3 or 5 candles that also close below VWAP but fail to break the low of the first OH candle, it indicates weakening bearish momentum. In such cases, if on the 10-minute timeframe the HM System turns bullish (RSI 9 > WMA 21) or price reclaims and sustains above VWAP, a reversal to the upside becomes likely. The same logic applies in reverse for OL formations. Notably, the 5-candle rule is particularly effective in identifying exhaustion points and potential reversals, especially in trending markets.

Lack of Confirmation Between Spot & Futures:

For OH/OL setups to be reliable, confirmation across both Spot and Futures is important. If the formation appears in only one and not the other, the resulting trend is often weak, inconsistent, or prone to false moves. Such setups can easily lead to intraday traps and should be traded with caution or preferably avoided.

Reversal near Bollinger Bands (UBB/LBB):

If price reaches the upper or lower Bollinger Band (UBB/LBB) on the 10-minute timeframe but fails to produce a strong breakout (i.e., no "BB blast"), it often signals exhaustion and a likely reversal. In such cases, especially when price reacts at a prior resistance/support or dynamic level like UBB/LBB, stop-loss hunting around VWAP is common. Therefore, it is prudent not to wait for VWAP-based confirmation and instead book profits near the reversal zone—particularly around previous resistance/support (PR/PS) or pivot levels.

Reversal from Previous Day's Support / Resistance:

While riding an OH/OL trend, always track previous day's key support and resistance levels. These zones are frequently retested intraday. If price fails to break a previous resistance (during an OL-based long) or fails to break a previous support (during an OH-based short), it is a warning sign of reversal. In such scenarios, it is advisable to exit the trade upon observing reversal signals on the 10-minute timeframe.

Reversal from Pivot, Trendline, or Dynamic Levels:

Apart from prior day levels, traders must also watch static and dynamic resistance/support zones such as the next pivot level (on 10-minute TF), trendline-based levels (drawn from higher timeframes like Daily), and dynamic indicators like the 20 SMA or UBB / LBB on the Hourly timeframe. If price approaches these levels and shows inability to break through—while trading in an OH/OL trend—it is often a signal to exit. Profit booking near such confluence zones helps avoid reversals and protects gains.

"Green Ice-Candy" Candle – Reversal Signal in Downtrend:

In a strong intraday downtrend (e.g., OH formation, price sustaining below VWAP, BB blast on lower TF, and HM System indicating sell), the appearance of a large bullish "ice-candy" type candle (a long green candle) on the 10/15-minute timeframe can signal a potential reversal. In such cases, the low of this candle often holds for the rest of the session, and price may reverse upward. Post-reversal, significant VWAP-based stop-loss hunting may occur. Hence, traders should exercise caution, avoid aggressive shorts, and reassess the trend upon such formations.

Two Reversals After Opening with OH/OL:

Two Reversals Toward Short after an OL Opening: When the market opens with an OL (Open = Low) candle that closes above VWAP—often after a gap-up—it initially signals strength. However, if the next 2–3 candles quickly reverse and close below VWAP, followed by a breach of the low of the first OL candle, it marks the first reversal toward a short bias. If price then attempts a recovery—moving back above VWAP and even sustaining above the high of the first OL candle—it may briefly suggest bullish continuation. But if this upward move again fails and price reverses for the second time, closing back below VWAP, it becomes a critical warning signal. This *second reversal toward short* after a failed bullish attempt typically indicates distribution and a potential strong intraday downtrend. In such cases, a short trade can be initiated near VWAP, as the market has shown inability to sustain higher levels and is likely to witness a sharp decline.

Two Reversals Toward Long after an OH Opening: A similar but opposite setup occurs when the market opens with an OH (Open = High) candle. If price initially reverses upward by breaching the high of the OH candle (first reversal toward long), but later fails and drops—breaking below the low of the OH candle and sustaining there—it signals temporary bearish control. However, if the market again reverses upward and reclaims VWAP (second reversal toward long), it indicates strong absorption of selling pressure. This *second reversal toward long* after a failed breakdown suggests accumulation and increases the probability of a strong intraday uptrend. In such scenarios, a long trade can be initiated near VWAP, as the market is likely to trend upward with momentum.

Key Insight: Double reversals—especially when they involve VWAP and breach of key OH/OL levels—often reflect a transition from weak hands to strong hands. The second reversal is typically the more reliable move, as it traps early participants and fuels a stronger directional trend.

RANGEBOUND TRADE SETUPS AND BREAKOUTS

Range-Bound Day Indication from First 30-Min / 1-Hour Candle:

The nature of the first candle on the 30-minute or 1-hour timeframe often provides a strong early indication of how the trading day may unfold. If the opening candle forms a **long spinning top**—characterized by a wide range with wicks on both sides—it reflects indecision between buyers and sellers. Such a structure typically suggests that neither side has clear control, increasing the probability of a **range-bound market** for the day.

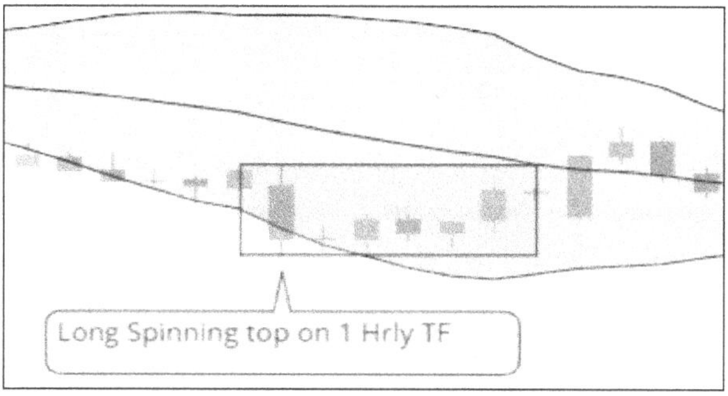

In these conditions, the market tends to oscillate within the high and low of the first candle, unless a decisive breakout occurs. A sustained move beyond the high or low of this initial candle—on a closing basis on the same timeframe—is required to shift the market from range-bound behaviour to a trending one. Until such a breakout happens, traders should assume sideways movement and avoid aggressive directional bets.

Additionally, during range-bound days, price action usually fluctuates around VWAP, frequently crossing and closing on either side of it. This further reinforces the absence of a strong trend. In such scenarios, range-trading strategies (like selling at resistance and buying at support) tend to be more effective than trend-following approaches.

Range-Bound Indication from First Hourly Long Candle:

When the first candle on the Hourly timeframe is a **large-bodied (long) candle**, it often reflects an initial burst of volatility or strong participation from both sides. However, contrary to what it may appear, such a candle frequently leads to a **range-bound trading day**, unless its high or low is decisively breached on a closing basis on the same timeframe.

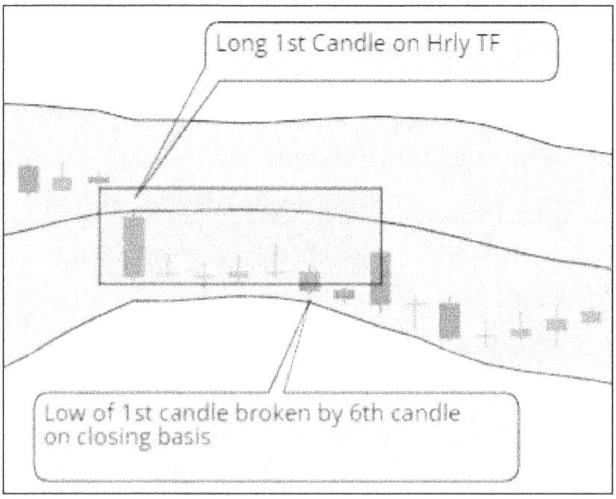

In such scenarios, the market typically respects the range defined by the high and low of the first Hourly candle, oscillating within this zone throughout the day. Traders should wait for a clear breakout (on a closing basis) beyond this range to consider directional trades. Until then, the market is more likely to behave sideways rather than trend strongly.

Additionally, during such range-bound conditions, price tends to fluctuate around VWAP, often closing on either side of it. This further reinforces the lack of directional conviction, making range-based strategies more effective than trend-following approaches for intraday trading.

Breakout of First 30-Min / 1-Hour Candle – Trend Day Indication:

When the first candle on the 30-minute or 1-hour timeframe forms a **long spinning top**, it reflects initial indecision in the market. However, this indecision often sets the stage for a decisive move. If any subsequent candle **breaches the high or low of this first candle on a closing basis**, it typically signals that the market has chosen a direction for the day.

A breakout above the high of the first candle indicates bullish strength, suggesting that the market is likely to trend upward for the remainder of the session. Conversely, a breakdown below the low of the first candle signals bearish dominance, indicating a probable downtrend for the day. Such breakouts often lead to momentum-driven moves, as the initial range gets resolved in one direction.

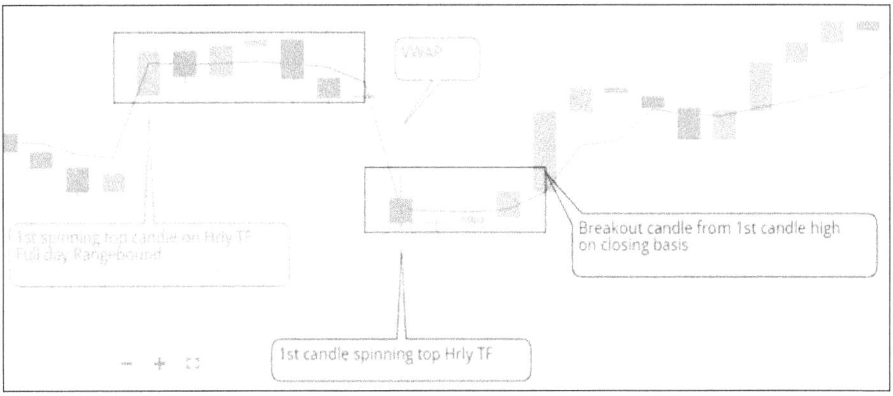

Therefore, the high and low of the first 30-minute or 1-hour candle act as **key intraday reference levels**. Once breached with conviction, traders can align their positions with the breakout direction, as the probability of a trending day increases significantly.

Hourly TF – Breakout from a Range-Bound Setup:

When the first Hourly candle forms a **long spinning top** and closes above VWAP, it initially indicates indecision, suggesting a likely range-bound environment. If this is followed by the 2nd and 3rd candles being **small-bodied (spinning top type)** and both closing above VWAP—irrespective of their colour—it reflects absorption of selling pressure and gradual strength building above VWAP.

This compression of price action above VWAP often precedes a directional move. In such a setup, a **long trade can be initiated on the 4th candle (typically post 12:15 PM)** near VWAP, as the market shows signs of holding strength and preparing for an upward move. The risk is relatively controlled in this structure, making it a favourable intraday opportunity.

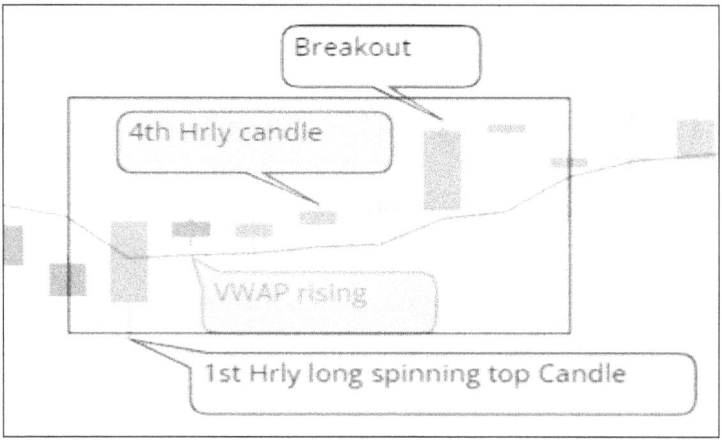

The **stop-loss** should be kept as one candle close below VWAP, ensuring protection against false breakouts. This setup effectively captures the transition from early indecision to a likely bullish breakout, with VWAP acting as a key support base.

3 STEP PATTERN FOR INTRADAY

The 3-step pattern is a structured intraday setup observed on the Hourly timeframe, typically offering high-probability trades around mid-session. In this pattern, the first three candles on the Hourly chart close progressively lower to the previous one indicating downward trend for intraday (or close progressively higher to the previous one indicating upward trend for intraday), with all three candles positioned consistently below (or above) VWAP. The colour of the candles is not significant; what matters is the directional closing sequence and alignment with VWAP.

Ideally, the 2nd and 3rd candles should be relatively small-bodied, indicating controlled movement and gradual build-up rather than exhaustion. Additionally, in case of lower low formations, the VWAP should be **sloping downward (for short trades)** and in case of higher (indicating upward trend for intraday), the VWAP should be **sloping upward (for long trades)**, also supported with confirmation from technical indicators like HM System or Ehler Fisher (EF) on the Hourly timeframe supporting the same directional bias.

Once this structure is established, a trade can be initiated on the **4th or 5th candle after 12:15 PM**, preferably near VWAP. This timing is crucial, as the market often shows directional expansion during the **12:30 PM to 1:30 PM window**. For a short setup, the expectation is a downward move, while the reverse conditions apply for a long setup. Only well-formed and clean 3-step patterns should be considered tradable, as partial or unclear formations may lead to false signals.

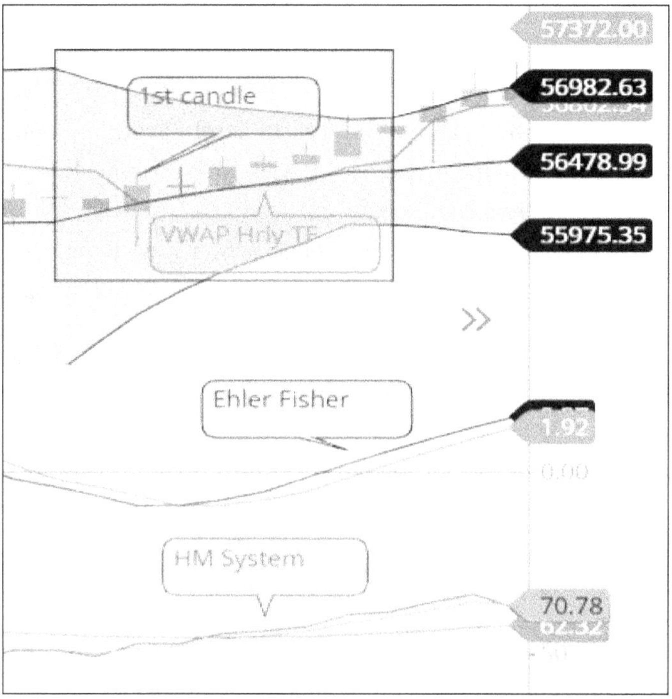

The **target** for this setup is typically the **20 SMA on the Hourly timeframe**. However, if the pattern forms close to the 20 SMA, then the next logical targets become the **Upper or Lower Bollinger Bands (UBB/LBB)**. A particularly strong version of this setup occurs when the pattern forms near the UBB/LBB and price action interacts closely with the band (touching, crossing, or moving along its slope). In such cases, the setup becomes more potent and can even justify option buying (CE/PE) due to expected momentum.

Exit Condition:

If, after entry, a subsequent candle shows signs of reversal—specifically, if price starts retracing and breaks below the midpoint (half level) of the 3rd or 4th candle—it indicates weakening momentum. In such a situation, it is advisable to exit the trade promptly, as the pattern may be failing and could lead to a reversal or consolidation.

BB TRAP

Bollinger Band (BB) Trap patterns represent one of the most insightful ways to understand failed breakouts at volatility extremes. Markets often tend to stretch beyond their natural range—moving outside the Upper or Lower Bollinger Bands (UBB/LBB)—creating an illusion of strong continuation. However, not every breakout sustains. When price fails to hold outside the bands and quickly re-enters the range, it signals exhaustion of the prevailing move and the possibility of a sharp reversal. This phenomenon is what we refer to as a BB Trap—where traders positioned on breakout expectations get "trapped," and the market moves in the opposite direction.

The real strength of BB Trap patterns lies in their ability to capture institutional behaviour and sentiment extremes. At the edges of the bands, markets are typically either overextended on the upside (euphoria) or oversold on the downside (panic). When such extremes coincide with reversal cues—like price re-entering the bands, VWAP shifts, or supporting indicators such as the HM System and Ehler Fisher—they provide high-probability opportunities for both intraday and positional trades. These setups become even more powerful when aligned with higher timeframe trends, OH/OL formations, or key support and resistance zones.

Across timeframes—from 5-minute intraday charts to Daily and Weekly setups—BB Trap patterns offer a structured framework to trade reversals with clarity. Whether it is a quick intraday reversal near VWAP or a multi-day positional shift from higher timeframe extremes, the underlying principle remains the same: identify exhaustion, wait for confirmation, and trade the reversion toward value. When applied with discipline and proper risk management, BB Trap strategies can consistently deliver favourable risk-reward opportunities while minimizing false breakout traps.

Bollinger Band (BB) Trap – Daily Timeframe (D TF):

A BB Trap on the Daily timeframe is a powerful reversal setup that occurs when price briefly moves outside the Bollinger Bands (UBB/LBB) but fails to sustain the breakout. Instead of continuation, such moves often lead to sharp reversals—especially when supported by price action and momentum indicators.

On the short side, when a daily candle forms completely outside the Upper Bollinger Band (UBB), it reflects an overstretched bullish move. If the next day breaks the low of this candle and, on lower timeframes (like hourly), price moves below VWAP with confirmation from the HM System (at least on the 10-minute timeframe in sell), it signals a potential BB Trap. In such cases, an intraday short trade can be initiated near VWAP, with targets such as the 20 SMA on the hourly timeframe or nearby pivot/previous day support levels.

However, for a positional BB Trap confirmation on the Daily timeframe, it is essential that a **subsequent candle closes back inside the band—below the UBB—and also breaches the 5 SMA low** on the Daily chart. Only then is the trap considered fully confirmed for a broader downtrend. The same logic applies in reverse for long trades when the setup forms outside the Lower Bollinger Band (LBB), supported by HM System buy signals.

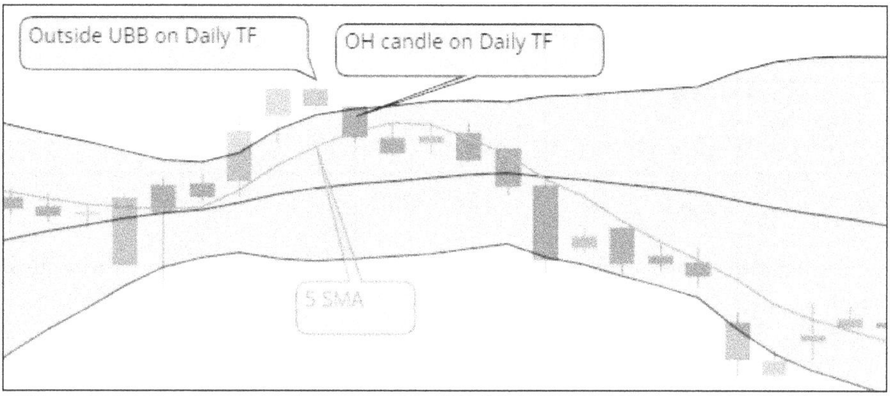

A high-probability variation occurs when a BB Trap near UBB aligns with an OH (Open High) formation, or near LBB aligns with an OL (Open Low) formation—this provides dual confirmation. Conversely, if a BB Trap near UBB is followed by an OL (or near LBB followed by an OH), it often indicates range-bound conditions rather than a trending move for the next few sessions.

BB Trap – Weekly Timeframe (W TF)

The BB Trap concept extends effectively to the Weekly timeframe, offering higher conviction positional trades. When a weekly candle forms completely outside the UBB, and the following candle breaks its low and moves below the 5 SMA low on the Weekly chart, supported by HM System sell signals (at least on the hourly timeframe), it confirms a bearish trap and presents a shorting opportunity.

Similarly, when a candle forms outside the LBB, and the next candle breaks its high and sustains above the 5 SMA high, supported by HM System buy signals, it confirms a bullish trap suitable for long positions.

Confirming BB Trap – 5 SMA Breach

A critical element in validating BB Trap reversals is the breach of the 5 SMA low/high on the respective timeframe.

When price moves below UBB and simultaneously breaches the 5 SMA low (in case of a bearish reversal), it indicates a shift in earlier trend, thus confirming BB trap pattern for a downtrend. Similarly, a move above LBB along with a breach of the 5 SMA high signals bullish reversal from an existing downtrend, thus confirming BB trap pattern for an uptrend.

This principle applies across timeframes:

- On **Daily TF** → use 5 SMA of Daily
- On **Weekly TF** → use 5 SMA of Weekly
- On **Monthly TF** → use 5 SMA of Monthly

Once this confirmation is in place, trades can be initiated near the 5 SMA level, with targets typically around the 20 SMA of the same timeframe.

An exception exists in high-conviction patterns like the Moh maya pattern (*discussed next in this Chapter*), where waiting for 5 SMA confirmation may lead to missed opportunities. In such cases, a positional short trade can be initiated near the close of the second candle, once it is evident that the candle will close below the low of the first candle formed outside the UBB.

Key Insight for BB Trap on Monthly, Weekly, Daily TF

BB Traps represent failed breakouts at extremes, where price exhausts itself beyond volatility bands and then reverses sharply. The edge lies in combining:

- Band behaviour (outside → back inside)
- 5 SMA breach for confirmation
- VWAP and lower timeframe alignment for entries

When used with discipline, BB Trap setups can offer high-probability reversal trades across intraday, positional, and even investment horizons.

Bollinger Band (BB) Trap – Intraday (10-Minute Timeframe):

The intraday BB Trap is a high-probability reversal setup that occurs when price temporarily moves outside the Bollinger Bands (UBB/LBB) but quickly fails to sustain that move and reverts back toward value (VWAP). This pattern can form on any intraday timeframe (5-minute to 2-hour), but is most effectively traded using the 10-minute chart, with confirmation from lower timeframes.

A typical BB Trap begins when the first candle after a gap-up/gap-down—or any strong intraday candle—forms **completely outside the UBB or LBB**. If price then reverses and sustains on the opposite side of VWAP, it indicates a failed breakout and potential trend reversal. For a long setup, price should move back above VWAP after forming outside LBB, supported by HM System buy signals (RSI 9 > WMA 21 or at least RSI 9 > EMA 3 on 5/10-min TF). For a short setup, price should fall below VWAP after forming outside UBB, supported by HM System sell signals (WMA 21 > RSI 9 or EMA 3 > RSI 9).

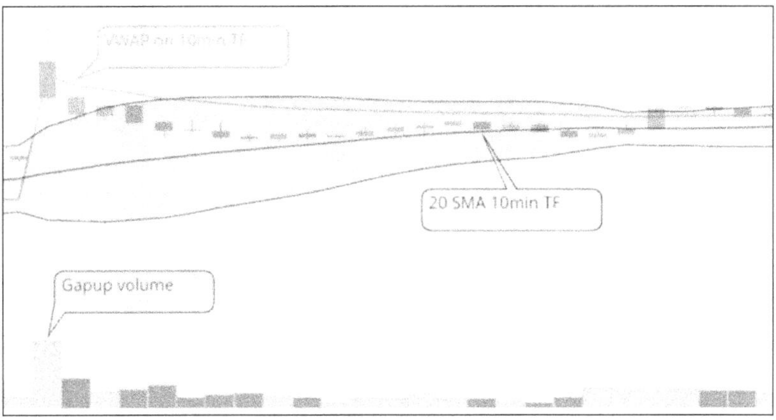

Execution and Trade Management

Trades are ideally initiated near VWAP after confirmation, not at the extreme band itself. The setup can also be monitored on the 30-minute timeframe for additional clarity on structure and momentum.

- *Targets:*
  - Short-term (<1 Hr TF): 9 SMA high/low
  - Higher TF (Hourly & above): 20 SMA
  - Extended targets: UBB/LBB, depending on trend continuation

Always remain mindful of previous day support/resistance, pivot levels, and dynamic zones, as price often reacts sharply at these levels.

- *Stop Loss:*
  - Conservative: 1 close above/below VWAP (opposite direction)
  - Practical: Day's high/low or 1 close beyond a 10-min pivot level, to avoid VWAP-based SL hunting

High-Conviction Variations and Cautions

A BB Trap combined with OH (Open High) or OL (Open Low) formation significantly enhances reliability and often results in smoother moves with minimal SL hunting. In such cases, OH favours short trades near UBB, and OL Favors long trades near LBB. When trading options, it is advisable to select strikes where OH/OL is also visible on the same timeframe, aligning price structure across instruments.

However, caution is necessary when price approaches key resistance/support or pivot levels. Even within a BB Trap setup, price may reverse sharply from these zones, leading to SL hunting. It is prudent to book profits near such levels rather than waiting for VWAP-based confirmation.

Trading with the Broader Trend

The most effective BB Trap trades are those aligned with the higher timeframe trend (Daily/Monthly). For example:

- If the broader trend is bearish, a BB Trap forming near UBB offers a strong shorting opportunity

- If the broader trend is bullish, a BB Trap near LBB favours long trades

When such setups are further supported by OH/OL formations, they become highly compelling. In these cases, stop loss should be placed beyond the OH/OL level (not VWAP) to avoid premature exits due to intraday noise.

Key Insight on BB Trap in Intraday setup

The intraday BB Trap is essentially a failed breakout at volatility extremes, where price quickly reverts to mean. The edge lies in combining:

- Band extremes (outside → re-entry)
- VWAP confirmation
- HM System alignment
- Higher timeframe trend direction

Executed with discipline, this setup can provide clean intraday reversals with favourable risk-reward and reduced probability of false breakouts.

Most Powerful BB Trap Setup – With Reversal Candle:

This is an advanced variation of the Bollinger Band Trap, where reversal candlestick patterns form at volatility extremes—either above the Upper Bollinger Band (UBB) or below the Lower Bollinger Band (LBB). Unlike the *Moh maya pattern* (*which typically involves a single large doji entirely outside the band without touching it*), this setup includes a broader class of reversal candles such as doji, spinning tops, hammers, and inverted hammers forming outside or at the edge of the bands. Such formations signal exhaustion of the prevailing trend and a high probability of reversal.

Structure indicating Strong Reversal

When a reversal candle forms near the top outside the UBB on the Daily or Weekly timeframe, it indicates that bullish momentum is likely exhausted. If the next candle shows signs of breaking or closing below the low of this reversal candle, it confirms bearish intent and a positional short trade can be considered.

Conversely, when a reversal candle forms near the bottom outside the LBB, and the next candle breaks or closes above its high, it signals a positional long opportunity.

For confirmation of reversal, the HM System should support the move:

- For longs (D/Hourly TF): RSI 9 turning upward and crossing above WMA 21 (even if still below 50)
- For shorts (D/Hourly TF): RSI 9 turning downward with WMA 21 above RSI 9 (even if RSI is still above 50)

If the pattern forms on the Weekly timeframe, it is advisable to wait for HM confirmation on the Daily timeframe. If it forms on the Daily timeframe, confirmation from the Hourly timeframe is sufficient.

High-Conviction Reversal, Supporting BB Trap:

The reliability of this pattern increases further if:

- The 2nd or 3rd candle after the reversal candle forms an OH/OL pattern, reinforcing directional bias
- The reversal candle appears clearly at the extremes of UBB/LBB, indicating strong rejection of prices

In such cases, the setup becomes highly convincing and often leads to clean directional moves.

Importantly, due to the strength of this pattern, waiting for additional confirmations like 5 SMA breach or VWAP crossover is not mandatory, especially on higher timeframes.

Intraday and Positional Application of BB Trap Pattern:

This pattern is effective across both intraday and positional trading:

- On Hourly or 2-Hour TF, it can lead to "jackpot" intraday trades, with momentum often extending into the next trading day
- On Daily/Weekly TF, it can signal multi-day or multi-week trend reversals

For intraday trades, entries can be taken without waiting for VWAP confirmation, given the strength of the signal.

MOH-MAYA PATTERN ON DAILY TF

The Moh maya Pattern is a rare but highly powerful reversal setup, typically observed during **extreme bearish phases**—often triggered by panic-driven events such as war, crisis, or global uncertainty. It generally forms **near market bottoms**, where sentiment is deeply negative and most participants have already exited or are trapped on the downside. This pattern can appear across **indices, stocks, commodities, or even crude**, and behaves similarly across instruments.

The defining feature of this pattern is the formation of a **Doji candle completely outside the Lower Bollinger Band (LBB)** on the Daily timeframe. This represents a state of extreme exhaustion, where despite aggressive selling, price fails to move decisively lower—indicating that the downtrend may be nearing its end. It is important not to trade on the day the Doji forms, as the signal is only preparatory in nature.

Confirmation and Trade Setup:

The confirmation unfolds on the next trading day (2nd day). If, on lower timeframes (especially Hourly), price begins to trade above VWAP and sustains strength, it signals early recovery. A stronger confirmation occurs when the 2nd day candle sustains above the high of the Doji for a few hours intraday, despite volatility, and eventually closes above the Doji's high and back inside the Bollinger Bands. Ideally, **this candle resembles a bullish engulfing structure, covering the Doji from near its low and closing strongly above it**.

For a safer approach, instead of entering intraday, a positional trade can be initiated near the close of the 2nd day (around 3:15–3:20 pm)—once it is evident that the candle will close above the Doji high. At this point, one may initiate a naked far OTM Call Option (monthly expiry) or take exposure in leading stocks, anticipating a gap-up opening on the 3rd day, which is a common outcome of this pattern.

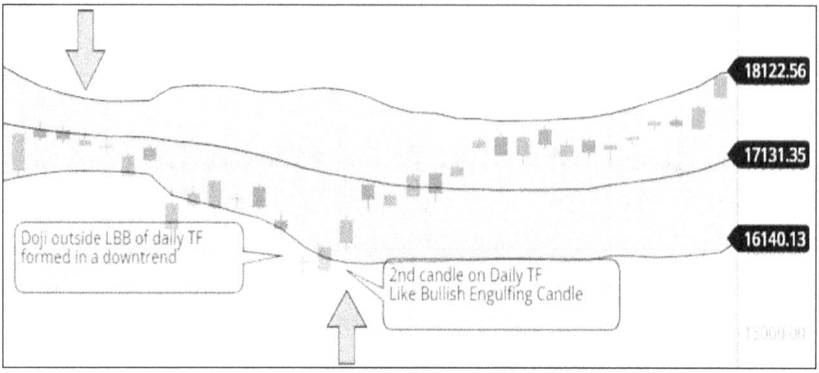

Risk Management and Profit Strategy:

- Stop Loss: A close below the Doji candle's closing price
- Initial Profit Booking:
    - Book ~50% profits if the position doubles (often possible on Day 2 intraday or Day 3 gap-up)
- Further Profit Management:
    - Ride the remaining position until price approaches the 20 SMA on Daily TF
    - Near this level, book an additional 25–30% profits, as it often acts as resistance

From the 3rd day onward, caution is required. If price nears major resistance zones like the 20 SMA, it is prudent to hedge the position. A simple strategy is to create a Bull Call Spread by selling a call option near resistance while holding the original long call. If price continues upward with strength (e.g., gap-up or strong bullish candle), the position can be held toward the Upper Bollinger Band (UBB). If reversal signs emerge—supported by indicators like HM System turning bearish on lower timeframes—further adjustments or exits should be considered.

Indicator Support and Key Insights:

The HM System on the Daily timeframe typically supports this pattern:

- As long as RSI 9 remains above WMA 21, the bullish momentum can be sustained

- Any reversal signal on lower timeframes (like Hourly) should be monitored closely post-entry

Target: If formed outside LBB → potential move toward UBB on Daily TF (and vice versa, though bullish Moh maya is more common)

Important Caution about Moh-Maya:

An "Imperfect Moh maya Pattern" occurs when the Doji touches or partially overlaps the LBB instead of forming completely outside it. In such cases, the pattern may still work, but with reduced reliability and follow-through.

Key Insight:

The Moh maya Pattern reflects a psychological turning point in the market, where extreme fear transitions into opportunity. It captures the moment when:

- Sellers are exhausted
- Smart money begins accumulation
- Price prepares for a sharp reversal

When identified correctly and executed with discipline, it can deliver exceptional risk-reward trades, especially through option strategies capturing gap-up momentum and volatility expansion.

BIG BANG PATTERN FOR TRADING & INVESTMENT

The Big Bang Pattern is a powerful reversal–continuation structure that can override even strong-looking setups like OH/OL formations. It typically **emerges in a declining market** and is most effective when it forms near key mean-reversion zones such as VWAP, AVWAP, 20 SMA, or the Bollinger Bands (UBB/LBB). The essence of this pattern lies in sudden, sharp opposing moves around a key average, which trap traders on both sides before the dominant trend resumes.

For intraday trading, this pattern is best observed on the 30-minute or hourly timeframe. During an ongoing trend (for example, a downtrend), price sustains below VWAP for a considerable period. Then, a single strong counter-trend candle abruptly pushes price above VWAP, creating a temporary bullish sentiment. However, this move is immediately negated by the next candle closing back below VWAP, re-aligning with the original trend. This swift two-step reversal confirms that the **prior trend remains intact** and that the **intermediate move was a trap**. A trade can be initiated near VWAP or at the close of the second candle, in the direction of the dominant trend. Confirmation from the HM System (e.g., RSI 9 below WMA 21 for short trades) adds conviction. The stop-loss should be placed at the high (or low) of the counter-trend candle that temporarily breached VWAP.

For positional trading or investment, the same structure applies on higher timeframes such as daily, weekly, or monthly charts, but instead of VWAP, the pattern forms around broader averages like AVWAP, 20 SMA, or 50 SMA.

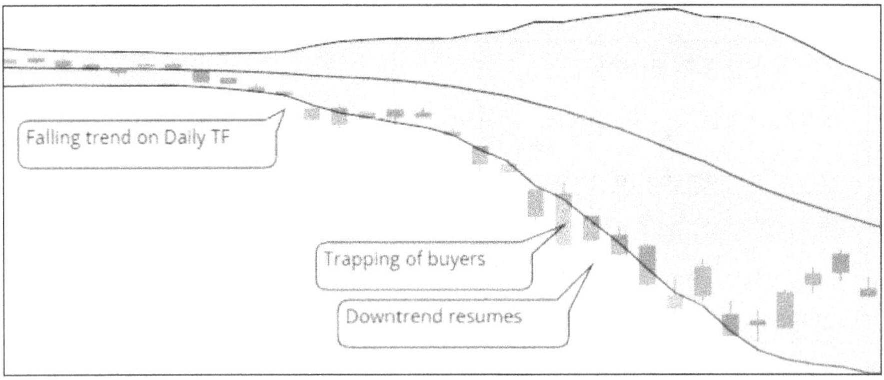

When such a sharp false breakout and immediate reversal occur near these key levels, it signals continuation of the prevailing macro trend after shaking out weak hands. Given its deceptive nature and strong follow-through potential, the Big Bang Pattern can be a highly reliable setup when traded with discipline and supported by trend-confirming indicators.

K WAVE PATTERN

The **K-Wave pattern** is a high-impact trading setup known for producing explosive moves, often delivering outsized returns—especially for Option buyers. K-wave is a smaller version of Killer Wave (*discussed next*).

When K-Wave is identified correctly, even low-priced Options can expand significantly due to sharp directional momentum. This pattern tends to replicate across broader market constituents—if observed in indices like Nifty or Bank Nifty, similar behaviour is often seen in their respective stocks.

Sell-Side K-Wave Setup for Intraday:

This setup typically emerges after a **gap-up opening** (though not mandatory). On the 10-minute chart, the **first candle closes just above the Upper Bollinger Band (UBB)**, indicating an initial exhaustion spike. This is followed by the next **three candles (2nd, 3rd, and 4th)** closing **below VWAP**, irrespective of their shape or colour. These candles usually show indecision with long wicks on either side of VWAP, often resembling hammer or spinning-top formations.

A slight **downward slope in VWAP during the first 30–40 minutes** adds further confirmation. The presence of an AVWAP above UBB strengthens the conviction for a bearish K-Wave. From the 5th to 8th or 10th candle, once the low of the first four candles is breached on a closing basis, the pattern confirms—and typically leads to a strong downside move.

Interestingly, traditional indicators like HM System or Ehler Fisher may appear misleading during the initial phase, sometimes signalling bullishness—these should be ignored in favour of price structure for this setup. Expect volatility with frequent long wicks and SL hunting around VWAP throughout the move.

Execution:

- Entry: Near VWAP on or after the 5th candle; if missed, re-enter on pullbacks to VWAP
- Target: 20 SMA or Lower Bollinger Band (LBB)
- Stop Loss: High of the 1st candle (system SL) or exit on one candle close above VWAP

Buy-Side K-Wave Setup for Intraday:

The bullish version is a mirror image and usually forms after a **gap-down opening**. Here, the **first candle closes just below the Lower Bollinger**

Band (LBB), signalling a potential exhaustion on the downside. The next **three candles close above VWAP**, again showing indecision with wicks but maintaining strength above VWAP.

A **slight upward slope in VWAP during the initial 30-40 minutes** supports the bullish bias. If an AVWAP is visible below LBB, it further reinforces the setup. Between the 5th and 8th candle, once the high of the first four candles is breached on a closing basis, the K-Wave pattern confirms for a strong upside move.

As with the sell-side setup, indicators like HM System and Ehler Fisher may give contradictory signals early on and should not override price action in this case. Expect intraday volatility with intermittent pullbacks and wick-based SL hunting.

Execution:

- Entry: Near VWAP on or after the 5th candle; or on later pullbacks to VWAP
- Target: 20 SMA or Upper Bollinger Band (UBB)
- Stop Loss: Low of the 1st candle (system SL) or exit on one candle close below VWAP

Key Insight:

The K-Wave pattern is a **pure price-action-driven setup**, where early-session structure and VWAP positioning matter more than lagging indicators. Patience during the first 30–40 minutes and disciplined execution near VWAP are critical to capturing the full potential of this high-reward intraday opportunity.

KILLER WAVE PATTERN

The **Killer-Wave pattern** is an advanced and highly potent version of the K-Wave setup, unfolding on the **1-hour timeframe** and typically delivering **multi-session trending moves**. Its impact is significantly larger, often resulting in substantial expansion in Option premiums. When this pattern appears in indices like Nifty or Bank Nifty, it tends to cascade into their constituent stocks as well. Since it forms near key dynamic levels such as **Upper / Lower Bollinger Bands (UBB/LBB)** or the **20 SMA**, its influence can extend **over 2–3 trading days** (and if observed on lower timeframes like 10 minutes, it may play out intraday or into BTST setups). These days are often accompanied by a **rise in volatility (VIX)**, supporting strong directional moves.

Sell-Side Killer-Wave Setup:

This setup typically forms near resistance zones such as UBB, 20 SMA, or even LBB (in pullback scenarios). On the hourly chart, the first three candles (9:15 AM to 12:15 PM) consistently close below VWAP and below the close of the previous candle, establishing a clear bearish structure. During this phase, VWAP develops a gradual downward slope, and importantly, both HM System and Ehler Fisher on the 1-hour timeframe must confirm a sell bias—this is crucial, as lack of confirmation may indicate a trap rather than a trend.

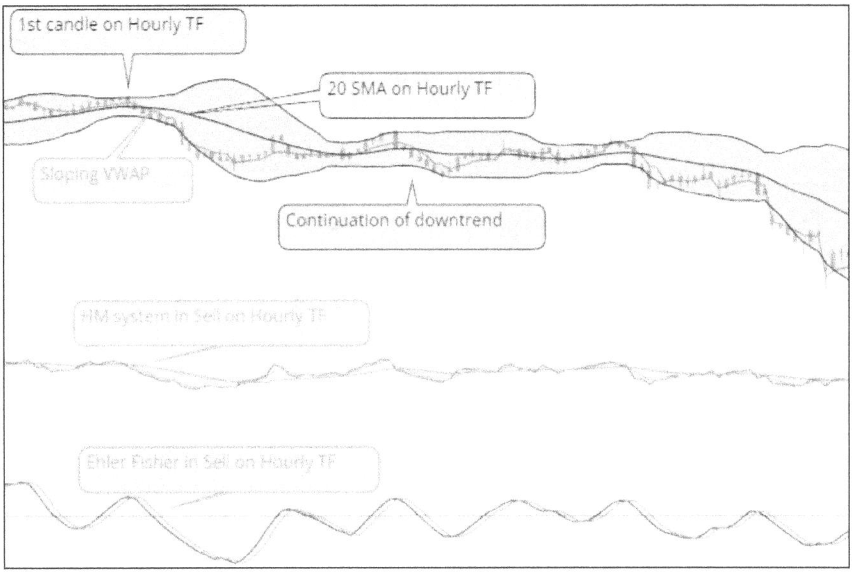

With three hours of structured selling already in place, the real momentum typically unfolds between the 4th and 5th hourly candles (approximately 12:15 PM to 2:15 PM). At this stage, the market often enters a strong downtrend, where each subsequent candle fails to close above the previous candle's close, reinforcing bearish continuation. Expect volatile price action with long wicks and intermittent SL hunting around VWAP, but the broader direction remains intact.

Execution:

- Entry: Near VWAP on the 4th candle (around 12:20–12:30 PM); if missed, re-enter on pullbacks to VWAP

- Targets:
  - UBB → 20 SMA
  - 20 SMA → LBB
  - Continue riding along LBB in strong trends
- Stop Loss: One candle close above the previous candle's close; alternatively, exit on a close above VWAP

Buy-Side Killer-Wave Setup:

The bullish version is a mirror image and forms near support zones such as LBB, 20 SMA, or even UBB (in continuation scenarios). On the hourly timeframe, the first three candles close above VWAP and above the close of the previous candle, building a strong bullish base. VWAP trends with a gentle upward slope, and both HM System and Ehler Fisher must confirm a buy signal—without this alignment, the setup may lack conviction.

The momentum phase begins between the 4th and 5th candles, where the market typically accelerates upward. In such cases, each hourly candle continues to close higher than the previous one, indicating sustained buying pressure. Similar to the sell-side, expect long wicks and occasional volatility, but the primary trend remains upward.

Execution:

- Entry: Near VWAP on the 4th candle (around 12:20–12:30 PM); or on later pullbacks to VWAP
- Targets:
  - LBB → 20 SMA
  - 20 SMA → UBB
  - Continue riding along UBB in strong trends
- Stop Loss: One candle close below the previous candle's close; alternatively, exit on a close below VWAP

Key Insight:

The Killer-Wave pattern is a structure-driven, multi-hour breakout-continuation setup, where alignment of price structure, VWAP slope, and higher-timeframe indicators creates a high-probability environment. Unlike shorter intraday patterns, this setup allows traders to ride extended trends with conviction, provided discipline is maintained around VWAP-based entries and structured stop-loss placement.

THE W PATTERN

A W-pattern on the short side is a classic intraday trapping structure that often precedes a strong downward move. It typically forms when the market initially trends downward while sustaining below VWAP, followed by a temporary reversal where price moves above VWAP and approaches the opening price of the first candle. However, it fails to decisively breach this level on a closing basis (CLBS) and reverses again. The price then declines for a few candles below VWAP before staging a second upward move, once again approaching the same opening price level—thereby forming a "W" structure on the chart.

This repeated failure to break the opening price level (acting as a resistance zone) is a key signal. If, after the second attempt, price begins to reverse downward again, it often indicates exhaustion of buying momentum and a high probability of a strong downward move. A **short trade can be initiated** near this resistance level (i.e., the opening price of the first candle), with the expectation that price will move toward the next support or pivot level. Stop-loss should be placed as one candle close above the resistance level (open price of the first candle).

However, caution is essential. If during the second attempt, price sustains above VWAP and successfully closes above the resistance level (opening price of the first candle) with strength, it **invalidates the short setup** and instead **signals a potential bullish breakout**. In such cases, a long trade may be considered on a pullback near VWAP, with stop-loss placed either below VWAP or below the breakout level (former resistance) on a closing basis. This scenario reflects a shift from a failed resistance pattern to a breakout continuation, often leading to a strong upward move.

This pattern is known for causing significant stop-loss hunting on both sides of VWAP before the actual directional move unfolds. Hence, patience and confirmation—especially around VWAP behaviour and closing levels—are critical for effectively trading this setup.

THE M PATTERN

An M-pattern on the long side is a mirror image of the W-pattern and is often a trap-then-reversal structure that precedes a strong upward move. It typically begins with the price rising and sustaining above VWAP, reflecting early bullish momentum. This is followed by a pullback where price moves below VWAP and declines toward the opening price of the first candle, but crucially fails to breach this level on a closing basis (CLBS). This level starts acting as a key support zone.

Subsequently, price rebounds again above VWAP, forming the second leg of the structure, and then once more reverses downward, sustaining below VWAP and revisiting the same support level near the opening price of the first candle—thereby completing the "M" formation. The critical observation is that despite two attempts, price fails to break below this support level, indicating absorption of selling pressure.

If, after the second test, price begins to pull back upward from this level, it presents a **high-probability long opportunity** near the opening price of the first candle. The expectation is that price will now move upward toward the next resistance or pivot level. The stop-loss should be maintained as one candle close below the support level (i.e., below the opening price of the first candle).

Breakdown Caution:

Traders must remain alert for a potential failure of this setup. If, during the second downward move, price sustains below VWAP and closes decisively below the support level (opening price of the first candle), it **invalidates the long setup** and instead **signals a bearish breakdown**. In such a case, a short trade may be considered on a pullback toward VWAP, with stop-loss placed above VWAP or above the breakdown level on a closing basis. This transition often leads to a sharp downward move as trapped buyers exit.

This pattern is known for causing extensive stop-loss hunting on both sides of VWAP during its formation. Hence, patience, confirmation on closing basis, and alignment with VWAP behaviour are essential before initiating trades.

PATTERN CONFIRMING CONTINUATION OF BULLISH TREND

When the price has already been showing strength—evidenced by price sustaining above the **20 SMA on the Hourly timeframe for the past 2–3 days** (i.e., no hourly close below the 20 SMA)—it establishes a strong bullish foundation. In such a context, if on a new trading day, the first Hourly candle is large, forms above the 20 SMA, closes above VWAP, and importantly breaks above the highs of the previous 1–2 days, it signals a decisive continuation of bullish momentum over a period of few successive days.

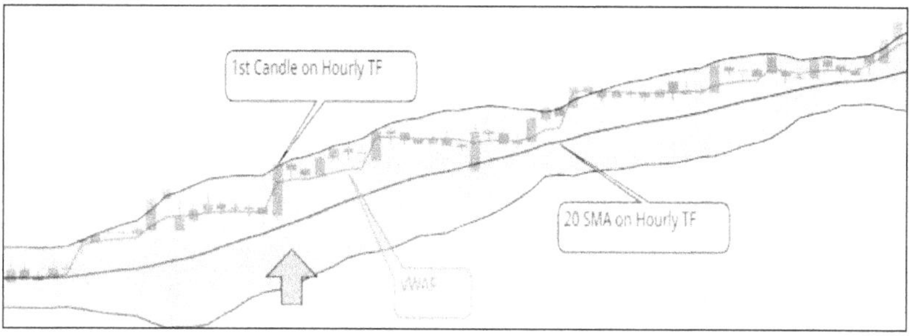

This setup typically indicates trending intraday bullish trend, where price may continue to move strongly upward—often even riding along the Upper Bollinger Band (UBB) without showing meaningful reversals. The breakout of prior highs combined with sustained positioning above VWAP reflects strong institutional participation and directional conviction.

For intraday trading, the ideal approach is to initiate long positions near VWAP on pullbacks, with the expectation of riding the trend throughout the day. In such high-conviction setups, traders may also consider aggressive participation through futures or even naked call (CE) buying, given the strength and continuity of the move.

This pattern tends to occur infrequently (typically 1–2 times a month), but when it does, it often impacts the broader market. For instance, if observed in Nifty, it is likely to reflect across constituent stocks; similarly, if it appears in Bank Nifty, the momentum usually extends across banking stocks as well.

INTRADAY TREND MOMENTUM

When the market trades in a tight range for two or more days, the Bollinger Bands on the Hourly timeframe tend to contract and narrow, forming a structure that resembles a funnel or the mouth of a balloon. This phase reflects low volatility and underlying accumulation or distribution. Such compression often precedes a sharp expansion in volatility, known as a **BB Blast**, which occurs when price breaks out above the Upper Band (UBB) indicating bullish momentum or when price breaks out below the Lower Band (LBB) on a closing basis indicating bearish bias.

Traders should actively monitor this narrowing phase, as it provides an early setup for a potential breakout. Once the bands are sufficiently compressed, a **BB Blast on the Hourly timeframe** can be anticipated.

To capitalize on this, traders may use the 30-minute timeframe for entry, initiating positions once a breakout is visible there, even before full confirmation on the Hourly chart.

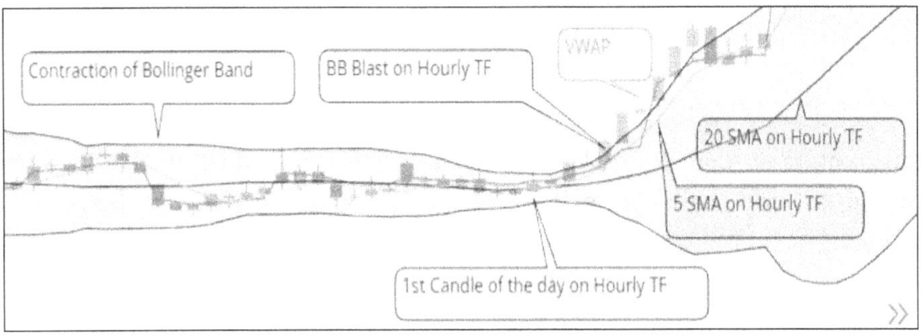

The stop-loss can be maintained as one candle close below the 5 SMA on the 30-minute timeframe for riding a bullish trend (and above 5 SMA in case of a bearish bias). For execution refinement, Option buyers may track exits on the

10-minute timeframe, while option sellers can continue to manage risk using the 30-minute structure.

Additionally, if the market has already been trending for 2–3 days, it increases the likelihood of intraday volatility expansion, as the BB tends to narrow before another directional move. When the eventual blast occurs—especially with strong price action—it can lead to sustained momentum throughout the session.

A particularly powerful scenario emerges when a **BB Blast occurs on the Hourly timeframe during an expiry day**. Such setups can result in a "jackpot" trading session, characterized by strong, uninterrupted trends. Traders should aim to ride the move at least until 1:30–2:00 PM, and extend further only if the option position has moved significantly in-the-money (ITM), typically by 100–200 points, as options tend to behave more like futures later in the session on expiry days, amplifying gains.

INTRADAY SETUP AROUND 1PM

This setup is built around early-session structure, VWAP behaviour, and confirmation from momentum indicators. When the first 30-minute candle forms an **OL (Open = Low)** and closes above VWAP, followed by a series of small candles that remain tightly range-bound near VWAP (but consistently above it), it reflects quiet accumulation. If VWAP stays relatively flat up to around 1 PM, and momentum indicators such as the HM System (RSI 9 > WMA 21 and RSI > 50) and Ehler Fisher support bullishness, it signals latent strength. In such conditions, a **long trade can be initiated near VWAP around 1 PM**, anticipating a strong directional move for the remainder of the intraday session. The stop-loss should be placed at one candle close below VWAP.

For execution, aggressive traders may consider far out-of-the-money call options (300–400 points away from ATM in Index options), preferably aligned with the strike where the OL formation occurred in the first candle. However, if volatility (VIX) is compressing during the day, option buying may not be ideal—in such cases, trading via Futures is more prudent.

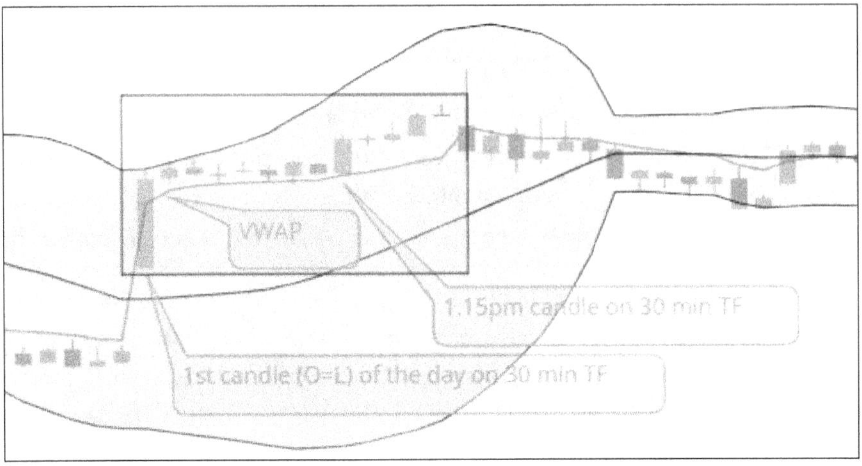

A similar but inverse setup applies for bearish conditions. If the first 30-minute candle forms an **OH (Open = High)** and closes below VWAP, followed by multiple small candles clustering just below VWAP with a flat VWAP trajectory, it indicates distribution. With HM and Ehler Fisher confirming bearish momentum (RSI 9 < WMA 21 and RSI < 50), a short trade can be initiated near VWAP around 1 PM. The stop-loss in this case should be one candle close above VWAP. Traders may consider far OTM put Options or futures depending on volatility conditions.

TREND REVERSAL PATTERN WITH CANDLESTICK

This setup focuses on **reversal candlestick patterns**—such as **Doji, Spinning Top, Hammer, or Inverted Hammer**—forming **near the extremes of Bollinger Bands (UBB / LBB)**, either **slightly outside or within the bands**. Unlike the Moh maya Pattern this formation does not require the candle to be completely outside the bands without touching them (or the Powerful BB Trap in which the reversal candle pattern may be fully outside the UBB/LBB or the low/high of the reversal candle may just touch the band). Instead, it captures reversal intent when price reaches the top of an uptrend near UBB or the bottom of a downtrend near LBB, even if the candle partially overlaps or forms within the band.

Such candles reflect indecision and exhaustion at extreme levels. When they appear at the top or bottom of a trend, they often signal a potential reversal or pause in momentum.

Trade Confirmation and Execution:

When a reversal candle forms:

- Near UBB (top): Watch for the next candle to close below the low of the reversal candle → indicates a short setup
- Near LBB (bottom): Watch for the next candle to close above the high of the reversal candle → indicates a long setup

For higher timeframes (Daily/Weekly):

- If the pattern forms on Weekly TF, wait for HM System confirmation on Daily TF
- If it forms on Daily TF, confirmation from the Hourly TF is sufficient

HM Confirmation:

- Long: RSI 9 sloping upward and crossing above WMA 21 (even if below 50)
- Short: RSI 9 sloping downward with WMA 21 above RSI 9 (even if RSI is above 50)

Key Distinction from BB Trap Patterns:

Since this pattern may form inside or touching the bands, it is less aggressive than a BB Trap. Therefore, an additional layer of confirmation must be ensured:

- Wait for price to breach the 5 SMA level on the respective timeframe
    - Daily pattern → breach of 5 SMA (Daily)
    - Weekly pattern → breach of 5 SMA (Weekly)
    - Monthly pattern → breach of 5 SMA (Monthly)

This step ensures that the reversal has actual follow-through, reducing the chances of false signals.

Enhancements and Intraday Application:

The setup gains strength if:

- The 2nd or 3rd candle forms an OH (Open High) or OL (Open Low) pattern
- The reversal occurs near key support/resistance zones or pivots

For intraday trading:

- If formed on Hourly or 2-Hour TF, it can lead to strong next-day continuation ("jackpot" setups)
- Entries should be taken only after price confirms direction via VWAP (unlike powerful BB Trap, where VWAP confirmation may not be required)

Risk Management and Targets:

- Stop Loss: One candle close beyond the high/low of the second candle after the reversal candle
- Target: Primarily the 20 SMA of the respective timeframe, with possible extensions based on trend strength

Key Insight:

This pattern captures early signs of reversal at volatility edges, but with a more conservative confirmation approach compared to aggressive BB Trap setups. Its edge lies in combining:

- Reversal candle at UBB/LBB extremes
- Follow-through via next candle
- 5 SMA confirmation for trend shift
- Support from HM System and VWAP (for intraday)

When used with patience and confirmation, it becomes a reliable structure for both intraday and positional trading, offering controlled risk with meaningful reversal opportunities.

REVERSAL PATTERN IN INTRADAY DOWNTREND

In a strong intraday downtrend—where the market may have formed an OH pattern on the 10-minute timeframe, is trading consistently below VWAP, possibly supported by a Bollinger Band (BB) blast on lower timeframes, and even the Hourly timeframe shows sustained weakness with the HM System indicating a sell—price action typically reflects strong bearish momentum.

However, within such a dominant downtrend, the appearance of a **large bullish "ice-candy" candle** (a long green candle with strong body) on the 10/15-minute timeframe can act as an early signal of **trend exhaustion and potential reversal**. This candle reflects sudden aggressive buying or short-covering, indicating that sellers may be losing control.

A key observation in this setup is that the low of this large green candle often remains intact for the rest of the trading session, acting as a strong support level. Following this formation, the market may reverse upward, but instead of a smooth trend, it often results in volatile price action with frequent VWAP-based stop-loss hunting.

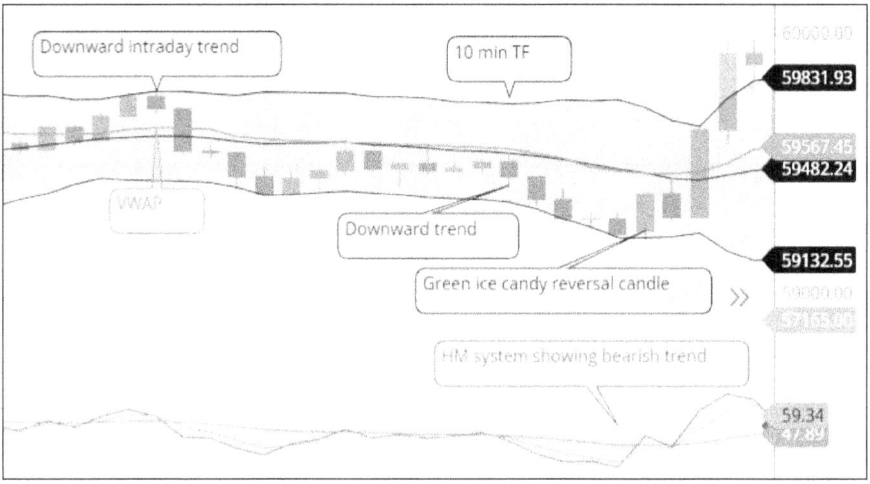

Therefore, traders should exercise caution in continuing short positions after such a candle appears. It is advisable to either **exit shorts or tighten stop-losses**, and reassess the market bias, as the structure may shift from a trending down market to a choppy or reversing environment.

REVERSAL PATTERN IN INTRADAY AFTER GAPUP / GAPDOWN

Gap up Rejection Setup on 10-Min TF – Low SL-Hunting Trend Day:

When the market opens with a **gap-up** and the first candle on the 10-minute timeframe touches the Upper Bollinger Band (UBB) but closes back inside the band, it often signals an early exhaustion of bullish momentum. If the second candle confirms weakness by closing below the close of the first candle and, more importantly, below VWAP, and thereafter price sustains below VWAP with both price and VWAP sloping downward, it establishes a clear intraday bearish bias.

In such a structure, the probability of stop-loss hunting around VWAP reduces significantly, as the market shows consistent directional intent. This creates a relatively "clean" trend environment. Traders can look to initiate short positions near VWAP on pullbacks, riding the downtrend through the session. A key characteristic of this setup is that subsequent candles continue to close below VWAP, reinforcing sustained selling pressure and offering high-conviction shorting opportunities.

However, even in a strong downtrend, vigilance is essential. If reversal patterns such as the 3-candle/5-candle rule or a green ice-candy candle appear (*discussed earlier in this Chapter*)—especially when supported by indicators like HM System or Ehler Fisher—it may signal weakening momentum. In such cases, it is prudent to exit early without waiting for a VWAP crossover. That said, a decisive close above VWAP remains a firm exit signal.

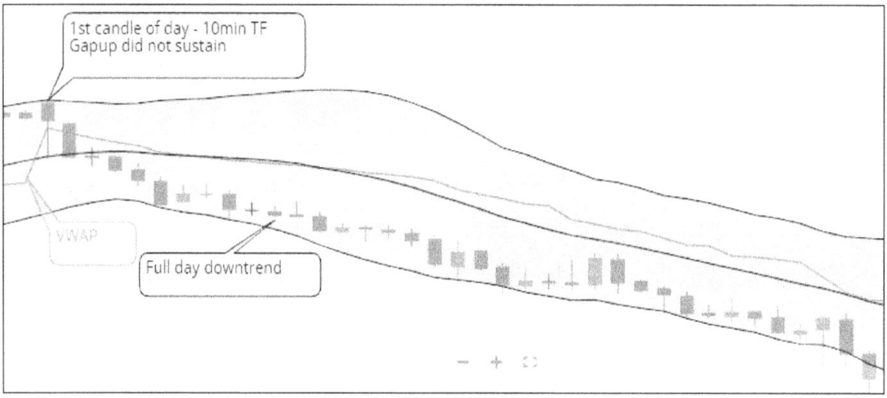

A similar setup on the **Hourly timeframe**—where the first candle after a gap-up touches a key level like the 20 SMA and then price breaks below VWAP—further strengthens the reliability of this pattern. When aligned across higher timeframes, this setup becomes even more compelling for intraday trending trades.

Gap down Rejection on 10-Min TF – Low SL-Hunting Trend Day (Bullish):

Likewise, when the market opens with a **gap-down** and the first candle on the 10-minute timeframe touches the Lower Bollinger Band (LBB) but closes back inside the band, it often signals early exhaustion of selling pressure. If the second candle confirms strength by closing above the close of the first candle and, more importantly, above VWAP, and thereafter price sustains above VWAP with both price and VWAP sloping upward, it establishes a clear intraday bullish bias.

In such a structure, the chances of stop-loss hunting around VWAP are relatively low, as the market demonstrates steady upward intent. This creates a smoother trending environment. Traders can look to initiate long positions near VWAP on pullbacks, aiming to ride the intraday uptrend. A key confirmation is that subsequent candles continue to close above VWAP, reflecting sustained buying interest.

That said, caution is still required during the trend. If reversal signals such as the 3-candle/5-candle rule or a green ice-candy candle emerge—especially when supported by indicators like HM System or Ehler Fisher—it may indicate weakening momentum. In such cases, it is advisable to exit the trade proactively without waiting for a VWAP breakdown. However, a decisive close below VWAP should always be treated as a firm exit signal.

A similar setup on the **Hourly timeframe**—where the first candle after a gap-down touches a key level like the 20 SMA and then price reclaims and sustains above VWAP—adds further strength to this pattern. When aligned across higher timeframes, this setup becomes a high-conviction intraday long opportunity.

PROBAILITY OF GAPUP / GAPDOWN

This setup is designed to capture **next-day gap openings** by reading the **late intraday structure of volatility (Bollinger Bands)** and **momentum (HM System)** on the **10-minute timeframe**. It works particularly well when the market transitions from low volatility (compression) to early expansion (pre-breakout) near the close.

Core Structure of the Setup:

During the **last 2–3 hours of trading**, if the market trades in a tight range within narrow Bollinger Bands, it reflects volatility compression—a phase where energy is building up for a directional move. As the session approaches the close, if the **Bollinger Bands begin to slightly expand** ("open their mouth"), it signals the start of volatility expansion, often leading to a breakout move that can carry into the next day.

This expansion must be supported by the **HM System** on the 10-minute timeframe to validate direction.

Expecting Gap-Up Opening (BTST Setup):

A BTST (long carry-forward trade) can be considered when:

- Market remains rangebound within narrow BB during the last 2–3 hours
- Near closing, BB starts widening slightly, indicating expansion
- HM System shows Buy signal in the last 1 hour:
    - RSI 9 > WMA 21
    - RSI above 50
    - Clear gap between RSI 9 and WMA 21 (strong momentum)

Action for BTST:

- Initiate BTST long position near market close
- Can consider Call Option (CE) buying, or shorting Put (PE) Options – subject to VIX rising / falling trend, before taking Options exposure (*rising VIX favours Options buying, and falling VIX shorting Options*)
- Can Long stocks or Futures

This setup indicates that the market is likely to open gap-up the next day, continuing the emerging bullish momentum.

Expecting Gap-Down Opening (STBT Setup):

A STBT (short carry-forward trade) can be considered when:

- Market remains rangebound within narrow BB during the last 2–3 hours
- Near closing, BB starts widening slightly
- HM System shows Sell signal in the last 1 hour:
    - WMA 21 > RSI 9

- RSI below 50
- Clear gap between WMA 21 and RSI 9 (strong bearish momentum)

Action for STBT:

- Initiate STBT short position near market close
- Can consider Put Option (PE) buying or selling Call (CE) Options, subject to VIX rising / falling trend (*rising VIX favours Options buying, and falling VIX shorting Options*)
- Can Short stocks or Futures

This suggests a likelihood of a gap-down opening the following day.

Key Insight:

This setup is essentially about identifying the shift from:

- Consolidation → Expansion
- Indecision → Directional Momentum

When BB compression releases with HM confirmation, it often leads to overnight continuation moves, reflected as gap openings.

Caution:

- Always assess VIX behaviour before taking Option trades (*rising VIX favours Options buying, and falling VIX shorting Options*)
- Stronger signals occur when aligned with higher timeframe trend (Daily/ Weekly)
- Avoid taking positions if major resistance /support is immediately overhead /underneath, as it may limit next day's likely gap follow-through.

NEXT DAY GAPUP / GAPDOWN

This variation of BTST / STBT is based purely on **trend reversal in intraday with momentum (supported with HM System)** during the final phase of the trading session. It captures a very practical market behaviour: when a strong intraday trend weakens and reverses slightly near the close, the next day likely opens in the opposite direction.

Expecting Next Day Gap-Up after Downtrend in Intraday (BTST Setup):

A BTST (long carry-forward trade) can be considered when:

- The market has been in a clear downtrend for most of the day (last 2–3 hours)
- HM System consistently indicates sell throughout the day:
  - RSI below 50
  - WMA 21 > RSI 9
  - Clear gap between WMA 21 and RSI 9 (strong bearish momentum)
- Trend Reversal in Intraday: Before market close in intraday (last 30–60 minutes), HM System shows a shift to buy (on 10mins TF):
  - RSI 9 crosses above WMA 21
  - There is a visible gap between RSI 9 and WMA 21
  - RSI may still be **below 50** (early-stage reversal)

Interpretation: The trend reversal in intraday – just before close of session, indicates short-covering and early buying interest, suggesting that the market may reverse upward the next day, often opening with a gap-up.

Action for BTST for next day Gap up:

- Initiate BTST long position near closing
- Can consider Call Option (CE) buying, or shorting Put (PE) Options – subject to VIX rising / falling trend, before taking Options exposure (*rising VIX favours Options buying, and falling VIX shorting Options*)
- Can Long stocks or Futures

Expecting Next Day Gap-Down after Uptrend in Intraday (STBT Setup):

A STBT (short carry-forward trade) can be considered when:

- The market has been in a clear uptrend for most of the day (last 2–3 hours)
- HM System consistently indicates buy throughout the day:
    - RSI above 50
    - RSI 9 > WMA 21
    - Strong gap between RSI 9 and WMA 21 (bullish momentum)
- Trend Reversal in Intraday: Before market close in intraday (last 30–60 minutes), HM System shows a shift to sell:
    - WMA 21 crosses above RSI 9
    - Clear gap between WMA 21 and RSI 9
    - RSI may still be above 50 (early-stage reversal)

Interpretation:

This reflects profit booking and weakening bullish momentum, increasing the probability of a gap-down opening the next day.

Action for STBT for next day Gap down:

- Initiate STBT short position near closing
- Can consider Put Option (PE) buying or selling Call (CE) Options, subject to VIX rising / falling trend (*rising VIX favours Options buying, and falling VIX shorting Options*)
- Can Short stocks or Futures

Key Insight:

This setup works on the principle of late-session momentum shift:

- Strong trend during the day
- Followed by opposite signal near the close

This often leads to overnight continuation of the reversal move, expressed as a gap in the next session.

Practical Notes:

- The signal is early reversal, not a full trend change—hence the importance of timing (last hour)
- Works best when supported by price action (reversal candles, VWAP behaviour, or exhaustion moves)
- Always evaluate VIX before taking Option trades (*rising VIX favours Options buying, and falling VIX shorting Options*)
- Avoid if price is stuck near major support /resistance, as it may limit gap follow-through
- This setup has been observed to deliver ~80–85% directional accuracy, especially when: the prior trend is strong & extended and the trend reversal signal near close of the session in intraday is clear and decisive.

TRADING GAPUP / GAPDOWN

This pattern captures a **failed gap move** on the **Hourly timeframe**, where the market opens with a strong bias (gap-up or gap-down) but **fails to sustain that direction**, leading to a **powerful intraday reversal**. It is particularly effective because it combines opening sentiment (gap), dynamic levels (VWAP/20 SMA), and early confirmation (first two hourly candles).

Gap-Up Failure: Short Trade for Intraday:

When the market **opens gap-up**, it initially reflects bullish sentiment. However, if that strength fails early, it often results in a **sharp downside move**.

Setup:

- 1st Hourly Candle: Forms after gap-up and closes above VWAP / 20 SMA
- 2nd Hourly Candle: Fails to hold strength and closes below VWAP / 20 SMA

Interpretation:

The inability to sustain above VWAP/20 SMA indicates that the gap-up was not supported by strong buying, leading to distribution and reversal.

Action:

- Initiate short trade near VWAP / 20 SMA on Hourly TF
- Expect a significant intraday down move

Gap-Down Failure: Long Trade for Intraday:

When the market **opens gap-down**, it signals bearish sentiment. But if selling pressure weakens early, a **strong upside reversal** can follow.

Setup:

- 1st Hourly Candle: Forms after gap-down and closes below VWAP / 20 SMA
- 2nd Hourly Candle: Reclaims strength and closes above VWAP / 20 SMA

Interpretation:

This indicates absorption of selling pressure and short covering, often leading to a strong upward move.

Action:

- Initiate long trade near VWAP / 20 SMA on Hourly TF
- Expect a meaningful intraday uptrend

Gap Sustainability Rule (Critical Filter):

- If the gap sustains for ~30 minutes, it provides initial confirmation of direction
- If the gap sustains for a full hour, it becomes highly convincing, and reversal trades should be avoided

In other words:

- Sustained gap → trend continuation
- Failed gap → reversal opportunity

Sustained Gap up, Bullish Trend:

In an intraday scenario, if the market opens **gap-up** and on the hourly timeframe the price sustains above VWAP consistently for the **first three hours**, it reflects strong buying interest and absorption of any early selling pressure. This kind of structure indicates that institutions are supporting higher prices, and the market is building a base for a directional move.

Typically, after around **12:30 pm**, such a setup can lead to a **sharp upward expansion**, often resulting in a strong trending move into the latter half of the session. In such cases, traders may look to initiate long positions near VWAP on pullbacks, riding the trend with confidence.

Risk management remains critical. For bullish trades, one may consider a stop-loss based on a close below VWAP or violation of early session structure. In case of Options trade, corresponding Futures Chart must be analysed for trading aforesaid pattern.

Sustained Gap down, Bearish Trend:

Conversely, if the market opens **gap-down** and the price remains below VWAP **for the first three hours** on the hourly timeframe, it signals persistent selling pressure and lack of buying strength. This sustained weakness usually precedes a significant downward move post mid-day, again typically after 12:30 pm. The inability of price to reclaim VWAP during the initial hours reflects bearish control, and traders can look to initiate short positions near VWAP retracements.

Risk management remains critical. For bearish trades, a prudent stop-loss would be a breach of the high of the first candle or a 30-minute close above VWAP. In case of Options trade, corresponding Futures Chart must be analysed for trading aforesaid pattern.

Key Insight:

This setup is built on a simple but powerful principle: *"A failed move often leads to a fast move in the opposite direction."*

The combination of:

- Gap opening (sentiment shock)
- VWAP / 20 SMA on Hourly TF (fair value zones)
- Early failure (2nd candle reversal),

creates a high-probability intraday reversal structure.

However, sustained positioning relative to VWAP in the first half of the day often dictates the directional bias for the second half, making it a high-probability intraday framework when combined with disciplined execution.

Practical Tips:

- Stronger signals occur when supported by volume spikes or reversal candles
- Align trades with higher timeframe context (Daily trend) for better conviction
- Avoid trades if price is stuck near major support/resistance zones

FAILED GAPUP / GAPDOWN IN INTRADAY

A powerful intraday setup emerges when the market opens with a **sharp gap** and the first 10-minute candle shows a strong rejection from the extremes of the Bollinger Bands. This pattern reflects aggressive early panic (or euphoria) being quickly absorbed, often leading to a directional move for the rest of the session.

Trading Reversal from Failed Gap down:

In a gap-down scenario, if the market opens with a significant gap-down such that the **open and low are outside the Lower Bollinger Band (LBB)**—and especially if an **OL (Open = Low)** is formed—the setup gains additional strength.

Now, if the first 10-minute candle is large, with approximately three-fourths of its body outside the LBB and the remaining one-fourth closing back inside the band and above VWAP, it signals strong buying absorption at lower levels. Despite the initial panic, price reclaiming VWAP indicates underlying strength.

In such a case, the HM system on the 10-minute timeframe typically begins to show early signs of reversal—RSI 9 crossing above WMA 21 (even if RSI is still below 50), while the Ehler Fisher indicator starts rising sharply, often like a "sword," even if it remains below the zero line. This combination suggests that downside is likely exhausted for the day, and the market is unlikely to fall further unless price decisively closes below VWAP.

Basis aforesaid observations, a **trade on bullish side reversal** can be initiated with conviction on the second candle near VWAP, or on any intraday pullback towards VWAP. The stop-loss should be a single candle close below VWAP on the 5-minute timeframe, though notably, SL hunting is rare in this structure due to the strength of reversal. The trade can be executed via futures or even a covered call strategy on the long side, targeting the next pivot level or resistance zone.

Trading Reversal from Failed Gap up:

The reverse applies in a gap-up scenario. If the market opens strongly higher with the **open and high outside the Upper Bollinger Band (UBB)**—and particularly if an **OH (Open = High)** is formed—followed by a large first candle where three-fourths of the body is outside the UBB and the remaining portion closes inside the band and below VWAP, it indicates strong selling pressure at higher levels. In this setup, HM typically signals weakness—WMA 21 above RSI 9 (even if RSI remains above 50), and Ehler Fisher indicator begins to fall sharply.

Here, the market is unlikely to rise further unless price reclaims VWAP. A short trade can be initiated near VWAP on the second candle or on retracements, with a stop-loss as a close above VWAP on the 5-minute timeframe. This setup also tends to avoid frequent SL hunting due to its clarity. Traders may consider shorting futures or implementing a covered put strategy, targeting the next pivot or support level.

Overall, this pattern captures a critical market behaviour: extreme opening moves that get rejected quickly often lead to strong intraday reversals, especially when supported by VWAP reclaim/loss and confirming momentum indicators.

SUSTAINED GAPUP / GAPDOWN

Gap openings often set the tone for the entire trading day. However, the real signal lies not just in the gap, but in how price behaves after the open—especially in relation to the previous day's range and the first hourly candle structure. The following scenarios provide high-probability intraday directional cues:

Gap up Fails and Slips Below Last Hourly Candle of Previous Day:

When the market opens gap-up but fails to sustain strength, and the first hourly candle closes below the previous day's last hourly close, it indicates immediate rejection of higher levels.

If this first hourly candle also forms an OH (Open = High), it further confirms selling pressure right from the top. This is a clear sign of weakness, and an intraday short trade can be initiated immediately on the close of the first hourly candle, as the market is likely to trend downward for the rest of the session.

Gap down Fails and Surges Above Last Hourly Candle of Previous Day:

Similarly, it may also be observed that when the price opens gap-down but quickly recovers, and the first hourly candle closes above the previous day's last hourly close, it reflects strong buying absorption at lower levels.

If this first hourly candle also forms an OL (Open = Low), it strengthens the bullish bias. In such a case, an intraday long trade can be initiated on the close of the first hourly candle, anticipating upward continuation.

Gap up Above Previous Day's High - Strong Bullish Bias:

A particularly strong trending setup occurs when the market opens beyond the entire range of the previous day. If the **previous day witnessed a full-day decline**, but today the price **opens above the high of the previous day's daily candle**, it signals a complete shift in sentiment—from bearish to aggressively bullish.

Such a setup often leads to a **full-day uptrend**, with price sustaining strength throughout the session. A conviction long trade can be initiated, either at the open or on a pullback towards VWAP later in the day. The stop-loss should be a one-candle close below VWAP.

Gap down Below Previous Day's Low - Strong Bearish Bias:

Similarly, if the previous day saw a **strong upward trend**, but the current day **opens below the low of the previous day's candle**, it reflects a sharp reversal in sentiment.

This setup typically results in a **full-day downtrend**, with persistent selling pressure. A conviction short trade can be initiated, with the stop-loss as a one-candle close above VWAP.

Insight:

In essence, gap openings that invalidate the prior day's structure tend to produce strong directional moves, while gaps that fail to sustain often lead to reversals. Understanding this distinction allows traders to align early with institutional flows and capture high-momentum intraday trends.

STUDY THE CHART PATTERNS

Chart patterns, when studied and applied with discipline, offer a powerful edge in understanding market behaviour. Unlike indicators, which are inherently lagging and derivative in nature, chart patterns are the direct visual representation of price and volume interaction—capturing the real-time psychology of market participants. Every formation—whether it is OH/OL, BB Trap, K-Wave, Moh Maya, or intraday reversal structures like W and M patterns—reflects a shift in control between buyers and sellers. When these patterns are interpreted in the context of timeframe alignment, VWAP positioning, and broader trend structure, they provide high-probability trading opportunities with defined risk and reward.

The uniqueness of these patterns lies in their repeatability across timeframes and instruments, as well as their ability to adapt to varying market conditions—ranging from trending to range-bound, and from high volatility to compression phases. Patterns such as BB Blasts, Killer Waves, and Gap-based setups help identify momentum-driven moves, while formations like time-based consolidations, reversal candles near bands, and trap patterns help capture turning points in the market. Importantly, the integration of supporting tools like HM System, VWAP, Bollinger Bands, and AVWAP enhances conviction—but the primary decision-making anchor remains the pattern itself.

Ultimately, mastering chart patterns is less about memorizing setups and more about developing the ability to read market structure with clarity and patience. **Not every pattern will play out perfectly, and false signals or traps are an inherent part of trading.** However, consistent application, proper risk management, and alignment with higher timeframe context can significantly tilt probabilities in the trader's favour. Over time, these patterns evolve from being mere visual formations to becoming a structured language through which the market communicates its intent—enabling traders and investors to act with confidence, precision, and discipline.

Chapter – 13

Intraday Trading

Watch Out Technicals

Introduction to Intraday Trading:

Intraday trading refers to the practice of buying and selling financial instruments within the same trading day, with all positions typically squared off before market close. The objective is to capitalize on short-term price movements, driven by momentum, liquidity, and intraday sentiment. Unlike positional or long-term trading, intraday trading demands quick decision-making, discipline, and precise timing, as price movements are faster and often more volatile.

Intraday dynamics reveal that meaningful moves—both rises and falls—often materialize after 12:30 PM, once the market has absorbed global cues and early volatility. The opening phase is typically dominated by retail participation, while the closing phase reflects smart money action. This is why initiating trades post 12–12:15 PM significantly improves probabilities, as the market stabilizes, traps are cleared, and trend clarity emerges. Traders who align with this timing often experience higher consistency in outcomes.

The success of intraday trading largely depends on understanding and applying key technical indicators and price action principles. Some of the most significant tools include VWAP and AVWAP for identifying fair value and trend direction, moving averages (such as 20 SMA / EMA) for dynamic support and resistance, and previous day support/resistance (PR/PS) for key reaction levels. Additionally, pivot points, Bollinger Bands, and volume behaviour help in assessing momentum, range conditions, and potential breakout or reversal zones. Combining these tools provides a structured framework for identifying high-probability entry and exit points.

Equally important are the watch-out factors in intraday trading. Traders must be cautious during range-bound or low-momentum conditions (such as flat VWAP), avoid chasing trades far from key averages, and be mindful of false breakouts and stop-loss hunting, especially around VWAP or major levels. Market behaviour around opening hours, mid-day consolidation, and closing sessions also plays a crucial role. Above all, strict risk management, proper position sizing, and adherence to stop-loss discipline are essential to sustain and grow in intraday trading.

Let us look at the various aspects of intraday trading.

INTRADAY TRADE SETUPS

Intraday trading involves taking positions within the same trading session, aiming to capture short-term price movements driven by momentum, liquidity, and market sentiment. Unlike positional or investment approaches, intraday trading demands quick decision-making, precise timing, and strict risk management, as price fluctuations can be sharp and fast within the day.

A successful intraday approach is built around identifying high-probability trading zones rather than chasing price. Key technical frameworks such as **VWAP, AVWAP, Pivot Points (including CPR), Moving Averages, Bollinger Bands, and Support/Resistance levels** help in understanding **intraday trend, momentum, and likely reversal or breakout areas**. These tools, when used in combination with price action, enable traders to align their trades with the prevailing market direction.

The discussions above focus on developing a structured intraday trading methodology—emphasizing entries near important levels, confirmation through smaller timeframes, and avoiding trades in uncertain or range-bound conditions. By combining trend identification, level-based trading, and disciplined execution, traders can improve their ability to participate in high-conviction intraday opportunities while managing risk effectively.

A structured intraday approach begins with reading overall market strength using indices like NIFTY 50 and NIFTY Bank. When the market is in red or near a major resistance zone, focus should shift to the **top losers**, but only when market breadth confirms weakness (declines significantly outweigh advances). Conversely, when the market is in green or near strong support, the **top gainers** become the focus—again, only when advances dominate.

The highest-probability trades emerge when such stocks also show **multi-timeframe confirmation**—a breakout/breakdown on the Weekly timeframe along with a range breakout/breakdown on the Daily timeframe. Entry can then be refined near VWAP with a disciplined stop loss based on a 10-minute close beyond VWAP.

Let us discuss below important aspects of intraday trading setups, *viz. entry – exit zone, reversal, various intraday tradable patterns* etc.

Intraday Entry Levels:

Intraday trades should ideally be initiated at three key levels:

1. Previous Resistance/Support (PR/PS)
2. 20 SMA on the hourly timeframe
3. VWAP / AVWAP on the hourly timeframe

Entries must be taken only when price shows a clear reversal from these levels, confirmed on a lower timeframe such as the 10-minute chart. This approach ensures better timing, tighter stop-loss, and improved risk-reward.

Additionally, intraday trades can also be initiated near pivot points or support/resistance levels derived from pivot analysis, as these levels often act as strong reaction zones for price movement.

Intraday Trade Setups:

Intraday trades can broadly be classified into directional (trend-based) trades and range-bound trades. Understanding the nature of the market is essential before selecting the appropriate trading approach. Some key intraday setups are outlined below:

1. Tradable Gap-Up / Gap-Down Setups:

When the market opens with a significant gap-up, it becomes tradable only if price sustains for at least one hour above VWAP, as well as above the key levels it has crossed during the gap (such as previous resistance/support or pivot levels). Additionally, no bearish reversal patterns (such as upper Bollinger Band traps,

Open High (OH) candles, K-wave formations, etc.) should be present. In such cases, a long trade can be initiated near optimal entry zones like PR/PS, VWAP, or pivot levels, with a stop loss placed at one close below the entry level.

Similarly, in case of a gap-down opening, price should sustain for at least one hour below VWAP and below the key levels it has broken. There should be no bullish reversal patterns (such as lower Bollinger Band traps, Open Low (OL) candles, etc.). If these conditions are met, the gap-down can be considered tradable, and a short trade may be initiated near key levels like PR/PS, VWAP, or pivot points, with a stop loss placed at one close above the entry level.

We have discussed in Chapter 12 about certain important gap up/ gap down setups which can be traded in intraday for trend reversal or sustained trained basis the technicals involved.

2. Pattern-Based Trades:

Intraday trades can also be initiated based on the formation of clear and reliable price patterns, such as OH/OL, Bollinger Band traps, K-wave, Killer-wave, or 3-step patterns. These trades are ideally taken near VWAP, which acts as a strong reference level for entry. The stop loss should be placed at one close above/below VWAP or based on the breach of the day's high/low, depending on the nature of the pattern.

Such pattern-based setups can be applied not only to indices but also to individual stocks, provided the pattern formation is clear and supported by price action. We have discussed about certain important trading patterns in Chapter 12.

3. PR / PS-Based Intraday Trades

In intraday trading, **Previous Resistance (PR) and Previous Support (PS)** act as critical decision zones, around which multiple trading opportunities can emerge:

- *First Reversal from PR/PS:*

  When price approaches and retests a PR/PS level and then begins to reverse from that zone, it presents a potential trade opportunity. If this reversal is supported by other confirming factors (such as indicator signals aligning with the direction of reversal), a trade can be initiated near the PR/PS level, with a stop loss placed at one close beyond the level. The target in such cases is typically the next pivot level or support/resistance zone in the direction of the move.

- *Second Retest of PR/PS:*

  If price approaches a PR/PS level, reverses initially (often towards VWAP), and then moves again to retest the same level, the probability of a breakout or breakdown increases significantly.

  For example, if price retests support, bounces, and then returns again to test the same support, a short trade can be initiated near VWAP, anticipating a breakdown. Similarly, if price retests resistance, pulls back, and then rises again for a second test, a long trade may be initiated near VWAP, anticipating a breakout.

  Such breakouts/breakdowns may occur either through a strong single candle (super candle) or via the two-candle rule—where the first candle breaches the level and the second candle confirms the move by closing decisively beyond the high/low of the first candle. If the second candle lacks strong confirmation, the setup may fall into a partial (75%) confirmation or indecision zone.

  The stop loss should be placed at one close beyond the PR/PS level, and the target would be the next pivot or key level in the breakout/breakdown direction.

- *Breakout/Breakdown on Breach of PR / PS:*

  When price approaches and retests a PR/PS level and decisively breaches it, supported by strong price action (either a super candle or confirmation via the two-candle rule), it indicates a clear breakout or breakdown. If this move is further supported by other confirming indicators, a trade can be initiated near the breached PR/PS level, with a stop loss placed at one close beyond the level.

  The expected move in such cases is generally strong, with the target being the next pivot or support/resistance zone in the direction of the breakout or breakdown.

4. Pivot-Based Support & Resistance Trades

Intraday trades can also be effectively initiated around pivot points and their associated support/resistance (R/S) levels, as these act as strong reaction zones. When both pivot levels and VWAP are in close proximity, greater importance should be given to pivot-based R/S, as VWAP often experiences stop-loss hunting near such confluence zones. It is advisable to wait for price to test and react at the pivot/R/S level before initiating a trade. Entries should ideally be taken near the pivot or R/S level, with a stop loss placed at one close beyond the respective pivot, support, or resistance level.

Within pivot-based trading, the following setups commonly emerge:

- *Crossover to the Next Pivot Level:*

  When price breaks a pivot level decisively, either through a strong momentum candle (super candle) or via the two-candle confirmation rule (where the second candle closes convincingly beyond the high/low of the first), it indicates a potential continuation move. If price is also sustaining above/below VWAP and supported by other confirming indicators, a trade can be initiated near the pivot level, with a stop loss at one close beyond the level.

  The target in such cases is typically the next pivot level in the direction of the breakout or breakdown. If the second candle lacks strong confirmation, the setup may fall into a partial confirmation (dilemma) zone.

- *Reversal from a Pivot Level:*

  When price approaches a pivot level, fails to breach it, and begins to reverse, it indicates rejection and a potential move in the opposite direction. If this reversal is supported by additional confirming signals, a trade can be initiated near the pivot level, with a stop loss placed at one close beyond it.

  The target in such cases would be the next pivot level in the direction of the reversal.

- *Pivot-Based Intraday Trading Setup:*

  On 10-min and Hourly timeframes, price typically moves from one pivot level to another, making pivot points highly effective for structuring intraday trades. However, when both Pivot/R-S levels and VWAP are in close proximity, greater preference should be given to Pivot/R-S levels. In such cases, it is advisable to wait for price to test the pivot or support/resistance zone, rather than entering near VWAP, to avoid VWAP-based stop-loss hunting.

  Trades should ideally be initiated near Pivot or R/S levels, with a stop-loss placed at one candle close beyond the respective level (above resistance or below support).

  - If the price opens just above the pivot and VWAP, there is a high probability (around 80%) of an intraday uptrend. However, the opening should be slightly above the pivot, not excessively higher—otherwise, it may lead to a Virgin CPR scenario, where price often retraces back to test the CPR levels.

  - When price is above VWAP and sustains above a higher pivot level on the 10-min timeframe, it signals bullish strength, and price is likely to move toward the next higher pivot level intraday. Conversely, if price is below VWAP and breaks below a pivot level, it indicates bearish momentum, with a high probability of price moving toward the next lower pivot level.

  - Higher timeframe pivot levels (Hourly, Daily, Weekly) are strongly respected during intraday trading. These levels are typically breached only with high momentum, such as a strong candle (super candle) or a gap-up/gap-down move, making them critical zones to monitor.

  Thus, in intraday trading, pivot levels act as high-probability decision zones. Aligning trades with VWAP direction and higher timeframe pivots, while prioritizing pivot-based entries, significantly improves trade reliability and reduces unnecessary stop-loss triggers.

Overall, pivot-based trading provides a structured framework for intraday entries and exits, especially when combined with price action and other confirming indicators.

5. Fractal Chaos Band – Breakout & Breakdown Trades

Intraday trades can also be initiated using Fractal Chaos Bands, which help identify expansion and breakout zones. When price breaks above the upper band or below the lower band with a strong momentum candle (super candle), or through the two-candle confirmation rule (where the second candle closes decisively beyond the high/low of the first), it indicates a potential breakout or breakdown.

If this move is supported by price trading above/below VWAP and aligned with other confirming indicators, a trade can be considered. Entries are best taken near nearby dynamic levels such as VWAP, 20 SMA, or pivot points, ensuring better risk-reward. The stop loss should be placed at one close beyond the respective Fractal Chaos Band (upper or lower).

In cases where the second candle does not provide strong confirmation (i.e., it closes within the range of the first candle), the setup may fall into a partial confirmation (dilemma) zone, and caution is advised.

The target for such trades typically extends until price, after moving outside the Fractal Chaos Band, re-enters the band, indicating exhaustion of the breakout move.

6. Bollinger Band (BB) Blast Trades

A Bollinger Band blast occurs when price breaks out of a compressed range and begins to expand sharply, moving along the Upper Band (UBB) or Lower Band (LBB). When such a move is supported by price sustaining above/below VWAP in the same direction, along with confirmation from other indicators, it signals a strong momentum-driven opportunity.

In such scenarios, an intraday trade can be initiated around the second or third candle after the blast, as this provides better confirmation of continuation. The stop loss may be placed at one close beyond the entry candle, or if price re-enters the Bollinger Band, or alternatively if price closes completely outside the band, depending on the trader's risk approach.

The target for such trades is generally maintained as long as price continues to ride the band, and profits can be booked when price begins to lose momentum—either by moving away from the band or showing signs of reversal/closure beyond the band structure.

7. Range-Bound Day or Breach of Intraday Range

When the CPR (Central Pivot Range) on a 10-minute timeframe is wide, and the first 30-minute or 1-hour candle is large with wicks on both sides, it typically indicates indecision and a range-bound market. In such conditions, the market is likely to remain sideways, making it more suitable for range-based strategies (such as short straddles, with proper risk management and sum-wise stop loss). It is also important to ensure that the VIX is not rising intraday, as increasing volatility may invalidate the range-bound setup.

However, if during the day the high or low of this initial large candle is breached, it often signals a shift from range-bound to trending behaviour. In such cases, a directional trade can be initiated near the breakout level (high/low of the first candle), with a stop loss placed at one candle close back inside the range (i.e., below the high for longs or above the low for shorts).

The target for such trades would typically be the next pivot level or key support/resistance zone in the direction of the breakout or breakdown.

8. Option Crossing and Sustaining Around AVWAP

When an option's price breaks below its AVWAP and sustains below it on a 10-minute timeframe, it indicates a bearish intraday bias. In such cases, the option—preferably when the first candle forms an Open High (OH) pattern—can be considered for short selling near the AVWAP, provided that VIX is stable or declining. The stop loss should be placed at one close above the AVWAP, and the target can be the next lower pivot or support level.

In general, option selling (shorting) using AVWAP is relatively easier and more reliable than buying, as long trades require strong momentum and supportive volatility conditions.

However, if an option breaks above its AVWAP and sustains above it, it may indicate a bullish setup. In such scenarios, a long trade can be considered—preferably when the first candle forms an Open Low (OL) pattern—with entry near the AVWAP, a stop loss at one close below AVWAP, and a target at the next higher pivot or resistance level.

9. Trading Top Gainers and Top Losers in F&O Stocks

Around 10:30 AM, identify the top three gainers and top three losers in the F&O segment and evaluate them for clear, tradable setups. Focus on stocks that show strong confirmation through patterns such as OH/OL formation, PR/PS breakout or breakdown, or a Bollinger Band blast, along with price sustaining above/below VWAP.

If these setups are further supported by additional indicators aligning in the same direction, a long trade can be initiated in a strong top gainer, and a short trade in a weak top loser, preferably near VWAP, with a stop loss placed at one close beyond VWAP.

For better risk management, one may also consider a hedged intraday approach by simultaneously taking a long position in a top gainer and a short position in a top loser, thereby balancing directional exposure while capitalizing on relative strength and weakness.

10. Net of 200 EMA for Intraday Trading

For intraday trading, a net of 200 EMA (based on high/low/close) can be effectively used on the 5-minute or 10-minute timeframe and may also be referenced on the hourly chart for added context. This EMA net acts as a dynamic zone of support and resistance, helping to identify high-probability entry points in alignment with price structure.

A long trade can be considered when price crosses above the 200 EMA net and sustains above VWAP, or when price retraces to the EMA net, holds above it, and begins to reverse upward—provided it remains above VWAP. Conversely, a short trade can be initiated when price falls below the EMA net **and sustains** below VWAP, or when it rallies toward the EMA net, faces rejection, and starts reversing downward while remaining below VWAP.

Trades should always be taken in the direction of the broader market trend as indicated by higher timeframes (daily, weekly, or monthly). The stop loss should be placed on a closing basis just beyond the EMA net. Additionally, if the market opens with a gap-up directly above the 200 EMA net on the 5- or 10-minute timeframe, it often signals strength—allowing for an immediate long entry near VWAP, with a stop loss placed on a closing basis below the EMA net.

STOP-LOSS IN INTRADAY TRADE SETUPS

Effective stop-loss management is crucial in intraday trading, especially in conditions where stop-loss hunting is likely. During SL hunting, price not only creates wicks across VWAP but may also close and sustain temporarily on the opposite side of VWAP, moving against the trade before reversing back in the original direction. For example, in a long trade, price may briefly close below VWAP, trade lower for some time, and then reverse upward again. To mitigate such scenarios, the following approaches can be adopted:

- *1/3rd Candle Stop Loss:*

  For trades based on OH/OL patterns or VWAP setups, instead of placing a wide SL at the candle's extreme, a 1/3rd candle SL can be used. This means placing the stop loss at a level one close beyond one-third of the candle range, which helps reduce risk and avoid unnecessary SL hits due to volatility around VWAP.

- *Preference to 20 SMA over VWAP:*

  For general intraday trades (excluding specific VWAP-based patterns like K-wave or BB Trap), it is often more reliable to initiate trades near the 20 SMA rather than VWAP. In such cases, the SL should be placed at one close beyond the 20 SMA, as it tends to be more stable and less prone to noise.

- *Preference to PR/PS or Pivot-Based R/S over VWAP:*

  When trading based on reversal or breakout / breakdown from Previous Resistance/Support (PR / PS) or pivot-based levels, priority should be given to these levels over VWAP. Entries should be taken near these strong zones, with SL placed at one close beyond the respective level, reducing the chances of VWAP-induced stop-loss hunting.

- *VWAP as SL in VWAP-Specific Patterns:*

  In trades based on clear VWAP-driven patterns (such as K-wave, BB Trap, etc.), VWAP itself can be used as a reference for stop loss, with one close beyond VWAP acting as the exit condition.

- *Stop Loss Based on Day's High/Low:*

  Certain intraday setups allow SL placement based on the breach of the day's high or low, such as trades based on first OH/OL candle or K-wave formations. This provides a logical structural stop aligned with price action.

- *Use of Deep ITM Options to Avoid SL hunting:*

  For option buying strategies based on VWAP, it is advisable to use deep ITM monthly expiry options, as they are less prone to erratic movements and SL hunting around VWAP. In contrast, OTM or weekly options tend to fluctuate sharply around VWAP, increasing the likelihood of premature stop-loss triggers.

By applying these techniques, traders can better manage risk, avoid false exits, and improve consistency in intraday trading.

STOP-LOSS HUNTING IN INTRADAY

Certain intraday conditions offer relatively stable price behaviour, where the probability of stop-loss (SL) hunting is minimal. Identifying such setups can significantly improve trade comfort and consistency:

1. **First Candle Hits UBB / LBB and Closes Inside (10-Min TF):**

   When the market opens with a gap-up or gap-down, and the first 10-minute candle touches the Upper/Lower Bollinger Band (UBB/LBB) but closes back inside the band, it signals initial exhaustion. If the second candle closes in the opposite direction and sustains below VWAP (in case of gap-up) or above VWAP (in case of gap-down), and both price and VWAP start sloping consistently in that direction, it indicates a steady trend with low SL-hunting probability.

   In such cases, trades can be initiated near VWAP during pullbacks. For example, after a gap-up, if price starts sustaining below VWAP with a downward slope, a short trade near VWAP can be relatively smooth. However, traders must remain alert—if any reversal pattern (such as multi-candle reversal or BB trap) emerges with supporting indicators, it is prudent to exit early without waiting for a VWAP breach.

2. **Bollinger Band (BB) Trap Setup (10-Min TF):**

   A BB trap forms when the first candle (post gap-up or gap-down) closes completely outside the Bollinger Band, followed by a sharp reversal where the next candle sustains on the opposite side of VWAP. This setup often provides high-probability intraday opportunities with minimal SL hunting.

   A long trade can be considered near the lower band (LBB) when price sustains above VWAP with confirmation from supporting indicators, while a short trade can be initiated near the upper band (UBB) when price sustains below VWAP.

   Targets typically progress through 9 SMA, 20 SMA, and then the opposite side band (UBB / LBB), while keeping an eye on key support / resistance and pivot levels for potential reversals. The stop loss should be placed at one close beyond VWAP in the opposite direction.

   When a BB trap coincides with OH/OL formation on the first candle, the setup becomes even more reliable and less prone to SL hunting. However, if price approaches a major PR/PS or pivot level and shows signs of reversal, caution is advised—profits should be booked early rather than waiting for a VWAP-based exit, as SL hunting may still occur near strong levels.

3. **Use of Deep ITM Options to Avoid SL Hunting:**

   For option buying strategies based on VWAP, using deep ITM monthly expiry options is advisable, as they exhibit stable price behaviour with minimal SL hunting near VWAP. In contrast, OTM or weekly options tend to fluctuate aggressively around VWAP, increasing the likelihood of premature stop-loss triggers.

   By focusing on these setups, traders can identify cleaner intraday trends with reduced noise, enabling better trade execution and improved risk management.

INTRADAY SKILL

The wide range of intraday setups and patterns discussed above ultimately converge on a few timeless principles: structure, confirmation, and discipline.

While each pattern—whether OH/OL formations, BB Traps, K-Waves, gap-based setups, or reversal structures—has its own nuances, they all represent different expressions of the same underlying market behaviour: the interaction between price, time, and participant psychology. No single setup guarantees success in isolation; rather, consistency emerges when these patterns are applied within a well-defined framework, supported by confluence factors such as VWAP positioning, higher time-frame context, and selective indicator confirmation.

A key takeaway is that intraday trading is less about prediction and more about reaction. The market continuously reveals its intent through price action—whether by sustaining above or below VWAP, respecting key support/resistance levels, or forming recognizable structures over time. The trader's role is to patiently wait for these conditions to align, execute with clarity, and avoid overtrading during uncertain or range-bound phases. Many of the patterns highlighted also emphasize timing within the day (such as post-12:15 pm moves or 1 pm breakouts), reinforcing that not just price, but *when* price behaves in a certain way, is equally critical.

Risk management stands at the core of all successful execution. Even the most powerful setups—be it a BB Blast, Killer-Wave, or Moh Maya pattern—can fail under certain market conditions. Hence, predefined stop-loss levels (often based on candle structure, VWAP, or key levels) must be strictly adhered to. Avoiding common pitfalls such as SL hunting zones, trading oversized candles, or ignoring higher time-frame signals can significantly improve trade quality. Equally important is the practice of partial profit booking and trailing positions, allowing traders to both protect capital and participate in extended moves.

Another important insight is the role of market context. Trending days, range-bound days, and high-volatility environments each demand a different approach. Patterns like range-bound spinning tops, BB squeezes, or gap-based continuations help identify the nature of the day early, enabling traders to adapt accordingly. Additionally, external factors such as volatility (VIX), global cues, and news flows can amplify or distort price action, making it essential to remain flexible rather than rigidly attached to any one setup.

In essence, mastery of intraday trading lies not in memorizing patterns, but in understanding their behaviour, context, and limitations. With disciplined execution, patience, and continuous learning, these setups can serve as powerful tools to navigate the markets effectively. Over time, the trader evolves from merely spotting patterns to interpreting the story behind them—transforming structured rules into intuitive decision-making.

Chapter – 14

Execution

With Knowledge, Skill & Discipline

Markets are living systems—constantly evolving, reacting, and adapting to a mix of information, sentiment, liquidity, and human behaviour. At times they trend with clarity, at times they move within ranges, and at other times they turn volatile and unpredictable. This dynamic nature of the market is what creates both opportunity and risk. Price does not move randomly; it reflects the collective actions of participants—retail traders, institutions, and smart money—each operating with different intentions and time horizons.

To navigate such an environment, it becomes essential to understand the underlying market dynamics—how price interacts with time, volume, volatility, and key levels. Tools like moving averages, VWAP, support/resistance, and chart patterns help decode this behaviour, but tools alone are not enough. True edge comes from learning how to interpret these tools in context, and more importantly, from developing the skill to apply them with consistency.

This skill is not acquired overnight. It is built gradually through practice, observation, patience, and discipline. A trader must train the eye to read charts, the mind to remain unbiased, and the execution to stay aligned with a defined plan. Over time, what initially feels complex begins to make sense, and decision-making becomes more structured and confident.

With this foundation in place, let us now discuss and focus on a few important aspects of trading and investment which every market participant must know and understand—as he or she plans to participate in the markets with the objective of generating consistent profits.

MARKET NATURE & PHILOSOPHY

Markets, by their very nature, are designed to grow over time. Broad indices like NIFTY 50 and BSE Sensex may move with varying character—sometimes sharply with momentum, sometimes gradually, and often within ranges—but their long-term trajectory remains upward. Even severe corrections triggered by events like wars, pandemics, or financial crises do not last indefinitely. Historically, major drawdowns have rarely persisted beyond 1–2 years, and the recovery phase tends to be faster and sharper than the decline. This reinforces a foundational belief: markets absorb shocks, consolidate, and eventually resume their upward journey.

Having said above about the broader macro trend in the markets, it is important to understand that the markets are dynamic, ever-evolving systems—there is no fixed behaviour, no permanent trend (in short or mid-term, even sometimes for years), and certainly no rigid rule that works in all conditions. A trader's greatest strength lies not in prediction, but in adaptability. If the market shifts from bullish to bearish—or vice versa—one must be quick to recognize the change and respond accordingly.

A trader's own mind is often his biggest adversary. Bias, ego, fear, and greed interfere with objective decision-making. Entering the market with a pre-defined bias is often counterproductive. Markets are dynamic, and success lies in the ability to adapt quickly as conditions change. A beginner trader, in particular, tends to get emotionally attached to their analysis, making it difficult to shift stance when the market moves against them. Over time and with experience, this rigidity softens, and adaptability becomes a natural strength. The market also plays a deeper role—it shapes behaviour. It challenges ego, humbles overconfidence, and gradually builds discipline. A trader's biggest battle is not with the market, but with their own mind. Developing a psychological edge—staying objective, flexible, and grounded—is essential for long-term survival.

Understanding price structure and adapting to changing market conditions is critical. What works in a low-volatility environment (VIX below 15) may fail in a high-volatility regime (VIX above 25–30). Each volatility zone demands a different strategy, risk appetite, and execution style.

Market dynamics are constantly evolving, and a trader must remain flexible. Rigid strategies often fail when conditions shift. The ability to read structure, recognise accumulation (smart money buying) and distribution (smart money selling), and adapt accordingly is what differentiates experienced traders from beginners.

At its core, the stock market operates like a business. It rewards those who think like businessmen—focused on opportunity, risk, and capital preservation. There is no holy grail in the market; no single strategy or pattern guarantees success. Instead, the market continuously offers opportunities, and a trader's job is to identify and act on them prudently. Think of the market as an ocean—vast, deep, and full of hidden opportunities waiting to be discovered.

PRICE ACTION & CHART READING

The foundation of trading lies in understanding price action. The first step in any trade is identifying the trend, and this begins with reading and interpreting price averages. Price is the ultimate truth, and its interaction with averages forms the foundation of chart reading. Understanding **price averages**—such as moving averages, VWAP, and AVWAP—is akin to learning the language of the market. A trader who understands how price behaves around these averages can "read" the market with clarity.

VWAP is a powerful tool but is applicable only to tradable instruments such as futures and stocks—not indices themselves. For example, VWAP can be effectively used on NIFTY Futures or Bank Nifty Futures, but not directly on the index values. Its universality, however, extends across asset classes—equities, commodities, crude, and even global markets—making it a versatile anchor for price action analysis.

A trader who understands how price behaves around averages can almost "communicate" with the market. Chart reading is therefore a critical skill—not just for identifying trends, but also for spotting reversals and continuations.

Price movement is not random—it is a function of volume dynamics. Momentum emerges when volume is aggressively deployed or withdrawn; sustained trends require strength, and that strength is built through consistent participation. For price to stabilize or reverse, it must interact with its averages—these act as equilibrium zones where the market rebalances itself.

In essence:

- Momentum drives movement
- Strength sustains trends
- Averages provide support and equilibrium

Understanding this interplay is central to mastering price action.

The primary reason most traders incur losses in their initial journey is not the market—it is their inability to read charts effectively and their failure to make timely adjustments. Chart reading is not just about identifying patterns but understanding context, structure, and behaviour. When this skill is weak, decisions become reactive rather than logical. consistent practice in reading charts, patterns, and formations is essential to build this skill. Chart reading is not a one-time skill—it is a craft that requires continuous practice.

The ability to identify trends, reversals, and patterns improves only through consistent observation and experience.

- The first step in any trade is always trend identification
- Chart reading helps detect both trend continuation and reversal
- Traditional candlestick patterns—such as spinning Top, Cup & Handle, Hammer, Inverted Hammer, Double Top, Triple Top, Flag, Doji, etc.—remain relevant and must be understood

An important observation is that patterns formed in indices or F&O stocks are also reflected in their corresponding options charts. This reinforces the idea that price behaviour is consistent across instruments, and understanding price action in one domain can be effectively applied in another.

Different market participants interpret price differently:

- A scalper focuses on micro-movements
- An intraday trader looks for structured setups
- An investor focuses on long-term trends

There is a common belief that "smart money defeats retail traders." In reality, the market rewards knowledge, not size. A knowledgeable trader—regardless of capital—can outperform an uninformed participant. The market ecosystem is fundamentally knowledge-driven.

Trading is a game of probability. While hedging represents structured knowledge and risk control, chart patterns and setups operate on probabilities, not certainties. No pattern works 100% of the time, and accepting this reality is crucial. The key is to develop a personal edge—rules and setups that one understands deeply and can execute confidently. "Be a genius in all, but a master in one" aptly applies here: broad awareness is useful, but specialization brings consistency.

To build this edge, one must continuously enhance understanding of price action, chart patterns, option behaviour, and calculation dynamics. Options, in particular, behave differently from futures—they evolve with time decay, volatility, and proximity to expiry. Ignoring this behaviour leads to mispricing risk and poor decision-making.

TIMEFRAME: SIGNIFICANCE & DISCIPLINE

Price action is always governed by the higher timeframe. Therefore, a structured approach involves analysing the higher timeframe first and then refining entries on the lower timeframe. For instance, if the hourly timeframe signals a buy, one should look for long opportunities on the 10-minute chart upon confirmation. Similarly, if the daily trend is bearish, short trades should be aligned with confirmation on the hourly timeframe.

This "top-down" approach—higher timeframe to lower timeframe—is a foundational rule of chart reading. It ensures that trades are aligned with the dominant trend, significantly improving probability and reducing noise-driven decisions.

An investor should primarily follow the Monthly timeframe, a positional trader the Daily timeframe, and an intraday trader the Hourly timeframe. Lower timeframes are merely execution tools, while higher timeframes define the direction. This multi-timeframe alignment ensures that trades are taken in harmony with the broader trend, significantly improving success probability.

Consistency in timeframe usage is critical. The timeframe used for initiating a trade or investment should be respected until exit. Lower timeframes, such as 10-minute charts, should only be used for refining entries or managing stop-loss levels—not for changing the core view.

If a trade initiated on a lower timeframe (like hourly) faces a reversal signal on a higher timeframe (like daily), the higher timeframe must take precedence. In such cases, positions should be adjusted promptly, and if required, reversed. This alignment ensures that the trader remains in sync with the dominant market force.

TREND ALIGNMENT & MARKET DIRECTION

One of the strongest principles in trading is to stay aligned with the broader trend. If the market is bearish across higher timeframes (daily, weekly, monthly), then every rise should be treated as a selling opportunity. Conversely, in a bullish structure, every dip becomes a buying opportunity.

Price always respects higher timeframes. A structured approach involves:

- Identifying trend on the monthly timeframe,
- Validating it on the weekly timeframe,
- Executing trades based on the daily timeframe.

For shorter positional trades (15–25 days), daily timeframe setups—supported by levels like 20 SMA, Bollinger Bands, or 200 EMA—become critical, with lower timeframe confirmation for precise entry.

RISK MANAGEMENT & CAPITAL ALLOCATION

Risk management is the backbone of long-term success. Capital preservation is the foundation of survival in markets. Without capital, opportunity becomes irrelevant.

- Never deploy 100% capital
- Option sellers should ideally deploy up to ~40% (preferably through pyramiding)
- Option buyers should limit exposure to ~10%

Trading is simple in concept but difficult in execution, largely due to psychological challenges. Emotions often work against the trader, making discipline and mental strength critical. Trading frequency must be controlled—5 to 6 high-quality trades per month are sufficient. Overtrading erodes both capital and psychological stability.

A practical discipline:

- If one good profit trade is achieved → stop for the day
- If two losses occur → stop for the day

This prevents emotional overtrading and preserves both capital and mental clarity.

Focus must always remain on controlling losses. Profits are a byproduct of disciplined risk management. Develop the habit of booking profits—whether small or large—because while losses are easy to accept, holding onto profits requires emotional maturity. A successful trader does not aim to catch the exact bottom or top but focuses on capturing the "meat" of the move—the most reliable and tradable portion.

Markets test behaviour more than knowledge. Aligning emotional control with price action is what separates consistent traders from inconsistent ones. Consistent profitability in trading is not just about technical setups—it is about aligning price action with emotional discipline. A trader must develop the ability to synchronize market behaviour (price action) with personal behaviour (emotional control). This convergence is what separates impulsive trading from professional execution.

Trading less but trading better is a hallmark of successful traders. Only high-conviction setups—those that align with one's tested patterns and understanding—should be executed. Profits from such trades are not only consistent but also psychologically satisfying.

If a trade requires continuous adjustment merely to avoid loss, the objective should shift to exiting at cost or minimal loss, rather than forcing profitability. It is often wiser to exit and re-enter with a fresh, clearer setup than to overmanage a flawed position.

A practical approach for beginners is to start with positional trades on higher timeframes, focusing on relatively safer and well-defined setups such as:

- Trading reversals at key support/resistance on the daily timeframe,
- OH/OL formations,
- BB Blast and BB Trap patterns.

STOCK INVESTMENT

Long-term investing in stocks is not merely about purchasing a good company; it is also about identifying the right timing, market structure, institutional participation, momentum, and the broader trend supporting the business and sector. While fundamentals help identify the quality and long-term potential of a company, Technical Analysis often helps investors understand *when* the market is beginning to recognize that value and where smart money may be gradually positioning itself.

Different market capitalization categories also behave differently and carry varying levels of risk and reward:

- **Large-cap stocks** are generally considered the safest category within equities because they are relatively stable, institutionally owned, and financially stronger businesses. However, being heavyweight companies, they may not always generate extremely high CAGR returns over long periods since "elephants cannot dance."
- **Mid-cap stocks** often provide a balance between growth potential and relative stability, while **small-cap stocks** tend to be more volatile, possess higher beta, and can generate exceptional returns during strong economic and sectoral cycles. However, small caps also carry significantly higher risk and sharper drawdowns during weak market conditions.
- The **SME segment** remains one of the riskiest yet potentially highly rewarding spaces in equity markets. Technical patterns in newly listed or thinly traded SME companies may not always behave reliably due to low liquidity, limited institutional participation, and immature price discovery. However, if such businesses possess strong fundamentals,

favourable industry tailwinds, government policy support, sectoral demand expansion, scalable business models, and capable promoters, they may eventually evolve into powerful multibagger opportunities. Institutional participation often drives sustained price appreciation in equities, but institutions usually accumulate gradually over extended periods within narrow consolidation ranges. This accumulation phase may continue for months or even years before the stock begins showing meaningful momentum. Hence, smart investors attempt to identify sustained breakouts from long consolidation bases using tools such as VCP structures, Bollinger Band squeezes, Relative Strength signals, accumulation patterns, and volume expansion to participate in the emerging trend early.

Investing styles may also differ based on an investor's philosophy, risk appetite, and time horizon:

- **Coffee Can** Investing focuses on identifying high-quality businesses with durable competitive advantages and holding them patiently over long periods while ignoring temporary market noise.
- **Growth Investing** emphasizes companies exhibiting strong earnings growth, expanding market share, innovation, and future scalability, while **Value Investing** focuses on fundamentally sound businesses trading below their intrinsic worth due to temporary pessimism or market inefficiencies.

Each approach carries its own significance and requires discipline, patience, and understanding of market cycles. However, irrespective of the investing style, understanding the broader sector, industry dynamics, government policies, management quality, demand outlook, balance sheet strength, and business fundamentals remains extremely important.

Foreign Institutional Investors (FIIs) and large institutional participants often identify promising businesses at a very early stage when there is little or no recognition from retail market participants. Such institutions usually accumulate shares gradually over an extended period of time while the stock trades quietly within a range or base formation. By the time the broader retail crowd begins noticing the stock and aggressively buying at elevated price levels after a substantial rally, a large part of the move may already have occurred.

Quite often, retail participants enter emotionally near euphoric stages when the stock has already run significantly, thereby exposing themselves to the risk of getting trapped during the subsequent profit-booking or distribution phase initiated by institutional investors. Hence, rising institutional participation — particularly increasing FII holding alongside strong promoter holding — while retail participation still remains relatively low or moderate, is often considered a constructive sign from a long-term investment perspective, especially when valuations and P/E (Price-to-Earnings) multiples are still reasonable. If such institutional accumulation is further supported by improving fundamentals such as consistent quarter-on-quarter growth in revenue, EBITDA, PAT, EPS, rising sales, improving margins, reduction in debt burden, lower promoter pledge, controlled expenses, and strengthening cash flows, it may indicate improving business quality and increasing market confidence in the company's long-term growth potential.

Thus, combining strong fundamentals with practical technical insights can significantly improve investment decision-making, entry timing, and risk management. Hence, one should invest in the "story" but trade the "price." Some of the major technical patterns that can give an edge to a stock investor are briefly discussed below (these technicals are already discussed under relevant Chapters, but are reiterated here in the context of stock investing):

1. ***Stock investing after market correction:*** One of the most powerful investment opportunities often emerges after a meaningful market correction or prolonged price decline. Strong fundamentally sound companies frequently revisit important anchored VWAP (AVWAP) zones anchored from major historical corrections, panic lows, or significant events. These AVWAP zones often act as dynamic institutional accumulation levels where price starts stabilizing and gradually absorbing supply. If the stock begins to sustain above such AVWAP zones with improving Relative Strength (RS), volume expansion, and trend reversal signals, it may indicate that larger market participants are slowly accumulating positions for the next major uptrend.
2. ***Reversal from oversold zones:*** Another highly useful investment setup emerges from historical oversold reversal zones. Many fundamentally

strong stocks repeatedly reverse from deeply oversold RSI zones such as RSI 9 or RSI 14 levels observed on daily, weekly, or monthly charts. These reversals become more reliable when accompanied by bullish candlestick patterns, higher lows, drying selling pressure, positive divergence, or strong support zones. Investors who patiently study the historical behaviour of a stock often notice recurring oversold regions from where institutional accumulation begins and medium- to long-term reversals emerge.

3. ***Accumulation exhibited in dry volume***: Compressed price structures with dry volume behaviour also provide powerful investment clues. Often, after a sharp correction or prolonged decline, a fundamentally strong stock may stop falling aggressively despite weak market sentiment. Volume gradually dries up, selling pressure weakens, and price starts moving within a narrow range. Sporadic bursts of buying volume begin appearing while supply continuously diminishes over time. Such structures may indicate silent accumulation by stronger hands. When this compression appears alongside Bollinger Band squeeze formations, VCP (Volatility Contraction Pattern), tightening price action, or narrow-range consolidation, the probability of a strong directional move increases substantially. Investors often watch for a successful breakout with 2 strong candle closes above the Upper Bollinger Band on daily charts, especially when similar compression structures are visible on higher time frames like weekly or monthly charts.

4. ***Moving averages***: Higher time frame moving averages also provide valuable long-term investment signals. Strong growth stocks frequently take support near the Monthly 20 SMA during healthy corrections within a broader secular uptrend. Reversals from Monthly 20 SMA zones with strong bullish price action and volume participation may indicate continuation of the larger trend. Similarly, long-term trend reversals often emerge when major moving averages begin converging after prolonged consolidation phases. Situations where the 20 SMA/EMA rises from below and gradually cuts through higher moving averages like the 50, 100, 200, or even 400 SMA/EMA, followed by sustained price action above these averages, may indicate the beginning

of a fresh long-term bullish cycle. Golden crossovers accompanied by improving Relative Strength and strong price-volume behaviour often attract institutional participation and trend-following investors.

5. ***Relative strength targeting alpha***: Relative Strength (RS) based investing is another powerful investing approach. Some stocks consistently outperform broader market indices or sectoral peers over long periods despite temporary corrections. Such stocks demonstrate leadership characteristics and often continue attracting institutional flows. Investors frequently use RS indicators, RS charts, and comparative performance analysis to identify stocks exhibiting superior strength against benchmark indices. A stock showing rising Relative Strength along with constructive price action, increasing volumes, sustained higher highs and higher lows, and breakout from consolidation zones may indicate leadership potential and continuation of momentum.

Therefore, investors must also carefully study price action, candlestick patterns, chart structures, accumulation-distribution behaviour, support-resistance zones, demand-supply dynamics, and volume analysis before taking investment positions. Understanding fake breakouts, bull traps, distribution phases, weak volume rallies, or exhaustion moves is equally important. Technical Analysis is not about certainty; rather, it is about improving probabilities and aligning with stronger market behaviour. Over time, investors gradually train their eyes to recognize repeated market structures and develop conviction in identifying sustainable trends and high-probability investment opportunities.

Ultimately, strong investing often lies at the intersection of sound fundamentals and intelligent technical execution. Even fundamentally strong companies may remain trapped within broad price ranges for years if institutional interest, sectoral momentum, or broader market participation remain absent. Therefore, once the fundamental checks are in place, Technical Analysis may help investors identify sustained breakouts, trend reversals, accumulation structures, momentum expansion, and institutional participation more effectively. The goal is not merely to buy a good company, but to participate in the right company at the right phase of its market cycle and patiently ride the broader uptrend while continuously managing risk and adapting to changing market behaviour.

INVESTMENT DISCIPLINE

Interestingly, investment is often more difficult than trading. While trading offers quicker feedback and exit flexibility, investing demands patience, deeper analysis, and conviction through drawdowns. Without strong chart reading and structural understanding, both paths become challenging.

While technicals guide entries and exits for stock investments, fundamentals of stocks should not be ignored. If a company shows signs of structural deterioration or faces major fundamental issues, decisive action must be taken to exit. Markets reward discipline, not attachment.

At a broader level, markets function like a business ecosystem. Capital flows toward strength and exits weakness. Recognizing this dynamic helps traders and investors align with sustainable opportunities rather than speculative noise.

Also, stocks move in cycles of accumulation and distribution, often appearing rangebound during these phases. Recognising these cycles provides an edge in anticipating future moves.

Effective capital allocation is the backbone of long-term investing success. It is prudent to deploy only 30–40% of total capital initially, while retaining the rest for strategic deployment—such as accumulating quality stocks near key levels like the 20 SMA or AVWAP on the monthly timeframe.

As highlighted above, one of the most powerful applications of AVWAP lies in long-term investing. When the market corrects deeply and price approaches its Monthly AVWAP—a zone that may appear once in several years—it often presents a rare opportunity. Historically, such zones appear once in 8–10 years and offer exceptional investment potential, particularly in market leaders, which tend to outperform sharply during recoveries. Investing in strong, large-cap market leaders near such levels can yield exceptional returns. Historically, such zones have led to significant upside moves within 150–200 trading sessions, as institutional money re-enters and drives recovery. These moments, often accompanied by fear and pessimism, are where disciplined investors build meaningful wealth.

Markets are not meant for perfect timing. Bottom fishing and top picking are largely controlled by institutional players ("smart money"). Retail traders should focus on capturing the middle portion of a move—the most reliable and tradable segment.

Averaging should not be done blindly in a falling market. Instead, it should be executed only after a meaningful correction has occurred, when price stabilises and begins to show signs of recovery. This disciplined approach ensures that capital is preserved and deployed at more favourable risk-reward zones.

Investment and trading demand very different starting points. Investment is best started early, allowing the power of compounding and time to work in your favour. Trading, on the other hand, should ideally begin later—after sufficient learning, observation, and skill development. Entering trading without preparation often leads to avoidable losses, whereas investing rewards patience even with limited initial knowledge.

At its core, profitability in both domains stems from one simple principle: focus on protecting capital. If the approach is consistently centred around saving losses, profits naturally follow over time.

EXECUTION EFFICIENCY & ORDER PLACEMENT

Execution quality plays a subtle but important role in trading outcomes.

Basket orders are useful when dealing with multiple trades in liquid instruments, but in less liquid strikes—especially deep ITM/OTM or far expiries—limit orders are more appropriate.

Liquidity must always be assessed through bid-ask spreads. A tight spread indicates tradability, while a wide spread signals risk. A disciplined trader places limit orders strategically—buying slightly below the ask price and selling slightly above the bid price—to optimise execution without unnecessary slippage.

EXIT WITH DISCIPLINE

If there is one principle that separates successful traders from the rest, it is the ability to exit well. Entry is relatively easy; exit is where discipline is tested. The first loss is always the smallest—delaying exit in hope or denial only magnifies the damage.

An effective trade is one where the exit is pre-defined and often located close to the entry point. This ensures that if the trade is wrong, the loss remains controlled. The market may forgive a poor entry, but it rarely forgives a poor exit. Hence, identifying a strong exit level often indirectly defines a strong entry as well.

Exit strategy must always aim to:

- Minimize loss when wrong
- Maximize profit when right

The focus should always be on identifying the **best exit point**, not just the best entry.

Market usually provides opportunities to exit gracefully. Recognising these moments and acting decisively leads to controlled outcomes. If one ignores these signals, the market eventually forces an exit—often at a much worse level.

Certain practical observations also add value in exit strategy—such as:

- Stocks hitting consecutive upper circuits often warrant profit booking due to exhaustion risk.
- Previous closing levels act as key reference points for future direction.
- High-probability trades are often those aligned with clear structure, strong levels, and multi-timeframe confirmation.

PLANNED RISK & STOP LOSS

A trader must learn to "know, plan, and trade their loss." Profitability is a by-product of controlled risk. When losses are managed effectively, gains naturally follow over time.

Every trade carry uncertainty—either profit or loss. However, a trader who understands how to manage downside risk stands a far better chance of becoming consistently profitable. Risk should be aligned with capital, adjusted thoughtfully, and accepted as part of the process.

A large portion of stop-loss hunting occurs due to **system-fed (visible) stop-losses**. To mitigate this:

- Prefer **close-based stop-loss (CLBS)** rather than trigger-based SL
- Place stops intelligently around structure, not obvious levels

STRUCTURED DECISION-MAKING FRAMEWORK

Trading is simple in concept but difficult in execution—primarily due to psychological challenges. Emotional discipline, patience, and adaptability are more important than any indicator or strategy.

Trading and investment decisions should always be rooted in logic, not intuition. Gut feeling has no consistent value in markets. A structured approach may include:

- Overbought and oversold conditions,
- Reversals near major static support and resistance,
- Dynamic levels like AVWAP, moving averages, or statistical bands,
- Advanced patterns such as Moh maya, BB Trap, BB Blast, or moving average convergence.

Among these, advanced tools like AVWAP (Anchored VWAP) offer deeper insights. By anchoring AVWAP at key emotional zones—such as points of maximum fear (market bottoms) and maximum hope (market tops)—traders can identify high-probability zones for entry, exit, and stop-loss. Using multiple AVWAP levels across time helps map the "stations" where price is likely to react, making it a powerful tool for both trading and investment decisions.

Higher timeframe confirmations add conviction, while lower timeframes refine execution.

The best trades are often those taken at key support and resistance levels—where risk is clearly defined and probability is favourable. In a rising market, identifying resistance may be relatively straightforward. However, in a falling market, identifying support becomes more complex and crucial. Multiple support levels must be analysed, and the most reliable level is often where repeated lows have formed.

Breakouts and breakdowns are often accompanied by gap openings. A gap-up above resistance (PR) or gap-down below support (PS) typically signals strong intent. Trades can be initiated in the direction of the breach, with stop loss placed just beyond the breakout level (1 close beyond PR/PS). However, sustainability is key—if a gap holds for 30 minutes, it provides early confirmation; if sustained for 1 hour, it becomes highly reliable. Additionally, for any breakout or reversal to be considered valid, at least two consecutive closes (**2 candle rule**) on the relevant timeframe are generally required.

Confidence also builds through familiarity. If a trader exits a position profitably and the market reverses, taking a trade again in the opposite direction on the same instrument becomes easier, as the behaviour of that instrument is already understood.

A crucial insight:

- Riding a confirmed trend generates steady returns
- But identifying and trading a failed trend or false breakout often yields significantly larger profits, as it traps the majority of participants

This contrarian edge—when executed with discipline—can be highly rewarding.

A key rule in trading is that confluence builds conviction. If two indicators confirm a trend, the third typically aligns soon after. However, confirmation should not come at the cost of delayed execution—while two candle closes (CLBS) on a relevant timeframe provide strong validation for breakouts or reversals, in fast-moving markets this may result in missed opportunities. Hence, a balance between confirmation and agility is essential.

Intraday behaviour also offers insight: if price approaches a support level, rebounds, returns to VWAP, and then revisits the same support again, it signals weakness. A second retest often leads to breakdown, making it an opportunity to initiate short trades near VWAP with high conviction. Further, for intraday directional decisions the following rule can be followed with conviction—on the Hourly timeframe, the 20-period moving average serves as a simple yet powerful trend filter:

- Sustaining above 20 SMA → bullish bias
- Sustaining below 20 SMA → bearish bias

Intraday trading is extremely demanding and often unforgiving for beginners. It is advisable to start with positional trading, where decisions are less reactive and more structured. Over time, as confidence and skill improve, one can gradually move to shorter timeframes. Consistency in trading comes not from frequent participation, but from selective participation. It is far more effective to take fewer, high-conviction trades rather than trading daily. Traders should develop and adhere to their own set of rules—focusing only on setups they deeply understand and trust. The principle is simple: *do less, but do the best.*

Timing within a trading day can significantly impact outcomes. Traders who initiate positions after around 12:15 PM often avoid early-session noise and traps. By this time, markets tend to stabilise, global cues are absorbed, and the day's direction becomes clearer—reducing unnecessary losses. Further, for intraday decision-making, the 1-hour and 30-minute timeframes (especially 30-minute for technical indicators like HM system) provide the best clarity. Entries should then be refined using the 10-minute timeframe. The 15-minute timeframe, despite its popularity, often becomes a trap zone due to excessive crowd participation.

A few practical insights that strengthen discipline:

- Previous day's levels and price behaviour are critical for next-day bias.
- No position is also a position—staying out is often better than forcing trades.
- The market always offers opportunities, but not every moment is tradable.

In reality, a trade is largely driven by chart reading (around 70%), while the remaining 30% involves understanding option behaviour, hedging, and execution mechanics.

Periods of low volatility often precede explosive moves. When markets remain rangebound for multiple sessions and Bollinger Bands contract into a narrow "funnel," it signals an impending breakout or breakdown—known as a BB Blast. This setup can be traded effectively using lower timeframes (like 30-minute charts) with defined stop-loss levels. On expiry days, such breakouts can become exceptionally powerful, offering "jackpot" opportunities due to heightened momentum and option behaviour. However, discipline is required to ride the trend and exit at the right time, typically around early afternoon unless momentum sustains strongly.

Certain periods, such as the last week of the financial year, behave differently. During such times, traditional candlestick patterns (like hammer, doji, or flag formations) often lose reliability. Instead, tools like Bollinger Bands and Anchored VWAP provide better insight into price behaviour. Markets also tend to remain rangebound on expiry during such periods, making non-directional strategies like short straddles or strangles more effective.

Additionally, when divergence appears between indices—such as Nifty being green while Bank Nifty is red—it signals lack of consensus, often leading to rangebound and non-trending conditions.

Markets also tend to exhibit the following recurring behavioural tendency during a week:

- A strongly trending week (uptrend) often sees reversal on Wednesday or Thursday
- A falling week often reverses similarly midweek

This tendency exhibited in a week, can be identified through tools like VWAP—if price starts sustaining below VWAP in an uptrend week, or above VWAP in a downtrend week, reversal probability increases sharply. If reversal does not occur on Wednesday, the probability intensifies on Thursday—especially in the second half, often creating **high-reward "jackpot" trades** due to low option premiums.

In extreme or war-like market conditions, traditional indicators often lose reliability. During such phases, simple moving averages—particularly 20 SMA and 50 SMA on higher timeframes—become the most dependable guides. For instance, if price breaks below the 50 SMA on the Weekly timeframe, it often signals a strong bearish phase where markets may either consolidate on the Monthly timeframe or drift lower until they align with the 20 SMA on the Monthly chart before reversing. In such situations, macro hedging strategies—like going long on assets such as crude oil or gold while shorting equity indices—can help manage risk during uncertainty. Adaptability in such environments is critical.

Markets do not always correct in price; sometimes they correct in time. During such phases, most stocks—except smaller speculative names—enter consolidation, moving sideways while averages catch up. Recognizing this phase prevents premature trades and helps align expectations with market reality.

Different trading styles focus on different aspects of the market:

- Momentum and swing traders focus on price movement,
- Option buyers focus on price expansion,
- Option sellers focus on time decay.

Options demand greater caution due to their asymmetric behaviour. Typically, call options premiums rise gradually in bullish markets, whereas put options premiums can spike sharply during market falls due to increased volatility. This makes selling put options riskier, especially during sudden reversals. Understanding this asymmetry is essential for both option buyers and sellers. Volatility, expiry, and momentum significantly influence option pricing, and ignoring these factors can result in disproportionate losses.

The price difference between futures and spot arises due to "time value" embedded in futures. This premium expands and contracts over time and eventually converges with spot price at expiry. Understanding this dynamic is crucial, as futures pricing often reflects forward expectations rather than current reality—something actively leveraged by institutional players.

On expiry day, an important nuance:

- Options are settled based on the average traded price (ATP) of the last 30 minutes (3:00–3:30 PM)
- This can create discrepancies between visible LTP and actual settlement price, especially for ATM/OTM strikes
- The likely settlement zone can often be estimated between 3:00–3:12 PM by tracking average price behaviour

Understanding the aforesaid mechanism is essential to avoid misjudging expiry-day closing price movements. This may lead an ATM to close as ITM on settlement. Therefore, heightened vigilance and careful judgment are essential—

otherwise, in options involving mandatory physical settlement, such situations can result in unpleasant and unexpected surprises.

Trading is not just technical—it is deeply psychological. A trader constantly battles their own thoughts, fears, and biases. The real challenge is aligning "emotion action" (execution) with "price action" (analysis). When trades are taken with clarity, conviction, and emotional control, consistency begins to emerge.

Each trader operates differently—scalpers, swing traders, and positional traders all interpret price differently based on their timeframe and objectives. Understanding one's own style and limitations is key to developing a stable approach.

While knowledge can be acquired through study, skill is developed only through consistent practice and market exposure. Chart reading, pattern recognition, and decision-making improve over time as the trader trains their eye and mind.

Technical analysis is often perceived as probabilistic—what some may call a guess work (*tukka in hindi*)—but its accuracy improves substantially with experience and practice. Over time, patterns, structures, and behaviour become more intuitive.

Market volatility, often tracked via India VIX, plays a critical role in strategy selection. When volatility rises toward higher levels (e.g., near 30), specific strategies perform better, while low volatility environments favour entirely different approaches. A trader must adapt strategies dynamically based on volatility regimes.

Hedging, however, is grounded in mathematics and structure. It provides a layer of protection and transforms trading from a speculative activity into a more calculated approach. This is why derivatives like futures and options were originally designed for hedging purposes.

Money in the market is ultimately made through conviction. Conviction does not mean stubbornness—it means clarity backed by analysis. When a trader identifies a setup with confidence and executes it with discipline, outcomes improve significantly.

The market is like an ocean—vast, deep, and full of hidden opportunities. Profitable trading requires the ability to "dive deep" and identify these hidden edges.

Since all human-created systems are inherently imperfect, inefficiencies and loopholes exist—and these are often where opportunities lie.

A trader's journey is about discovering these nuances, refining their approach, and building an edge through observation and experience.

RANGEBOUND MARKETS & TRADING OPPORTUNITY

A rangebound market is often the most favourable environment for a trader to generate consistent and relatively safer profits. Such conditions can be effectively identified using Bollinger Bands (BB), where price oscillates within a defined band. In this phase, trades can be structured systematically—buying near support zones and selling near resistance zones. These zones may be identified using static levels, dynamic indicators like moving averages, or through demand-supply analysis and overbought/oversold conditions.

This behaviour continues until the range is decisively broken. Once a breakout or breakdown sustains, the strategy shifts—from range trading to trend following. A sustained breakout invites long positions, while a sustained breakdown favours shorts, thereby transitioning from low-volatility accumulation to directional momentum.

The previous day's closing plays a crucial role in shaping the next day's trend. Additionally, when indices like Nifty and Bank Nifty move in opposite directions within a narrow range, it often signals a rangebound intraday market. In such scenarios, non-directional strategies like short straddles or strangles may be considered, provided volatility conditions are favourable.

Another practical rule is to allow the market to settle for the first 30 minutes after a gap-up or gap-down opening. This helps avoid early traps and provides clearer directional cues.

Understanding option behaviour—especially around volatility, premium decay, and expiry settlement—is essential for effective participation. I seriously recommend considering to read my comprehensive book on F&O trading: *The Intelligent F&O Trader – Volume I, II & III* available on all major online Indian and international platforms like Amazon, Flipkart, Barnes & Noble etc.

In extreme or war-like environments, traditional directional trades may become risky. Instead of aggressive positioning, hedged strategies offer better risk management—for example, combining index shorts with long positions in safe-haven assets like gold or crude.

Special caution is required during atypical periods such as the last week of a financial year. During such phases, conventional chart patterns often lose reliability, and markets tend to behave in a range-bound manner. In these conditions, tools like Bollinger Bands and AVWAP provide better insights than traditional candlestick patterns.

During extreme or uncertain environments (like geo-political issues, wars etc), directional conviction may be risky. In such cases:

- Prefer hedged strategies (e.g., short index with long gold/crude exposure)
- Avoid aggressive directional trades in highly volatile commodities during crisis phases

Volatility plays a critical role in options trading:

- When VIX is high (e.g., near 30), premiums expand, and when VIX is in rising mode – then directional breakout strategies may perform well. Therefore, rangebound trend targeting strategies should be avoided.
- When VIX is low (e.g., below 15), price movement compresses within a range and options premium decay—and when VIX is in falling mode–it creates ideal conditions for option sellers to play decay through strategies like short straddles and short strangles

GEOPOLITICAL, MACRO-ECONOMICS & DOMESTIC RISKS

A smart investor does not operate in isolation from the world around him. He remains closely attuned to geopolitics, macroeconomic trends, and the evolving landscape of industries. Shifts in technology, changing consumer preferences, and the natural cycle of sectoral rotation often redirect capital flows across asset classes, sectors, and economies. Alongside this, domestic factors—such as policy decisions, regulatory changes, and economic stability within a country—play a crucial role in shaping investment outcomes.

These forces directly influence asset prices by altering demand and supply dynamics. Disruptions in supply chains, fluctuations in raw material costs, or the emergence of new technologies can render existing business models less relevant, while simultaneously creating opportunities in new areas. At times, demand or supply shocks can trigger sharp movements in prices, reshaping market sentiment and expectations almost overnight.

Importantly, certain macro-economic developments often build gradually and may take time before markets begin to fully price them in. In other instances, events unfold suddenly—causing abrupt dislocations that can disrupt established trends and invalidate prior assumptions. For a trader or investor, the challenge lies not in predicting the exact timing of these shifts, but in recognizing their emergence early and adapting swiftly. Agility, awareness, and the willingness to recalibrate one's view are essential traits for navigating an ever-changing market environment.

APPROACHING MARKETS WISELY

The market offers equal opportunity to both small and large participants. The key lies in staying open-minded, continuously learning, and preserving capital to take advantage of these opportunities. A single well-executed trade can sometimes be life-changing, but only if one is prepared and disciplined.

Ultimately, successful trading is built on simplicity, discipline, and consistency:

- Trade selectively, not frequently
- Follow a defined set of setups with conviction
- Respect higher timeframe structure
- Align with volume, momentum, and averages
- Control losses—profits will follow
- Respect exits more than entries
- Trade less, but trade better
- Stay patient and let the market confirm your bias

Markets reward those who wait for clarity, act with discipline, and remain aligned with the underlying structure rather than reacting to noise.

Most traders incur repeated losses due to a few recurring mistakes. Identifying and correcting these is critical for progress.

- Beginners often develop bias and resist adapting to changing conditions
- With experience, flexibility and objectivity improve

Chart reading, pattern recognition, and execution are all skills that improve only with deliberate practice over time.

Markets are vast—like an ocean—with countless visible and hidden opportunities. Success lies in the ability to identify, wait for, and act upon these opportunities with discipline.

- Keep an open mind—markets offer opportunities to both small and large participants
- Preserve capital to capitalize on these opportunities
- Even a single well-executed trade can be transformative

Ultimately, the journey in trading is not just financial but also personal. It teaches humility, patience, and resilience. There are no guarantees—only probabilities—but with the right mindset, skill, and discipline, consistent profitability becomes achievable.

CONCLUSION

In essence, the crux of the matter is that successful trading and investing is not about chasing signals, but about developing a structured understanding of price action, context, and discipline.

Markets operate through cycles of trend, range, momentum, and volatility—each demanding a different approach, strategy, and mindset. By aligning trades with higher timeframe direction, respecting key levels like VWAP, moving averages, and support/resistance, and combining this with pattern recognition, volume insight, and risk management, a trader gradually builds conviction and consistency.

Equally important is adaptability—markets are dynamic, and rigid views often lead to losses. Hence, prudence, patience, and continuous learning remain the cornerstone.

Ultimately, there is no holy grail—only probability, preparation, and execution—and those who learn to manage risk, control emotions, and act with clarity are the ones who sustain and succeed over the long term.

Final Word

With this, we come to the close of this book.

Whether you are an **investor or a trader**—and whether your style is intraday, swing, positional, or scalping—one truth remains constant: **technical analysis is not optional, it is essential**. Investors, in particular, must not underestimate its power. While fundamentals help identify what to buy, technical analysis helps determine when to buy, when to exit, and how to manage risk effectively. The combination of both creates a far more complete and practical approach to participating in the markets.

A sound understanding of technical analysis provides a meaningful edge. It equips you to identify better entry points, exit at appropriate levels, anticipate potential reversals, and plan trades with clarity and conviction. More importantly, it gives you the confidence to navigate market corrections, avoid emotional decision-making, and prevent being stuck in positions taken at the wrong levels. Over time, this discipline and structured approach can make a significant difference in your overall performance and consistency.

I sincerely hope that this book has helped you appreciate the true significance of technical analysis and has added a valuable tool to your investing and trading arsenal. My endeavour has been to simplify complex concepts and present them in a practical, usable manner—so that retail participants can make more informed and confident decisions in their day-to-day market journey.

If you are interested in gaining a deeper understanding of Futures & Options—their concepts, dynamics, and practical trading strategies—I would encourage you to explore my book: ***The Intelligent F&O Trader – Vol I, II & III.*** These volumes are designed to provide comprehensive, real-world insights and actionable strategies suited for different market conditions.

If you have found value in this book, I would humbly request you to share your feedback on the platform from where you purchased it. Your support and feedback will help in reaching and benefiting many more participants in the market.

Wishing you clarity in thought, discipline in action, and success in your market journey.

I would love to hear from you—please feel free to write to me at intelligentmoneywise@gmail.com

Wishing you all the very best for your trading and investment career!

Abbreviations

- ADX – Average Directional Index
- ATR – Average True Range
- AVWAP – Anchored Volume Weighted Average Price
- BB – Bollinger Bands
- BD – Breakdown
- BO – Breakout
- BTST – Buy today, sell tomorrow
- CMP – Current Market Price
- CPR – Central Pivot Range
- DMA – Daily Moving Average
- DII – Domestic Institutional Investor
- EBITDA – Earnings Before Interest, Taxes, Depreciation and Amortization
- EMA – Exponential Moving Average
- EPS – Earnings Per Share
- ETF – Exchange Traded Fund
- F&O – Futures and Options
- FII – Foreign Institutional Investor
- HOD – High of the Day
- H&S – Head and Shoulders
- IOC – Immediate or Cancel

- IPO – Initial Public Offering
- ITM – In The Money
- LOD – Low of the Day
- LTP – Last Traded Price
- MACD – Moving Average Convergence Divergence
- MFI – Money Flow Index
- M2M – Mark to Market
- OHLC – Open, High, Low, Close
- OI – Open Interest
- OTM – Out of The Money
- P&S – Point and Figure Chart
- PAT – Profit After Tax
- PCR – Put Call Ratio
- POC – Point of Control
- PR – Pivot Resistance
- PS – Pivot Support
- QOQ – Quarter-on- Quarter
- R:R – Risk Reward Ratio
- ROC – Rate of Change
- ROI – Return on Investment
- RS – Relative Strength
- RSI – Relative Strength Index
- R/S – Resistance / Support
- SIP – Systematic Investment Plan
- SL – Stop Loss

- SMA – Simple Moving Average
- SRT – Spot-to-Range Trend
- STBT – Sell today, buy tomorrow
- TF – Time Frame
- VCP – Volatility Contraction Pattern
- VIX – Volatility Index
- VWAP – Volume Weighted Average Price
- WMA – Weighted Moving Average
- YOY – Year-on-Year

Subject Index

www.ingramcontent.com/pod-product-compliance
Lightning Source LLC
LaVergne TN
LVHW022155200926
848481LV00006B/1752
9798904795412